THE LEGAL AUTHORITY OF ASEAN AS A SECURITY INSTITUTION

The Association of Southeast Asian Nations (ASEAN) has achieved deeper regional market integration to lay a socio-economic foundation for the development of a regional community, yet inter-state trust is by no means assured as Southeast Asian nations remain steadfast in maintaining their political regime stability against external interference. However, through its institutional practices, ASEAN has emerged as a distinct model of security institution, while the region's contemporary security landscape has diversified with various non-traditional security issues. By looking beyond the veneer of diplomacy and prevailing political circumstances, this book examines the legal nature and form of ASEAN's authority to address diverse regional security issues. It provides a fresh perspective on ASEAN's role as a security institution. With an interdisciplinary analysis, this book reveals the normative role that ASEAN plays in facilitating the processes of norm development, localisation and internalisation as it deals with contemporary security challenges confronting Southeast Asia.

HITOSHI NASU is Professor of International Law at the University of Exeter. He is an expert of public international law, especially in the fields of international security law and the law of armed conflict. He is the author of *International Law on Peacekeeping* (2009) and co-editor of *Human Rights in the Asia-Pacific Region: Towards Institution Building* (2011), *Asia-Pacific Disaster Management* (2013), *New Technologies and the Law of Armed Conflict* (2014), and *Legal Perspectives on Security Institutions* (2015).

ROB MCLAUGHLIN is Professor of Military and Security Law at the University of New South Wales – Canberra, and Honorary Professor at the Australian National University. His fields of research focus around law of armed conflict, law of the sea, and military operations, military administrative, and military discipline law. He served more than twenty years in the Royal Australian Navy. He is the author of *United Nations Peace Operations in the Territorial Sea* (2009) and *Maritime Crime: A Manual for Criminal Justice Practitioners* (2017), co-author of *Multinational Rules of Engagement Handbook* (2009) and *Handbook on the Use of Force by Private Security Companies* (2016), and co-editor of *New Technologies and the Law of Armed Conflict* (2014).

DONALD R. ROTHWELL is Professor of International Law at the ANU College of Law, Australian National University. His research has a specific focus on law of the sea, international polar law, and implementation of international law within Australia as reflected in 24 books, and over 200 articles, book chapters and notes in international and Australian publications. Rothwell is co-editor of the *Australian Year Book of International Law* and editor-in-chief of the *Brill Research Perspectives in the Law of the Sea*. From 2012 to 2018 he was Rapporteur of the International Law Association (ILA) Committee on Baselines under the International Law of the Sea.

SEE SENG TAN is Professor of International Relations at Nanyang Technological University, Singapore. He is the author of *Multilateral Asian Security Architecture: Non-ASEAN Stakeholders* (2015) and *The Making of the Asia Pacific: Knowledge Brokers and the Politics of Representation* (2013), co-editor of *United States Engagement in the Asia Pacific: Perspectives from Asia* (2015), and editor of the four-volume *Regionalism in Asia* (2009).

INTEGRATION THROUGH LAW

The Role of Law and the Rule of Law in ASEAN Integration

General Editors
J. H. H. Weiler, European University Institute
Tan Hsien-Li, National University of Singapore

The Association of Southeast Asian Nations (ASEAN), comprising the ten member states of Brunei Darussalam, Cambodia, Indonesia, Lao PDR, Malaysia, Myanmar, Philippines, Singapore, Thailand and Vietnam, has undertaken intensified integration into the ASEAN Community through the Rule of Law and Institutions in its 2007 Charter. This innovative book series evaluates the community-building processes of ASEAN to date and offers a conceptual and policy toolkit for broader Asian thinking and planning of different legal and institutional models of economic and political regional integration in the region. Participating scholars have been divided up into six separate thematic strands. The books combine a mix of Asian and Western scholars.

Centre for International Law, National University of Singapore (CIL-NUS)

The Centre for International Law (CIL) was established in 2009 at the National University of Singapore's Bukit Timah Campus in response to the growing need for international law expertise and capacity building in the Asia-Pacific region. CIL is a university-wide research centre that focuses on multidisciplinary research and works with other NUS or external centres of research and academic excellence. In particular, CIL collaborates very closely with the NUS Faculty of Law.

THE LEGAL AUTHORITY OF ASEAN AS A SECURITY INSTITUTION

HITOSHI NASU
University of Exeter

ROB MCLAUGHLIN
University of New South Wales, Canberra

DONALD R. ROTHWELL
Australian National University, Canberra

SEE SENG TAN
Nanyang Technological University, Singapore

CAMBRIDGE
UNIVERSITY PRESS

CAMBRIDGE
UNIVERSITY PRESS

University Printing House, Cambridge CB2 8BS, United Kingdom

One Liberty Plaza, 20th Floor, New York, NY 10006, USA

477 Williamstown Road, Port Melbourne, VIC 3207, Australia

314–321, 3rd Floor, Plot 3, Splendor Forum, Jasola District Centre, New Delhi – 110025, India

79 Anson Road, #06–04/06, Singapore 079906

Cambridge University Press is part of the University of Cambridge.

It furthers the University's mission by disseminating knowledge in the pursuit of education, learning, and research at the highest international levels of excellence.

www.cambridge.org
Information on this title: www.cambridge.org/9781108705653
DOI: 10.1017/9781108669511

First published 2019

Printed and bound in Great Britain by Clays Ltd, Elcograf S.p.A.

A catalogue record for this publication is available from the British Library.

Library of Congress Cataloging-in-Publication Data
NAMES: Nasu, Hitoshi, author. | McLaughlin, Rob, author. | Rothwell, Donald, 1959– author. | Tan, See Seng, 1965– author.
TITLE: The legal authority of ASEAN as a security institution / Hitoshi Nasu, University of Exeter; Rob McLaughlin, University of New South Wales, Canberra; Donald R. Rothwell, Australian National University, Canberra; See Seng Tan, Nanyang Technological University, Singapore.
DESCRIPTION: Cambridge, United Kingdom ; New York, NY, USA : Cambridge University Press, 2019. | Series: Integration through law: the role of law and the rule of law in ASEAN integration | "Published within the context of a wide-ranging research project entitled, Integration Through Law: The Role of Law and the Rule of Law in ASEAN Integration (ITL), undertaken by the Centre for International Law at the National University of Singapore and directed by J. H. H. Weiler and Tan Hsien-Li." | Includes bibliographical references and index.
IDENTIFIERS: LCCN 2018056602 | ISBN 9781108705653 (alk. paper)
SUBJECTS: LCSH: ASEAN. | Security, International – Southeast Asia. | Law enforcement – Southeast Asia. | Southeast Asia – International status.
CLASSIFICATION: LCC KNE173 .N37 2019 | DDC 341.24/73–dc23
LC record available at https://lccn.loc.gov/2018056602

ISBN 978-1-108-70565-3 Paperback

CONTENTS

TABLES

This monograph is published within the context of a wide-ranging research project entitled, Integration Through Law: The Role of Law and the Rule of Law in ASEAN Integration (ITL), undertaken by the Centre for International Law at the National University of Singapore and directed by J. H. H. Weiler and Tan Hsien-Li.

The Preamble to the ASEAN Charter concludes with a single decision: 'We, the Peoples of the Member States of the Association of Southeast Asian Nations . . . [h]ereby decide to establish, through this Charter, the legal and institutional framework for ASEAN.' For the first time in its history of over four decades, the Legal and the Institutional were brought to the forefront of ASEAN discourse.

The gravitas of the medium, a Charter: the substantive ambition of its content, the creation of three interlocking Communities, and the turn to law and institutions as instruments for realisation provide ample justification for this wide-ranging project, to which this monograph is one contribution, examining ASEAN in a comparative context.

That same substantive and, indeed, political ambition means that any single study, illuminating as it may be, will cover but a fraction of the phenomena. Our modus operandi in this project was to create teams of researchers from Asia and elsewhere who would contribute individual monographs within an overall framework which we had

xi

designed. The project framework, involving several thematic clusters within each monograph, is thus determined by the framework and the place of each monograph within it.

As regards the specific content, however, the authors were free, indeed encouraged, to define their own understanding of the problem and their own methodology and reach their own conclusions. The thematic structure of the entire project may be found at the end of this Preface.

The project as a whole, and each monograph within it, display several methodological sensibilities.

First, law, in our view, can only be understood and evaluated when situated in its political and economic context. Thus, the first studies in the overall project design are intended to provide the political, economic, cultural and historical context against which one must understand ASEAN and are written by specialists in these respective disciplines. This context, to a greater or lesser degree, also informs the sensibility of each monograph. There are no 'black letter law' studies to be found in this project and, indeed, even in the most technical of areas we encouraged our authors to make their writing accessible to readers of diverse disciplines.

Comparative experience suggests that the success of achieving some of the more ambitious objectives outlined in Article 1 of the Charter will depend in no small measure on the effectiveness of legal principles, legal rules and legal institutions. This is particularly true as regards the success of establishing 'an ASEAN Community comprising the ASEAN Security Community, the ASEAN Economic Community and the ASEAN Socio-Cultural Community as provided for in the Bali Declaration of ASEAN Concord II'. Article 2(2) (n) stipulates the commitment of ASEAN member states to act in accordance with the principle of 'adherence to multilateral trade rules and ASEAN's rules-based regimes for effective implementation of economic commitments and progressive reduction towards elimination of all barriers to regional economic integration'. The ASEAN member states therefore envisage that rules of law and the Rule of Law will become a major feature in the future of ASEAN.

Although, as seen, the Charter understands itself as providing an institutional and legal framework for ASEAN, the question of the 'role of law and the rule of law' is not advocacy but a genuine enquiry in the various substantive areas of the project as to:

- the substantive legal principles and substantive rules of the various ASEAN communities;
- the procedural legal principles and rules governing institutional structures and decision-making processes;
- implementation, enforcement and dispute settlement.

One should not expect a mechanical application of this scheme in each study; rather, a sensibility that refuses to content itself with legal enactments as such and looks to a 'living' notion of law and institutions is ubiquitous in all the studies. Likewise, the project is sensitive to 'non law'. It variously attempts to locate the appropriate province of the law in this experience. That is, not only the role of law, but also the areas that are and should remain outside the reach of legal institutionalisation with due sensitivity to ASEAN and Asian particularism and political and cultural identities.

The project, and the monographs of which it is made, are not normatively thick. They do not advocate. They are designed, for the most part, to offer reflection, discuss the pros and cons, and in this way enrich public awareness, deepen understanding of different options and in that respect contribute indirectly to policy-making.

This decisive development of ASEAN has been accompanied by a growing Asian interest in various legal and institutional forms of transnational economic and political cooperation, notably the various voices discussing and showing an interest in an East Asia Integration project. The number of Free Trade Agreements (FTAs) and Regional Trade Agreements (RTAs) has increased from six in 1991 to 166 in 2013, with a further sixty-two in various stages of negotiations.

Methodologically, the project and many of the monographs are comparative in their orientation. Comparative law is one of the few real-life laboratories that we have in which to assess and understand the operation of different legal and institutional models designed to tackle similar objectives and problems. One should not need to put one's own hand in the fire to learn that it scorches. With that in mind a couple of monographs offer both conceptual reflection and pragmatic 'tool-boxing' on some of the key elements featuring in all regional integration systems.

Comparative law is in part about divergence: it is a potent tool and means to understand one's own uniqueness. One understands better the uniqueness of apples by comparing them to oranges. You understand better the specialness of a Toyota by comparing it to a Ford.

Comparative law is also about convergence: it is a potent tool and means to understand how what are seemingly different phenomena are part of a broader trend, an insight which may enhance both self-understanding and policy potentialities.

Although many studies in the project could have almost immediate policy implications, as would the project as a whole, this is not its only or even principal purpose. There is a rich theory of federalism which covers many countries around the world. There is an equally rich theory of European integration, which has been associated with the advent Union. There is also considerable learning on Free Trade Areas and the like.

To date, the study of the legal aspects of ASEAN specifically and other forms of Asian legal integration has been derivative of, and dependent on, theoretical and conceptual insight which were developed in different contexts.

One principal objective of ITL and these monographs will be to put in place the building blocks for an authentic body of ASEAN and Asian integration theory developed in, and with sensitivity to, the particularities and peculiarities of the region and continent. A theory and conceptual framework of Asian legal integration will signal the coming of age of research of and in the region itself.

Although the monographs form part of an overarching project, we asked our authors to write each as a 'standalone' – not assuming that their readers would have consulted any of the other titles. Indeed, the project is rich and few will read all monographs. We encourage readers to pick and choose from the various monographs and design their own menu. There is, on occasion, some overlap in providing, for example, back-ground information on ASEAN in different studies. That is not only inevitable but desirable in a project of this amplitude.

The world is increasingly witnessing a phenomenon of interlocking regional organisation where the experience of one feeds on the others. In some way, the intellectual, disciplinary and comparative sensibility of this project is a microcosm of the world it describes.

The range of topics covered in this series comprises:
The General Architecture and Aspirations of ASEAN
The Governance and Management of ASEAN: Instruments, Institutions, Monitoring, Compliance and Dispute Resolution
Legal Regimes in ASEAN
The ASEAN Economic Community ASEAN and the World
The Substantive Law of ASEAN

The Association of Southeast Asian Nations (ASEAN) has celebrated a fiftieth anniversary in 2017. Its history, development and achievements are all remarkable for an institution that started as an informal arrangement of geographically proximate states with diverse political, economic, cultural and religious traditions and interests. The volume of academic literature and policy study has grown, particularly since the end of the Cold War, with many devoted to the assessment of ASEAN's role in and contribution to regional security. Despite the significance of such literature to the understanding of ASEAN and its role in regional security, there is a need for fresh perspectives with a more objective, legal assessment of ASEAN's authority to address regional security issues.

The intention of this book is to present ASEAN as a distinct model of security institution, different to a collective security institution or an integrated regional institution, by critically evaluating the normative role of ASEAN in light of regional principles and application thereof in practice. We are keenly aware of the importance of understanding the historical, geopolitical and socio-cultural backgrounds to inform legal inquiries into ASEAN's authority in regional security and therefore sought guidance from a variety of regional security experts so that our legal inquiry is reflective of a robust and up-to-date assessment of the socio-political environment of the region.

The outcome of the four-year-long collaborative research is compiled in this book. While all the authors exercised oversight of this research project and in preparation of the final manuscript, primary responsibility for research and writing of each chapter was allocated as follows: Chapter 1 (Nasu); Chapter 2 (McLaughlin); Chapter 3 (Tan); Chapter 4 (Rothwell); Chapter 5 (Nasu); Chapter 6 (Nasu); and Chapter 7 (Nasu). Hitoshi Nasu, as the lead author, took the overall editorial responsibility including the drafting of the Introduction and Conclusion. A substantial part of Chapter 3 has been reproduced from: See Seng Tan and Hitoshi Nasu, 'ASEAN and the Development of Counter-Terrorism Law and Policy in Southeast Asia' (2016) 39 *University of New South Wales Law Journal* 1219–38, with permission granted by the executive editor of the journal.

We gratefully acknowledge the support provided by the Australian Research Council under its Discovery Grant funding scheme (Project Number: DP130103683) for this research project. We are also grateful to many experts for sharing information and their views on different regional security issues and various aspects of ASEAN's engagement therewith at different stages of our research, including: Termsak Chalermpalanupap (Institute of Southeast Asian Studies), Alistair Cook (S. Rajaratnam School of International Studies), Ralf Emmers (S. Rajaratnam School of International Studies), Teruhiko Fukushima (National Defence Academy of Japan), Euan Graham (Lowy Institute), Tsutomu Kikuchi (Aoyama Gakuin University), Wonhee

Kim (Korea Maritime Institute), Masahiro Kurosaki (National Defence Academy of Japan), Futoshi Matsumoto (Institute for International Policy Studies), Hiroshi Ohta (Waseda University), Willem Pretorius (Australia-Asia Program to Combat Trafficking in Persons), Ainsley Stinson (UN Office on Drugs and Crime), Ian Storey (Institute of Southeast Asian Studies), Hsien-Li Tan (Centre for International Law, National University of Singapore), Ranyta Yusran (Centre for International Law, National University of Singapore), Joseph H. H. Weiler (European University Institute) and two anonymous reviewers.

We also thank Australian National University law students, Kayjal Dasan, Megan Lingafelter, Senada Meskin, Madeleine Ellen Miller, Alexa Milosevic, Philippa Mowat, Parissa Tosif, Helen Trezise and Jeanette Zhang, for their research assistance on various aspects of ASEAN's engagement with regional security issues. Helen Trezise also worked with us reviewing the entire manuscript on style matters at the final stages of its preparation.

Finally, we thank our colleagues at the Australian National University and S. Rajaratnam School of International Studies and our respective families and friends for their support and encouragement.

All the online references are correct as at 1 September 2018.

Brunei Darussalam

Anti-Terrorism (Financial and Other Measures) Act 2002

Anti-Terrorism Order 2011

Anti-Terrorism (Terrorist Financing) Regulations 2013

Computer Misuse Act 2000 (amended in 2007)

Defence White Paper 2011: Defending the Nation's Sovereignty, Expanding Roles in Wider Horizons (2011)

Electronic Transactions Act 2001 (amended in 2008)

Maritime Offences (Ships and Fixed Platforms) Order 2007

Merchant Shipping (Safety Convention) Regulations 2003 (amended in 2004)

Trafficking and Smuggling in Persons Order 2004

Cambodia

Agricultural Sector Strategic Development Plan 2006–2010 (2006)

Agricultural Sector Strategic Development Plan 2014–2018 (2015)

Defense Policy of the Kingdom of Cambodia 2006: Security, Development and International Cooperation (White Paper, 2006)

Law on Anti-Money Laundering and Combating the Financing of Terrorism 2007

Law on Counter-Terrorism 2007

Law on the Prohibition of Chemical, Nuclear, Biological and Radiological Weapons 2009

Law on the Suppression of Human Trafficking and Sexual Exploitation 2008

Law on the Suppression of the Kidnapping, Trafficking, and Exploitation of Human Beings 1996

National Strategic Development Plan 2006–2010 (2006)

National Strategic Development Plan 2014–2018 (2014)

National Strategy for Food Security and Nutrition 2014–2018 (2014)

Rectangular Strategy for Growth, Employment, Equity and Efficiency in Cambodia (2004)

Rectangular Strategy for Growth, Employment, Equity and Efficiency Phase II (2008)

Rectangular Strategy for Growth, Employment, Equity and Efficiency Phase III (2013)

India

National Food Security Act 2013

Indonesia

Decree No. 62/2012

Decree No. 88/2002 on the National Plan of Action for the Elimination of Trafficking in Women and Children

Law on Combating Criminal Acts of Terrorism 2002

Law on the Crime of Money Laundering 2002 (amended by Law No. 8/2010)

Law on Electronic Information and Transactions 2008

Law on the Eradication of the Criminal Act of Trafficking in Persons 2007

Law on Food 1996
Law on Food 2012
Law on Immigration 2011
Law on Indonesian Waters 1997
Law on Nuclear Energy 1997
Law on the Prevention and Eradication of Crimes of Financing
of Terrorism 2013
Law on the Protection of Children 2002
National Long-Term Development Plan 2005–2025
Regulation No. 37/2002 on the Rights and Obligations of
Foreign Ships and Aircraft Exercising the Right of
Archipelagic Sea Lanes Passage through Designated Sea
Lanes
Regulation No. 68/2002 on Food Security

Lao PDR
Decree No. 327 on Internet-Based Information Control and
Management 2014
Law on Anti-Money Laundering and Counter-Financing of
Terrorism 2015
Law on Anti-Trafficking in Persons 2015
Law on Development and Protection of Women 2004
Law on Electricity 2008
Law on Electronic Transactions 2012
Law on Prevention and Combating Cyber Crime 2015
Law on the Protection of the Rights and Interests of Children
2007
Penal Code 1990 (as amended in 2005)
Strategy for Agricultural Development 2011 to 2020 (2010)

Malaysia

Anti-Money Laundering, Anti-Terrorist Financing and Proceeds of Unlawful Activities Act 2001

Anti-Trafficking in Persons and Anti-Smuggling of Migrants Act 2007 (amended in 2010 and 2015)

Atomic Energy Licensing Act 1984

Computer Crimes Act 1997

Internal Security Act 1960

Malaysian Maritime Enforcement Agency Act 2004

National Cyber-Security Policy (2006)

National Food Security Policy (2008)

Penal Code 1936

Penal Code (Amendment) Act 2003

Prevention of Crime Act 1959

Prevention of Terrorism Act 2015

Security Offences (Special Measures) Act 2012

Special Measures against Terrorism in Foreign Countries Act 2015

Myanmar

Anti-Trafficking in Persons Law 2005

Atomic Energy Law 1998

The Control of Money Laundering Law 2002

Electronic Transactions Law 2004

Mutual Legal Assistance in Criminal Matters Law 2004

Philippines

Act Providing and Use of Electronic Commercial and Non-Commercial Transactions, Penalties for Unlawful Use Thereof, and Other Purposes 2000

Act to Define the Baselines of the Territorial Sea of the
Philippines 1961 (amended in 1968 and 2009)
Anti-Money Laundering Act 2001
Anti-Trafficking in Persons Act 2003 (amended in 2012)
Atomic Energy Regulatory and Liability Act 1968
Executive Order No. 57/2011 'Establishing a National Coast
Watch System, Providing for Its Structure and Defining the
Roles and Responsibilities of Member Agencies in
Providing Coordinated Inter-Agency Maritime Security
Operations and for Other Purposes'
Human Security Act 2007
National Cyber Security Plan (2004)
Philippine Development Plan 2011–2016 (2011)
Terrorism Financing Prevention and Suppression Act 2012

Singapore
Computer Misuse and Cybersecurity Act 1993 (amended in
2007)
Maritime Offences Act 2003
Prevention of Human Trafficking Act 2015
Radiation Protection Act 2007 (amended in 2014)
Singapore's Cybersecurity Strategy (2016)
Terrorism (Suppression of Bombings) Act 2007
Terrorism (Suppression of Financing) Act 2002
United Nations (Anti-Terrorism Measures) Regulations 2001

Thailand
Anti-Money Laundering Act 1999, (No. 2) 2008, (No. 3) 2009
Anti-Trafficking in Persons Act 2008
Atomic Energy for Peace Act 1961, 2016

Law on Maritime Code 2005

Law on Prevention and Suppression against Human Trafficking 2012

Master Plan for Nuclear Power Infrastructure Development (2014)

Ordinance on Radiation Safety and Control 1996

Penal Code 1999 (amended in 2009 and 2015)

Resolution No. 63/NQ-CP (23 December 2009) on National Food Security

Agreement on the ASEAN Food Security Reserve, adopted 4 October 1979 (entered into force 17 July 1980)

APEC Economic Leaders' Declaration of Common Resolve, adopted at the 2nd APEC Leaders' Meeting, Bogor, Indonesia, 15 November 1994

APEC Leaders' Statement on Counter-Terrorism, adopted at the APEC Shanghai Summit, Shanghai, PRC, 21 October 2001

APEC Leaders' Statement on Fighting Terrorism and Promoting Growth, adopted at the 14th APEC Joint Ministerial Meeting, Los Cabos, Mexico, 26 October 2002

Arab Convention on the Suppression of Terrorism, adopted 22 April 1998 (entered into force 7 May 1999)

ASEAN Agreement on Disaster Management and Emergency Response, adopted 26 July 2005 (entered into force 24 December 2009)

ASEAN Agreement on Transboundary Haze Pollution, adopted 11 June 2002 (entered into force 25 November 2003)

ASEAN Convention against Trafficking in Persons, Especially Women and Children, adopted 21 November 2015 (not in force)

ASEAN Convention on Counter Terrorism, adopted 13 January 2007 (entered into force 27 May 2011)

ASEAN Declaration against Trafficking in Persons, Particularly Women and Children, adopted at the 10th ASEAN Summit, Vientiane, Lao PDR, 29 November 2004

ASEAN Declaration on Cooperation in Search and Rescue of Persons and Vessels in Distress at Sea, adopted at the 17th ASEAN Summit, Hanoi, Vietnam, 27 October 2010

ASEAN Declaration on Joint Action to Counter Terrorism, adopted at the 7th ASEAN Summit, Bandar Seri Begawan, Brunei Darussalam, 5 November 2001

ASEAN Declaration on Terrorism, adopted at the 8th ASEAN Summit, Phnom Penh, Cambodia, 3 November 2002

ASEAN Declaration on the Protection and Promotion of the Rights of Migrant Workers, adopted at the 12th ASEAN Summit, Cebu, Philippines, 13 January 2007

ASEAN Declaration on Transnational Crime, adopted at the 1st ASEAN Conference on Transnational Crime, Manila, Philippines, 20 December 1997

ASEAN Declaration to Prevent and Combat Cybercrime, adopted at the 31st ASEAN Summit, Manila, Philippines, 13 November 2017

ASEAN Economic Community Blueprint, adopted at the 13th ASEAN Summit, Singapore, 20 November 2007

ASEAN Integrated Food Security (AIFS) Framework and Strategic Plan of Action on Food Security in the ASEAN Region (SPA-FS) 2009–2013, adopted at the 14th ASEAN Summit, Cha-am Hua Hin, Thailand, 1 March 2009

ASEAN Petroleum Security Agreement, adopted 24 June 1986 (entered into force 2 April 1987)

ASEAN Petroleum Security Agreement, adopted 1 March 2009 (entered into force 22 March 2013)

ASEAN Plus Three Emergency Rice Reserve Agreement, adopted 7 October 2011 (entered into force 12 July 2012)

ASEAN Political-Security Community Blueprint, adopted at the 14th ASEAN Summit, Cha-am Hua Hin, Thailand, 1 March 2009

ASEAN Regional Forum Statement on Cooperation against Piracy and Other Threats to Security, adopted at the 10th ARF Meeting, Phnom Penh, Cambodia, 17 June 2003

ASEAN Regional Forum Statement on Cooperation in Ensuring Cyber Security, adopted at the 19th ARF Meeting, Phnom Penh, Cambodia, 12 July 2012

ASEAN Regional Forum Statement on Cooperation in Fighting Cyber Attack and Terrorist Misuse of Cyberspace, adopted at the 13th ARF Meeting, Kuala Lumpur, Malaysia, 28 July 2006

ASEAN Regional Forum Statement on Cooperative Counter-Terrorist Action on Border Security, adopted at the 10th ARF Meeting, Phnom Penh, Cambodia, 18 June 2003

ASEAN Regional Forum Statement on Information Sharing and Intelligence Exchange and Document Integrity and Security in Enhancing Cooperation to Combat Terrorism and Other Transnational Crimes, adopted at the 12th ARF Meeting, Vientiane, Lao PDR, 29 July 2005

ASEAN Regional Forum Statement on Non-Proliferation, adopted at the 11th ARF Meeting, Jakarta, Indonesia, 2 July 2004

ASEAN Regional Forum Statement on Strengthening Transport Security against International Terrorism, adopted at the 11th ARF Meeting, Jakarta, Indonesia, 2 July 2004

Cha-am Hua Hin Statement on EAS Disaster Management, adopted at the 4th East Asia Summit, Cha-am Hua Hin, Thailand, 25 October 2009

Charter of the Association of Southeast Asian Nations, 20 November 2007, 2624 UNTS 223 (entered into force 15 December 2008)

Charter of the United Nations, opened for signature 26 June 1945, 1 UNTS xvi (entered into force 24 October 1945)

Code for Unplanned Encounters at Sea, adopted at the Western Pacific Naval Symposium, Qing Dao, PRC, 22 April 2014

Comprehensive Nuclear Test Ban Treaty, adopted 10 September 1996, 35 ILM 1439 (1996) (not in force)

Convention for the Suppression of Unlawful Acts against the Safety of Maritime Navigation, adopted 10 March 1988, 1678 UNTS 221 (entered into force 1 March 1992)

Convention of the Organization of the Islamic Conference on Combating International Terrorism, adopted 1 July 1999 (entered into force 7 November 2002)

Convention on Cybercrime, adopted 23 November 2001, ETS No. 185, 2296 UNTS 167 (entered into force 1 July 2004)

Convention on Early Notification of a Nuclear Incident, adopted 26 September 1986, 1457 UNTS 133 (entered into force 27 October 1986)

Convention on Nuclear Safety, adopted 17 June 1994, 1963 UNTS 293 (entered into force 24 October 1996)

Convention on the Prohibition of Nuclear Weapons, adopted 7 July 2017 (not in force)

Declaration Constituting an Agreement Establishing the Association of South-East Asian Nations, adopted 8

August 1967, 1331 UNTS 235 (entered into force 8 August 1967)

Declaration of the 7th East Asia Summit on Regional Responses to Malaria Control and Addressing Resistance to Antimalarial Medicines, adopted at the 7th East Asia Summit, Phnom Penh, Cambodia, 20 November 2012

Declaration of the 8th East Asia Summit on Food Security, adopted at the 8th East Asia Summit, Bandar Seri Begawan, Brunei Darussalam, 10 October 2013

Declaration of the Fourteenth SAARC Summit, New Delhi, India, 3-4 April 2007

Declaration of the Fifteenth SAARC Summit, Colombo, Sri Lanka, 2-3 August 2008

Declaration of the Sixteenth SAARC Summit, Thimphu, Bhutan, 28-29 April 2010

Declaration of the Seventeenth SAARC Summit, Addu City, Maldives, 10-11 November 2011

Declaration on the Conduct of Parties in the South China Sea, adopted at the 8th ASEAN Summit, Phnom Penh, Cambodia, 4 November 2002

Declaration on the Elimination of Violence against Women and Elimination of Violence against Children in ASEAN, adopted 9-10 October 2013

Declaration on the Zone of Peace, Freedom and Neutrality, adopted at the Special ASEAN Foreign Ministers' Meeting, Kuala Lumpur, 27 November 1971

Defence Cooperation Agreement between Singapore and Indonesia, adopted 27 April 2007 (not in force)

e-ASEAN Framework Agreement, adopted 24 November 2000 (not in force)

East Asia Summit Declaration on Avian Influenza Prevention, Control and Response, adopted at the 1st East Asia Summit, Kuala Lumpur, Malaysia, 14 December 2005

European Convention on the Suppression of Terrorism, adopted 27 January 1977, 1137 UNTS 93 (entered into force 4 August 1978)

Final Act of the Paris Conference on Cambodia, UN Doc S/23177/Annex (30 October 1991)

Hanoi Declaration of 1998, Hanoi, Vietnam, 16 December 1998

International Convention for the Safety of Life at Sea, adopted 1 November 1974, 1184 UNTS 278 (entered into force 25 May 1980)

International Convention for the Suppression of Terrorist Bombings, adopted 15 December 1997, 2149 UNTS 256 (entered into force 23 May 2001)

International Convention for the Suppression of the Financing of Terrorism, adopted 9 December 1999, 2178 UNTS 197 (entered into force 10 April 2002)

Joint Communiqué of the 3rd ASEAN Ministerial Meeting on Transnational Crime, Singapore, 11 October 2001

Joint Communiqué of the 9th ASEAN Ministerial Meeting, Manila, Philippines, 24–26 June 1976

Joint Communiqué of the 50th ASEAN Foreign Ministers' Meeting, Manila, Philippines, 5 August 2017

Joint Declaration of ASEAN and China on Cooperation in the Field of Non-traditional Security Issues, adopted at the 6th ASEAN-China Summit, Phnom Penh, Cambodia, 4 November 2002

Joint Declaration of the ASEAN Defence Ministers on Partnering for Change, Engaging the World, adopted at

Telecommunications & IT Ministers, Mactan Cebu, Philippines, 15–16 November 2012

Manila Accord, signed 31 July 1963, 550 UNTS 344 (entered into force 31 July 1963)

Manila Declaration on the Prevention and Control of Transnational Crime, adopted at the 1st Asian Regional Ministerial Meeting on Transnational Crime, Manila, Philippines, 25 March 1998

Memorandum of Cooperation between the Government of the United States of America and the Government of the Republic of the Philippines on Maritime Counter-Piracy Training and Education, signed in Washington DC, US, 31 July 2009

Memorandum of Understanding between the Governments of the Member Countries of the Association of Southeast Asian Nations (ASEAN) and the People's Republic of China on Cooperation in the Field of Non-Traditional Security Issues, adopted in Bangkok, Thailand, 10 January 2004

Memorandum of Understanding on Cooperation against Trafficking in Persons in the Greater Mekong Sub-Region, adopted in Yangon, Myanmar, 29 October 2004

Model Protocol Additional to the Agreements between State(s) and the International Atomic Energy Agency for the Application of Nuclear Safeguards, IAEA Doc INFCIRC/540 (Corrected) (1 September 1997)

Niigata Declaration on APEC Food Security, adopted at the 1st APEC Ministerial Meeting on Food Security, Niigata, Japan, 17 October 2010

Organization of African Union Convention on the Prevention and Combating of Terrorism, adopted 14 July 1999, 2219 UNTS 179 (entered into force 6 December 2002)

Organization of American States Convention to Prevent and Punish Acts of Terrorism Taking the Form of Crimes against Persons and Related Extortion that are of International Significance, adopted 2 February 1971, 1438 UNTS 191 (entered into force 16 October 1973)

Phnom Penh Declaration on the East Asia Summit Development Initiative, adopted at the 7th East Asia Summit, Phnom Penh, Cambodia, 20 November 2012

Protocol against the Smuggling of Migrants by Land, Sea and Air, Supplementing the United Nations Convention against Transnational Organized Crime, adopted 15 November 2000, 2241 UNTS 507 (entered into force 28 January 2004)

Protocol for the Suppression of Unlawful Acts against the Safety of Fixed Platforms on the Continental Shelf, adopted 10 March 1988, 1678 UNTS 304 (entered into force 1 March 1992)

Protocol to Prevent, Suppress and Punish Trafficking in Persons Especially Women and Children, supplementing the United Nations Convention against Transnational Organized Crime, adopted 15 November 2000, 2237 UNTS 319 (entered into force 25 December 2003)

Regional Cooperation Agreement on Combating Piracy and Armed Robbery against Ships in Asia, adopted 11 November 2004, 2398 UNTS 199 (entered into force 4 September 2006)

Shanghai Accord, adopted at the 9th APEC Leaders' Meeting, Shanghai, PRC, 21 October 2001

Singapore Declaration, adopted at the 3rd Meeting of ASEAN Telecommunications & IT Ministers, Singapore, 19 September 2003

Singapore Declaration on Climate Change, Energy and the Environment, adopted at the 3rd East Asia Summit, Singapore, 21 November 2007

South Asian Association for Regional Cooperation (SAARC) Convention on Preventing and Combating Trafficking in Women and Children for Prostitution, adopted 5 January 2002 (entered into force 15 November 2005)

South Asian Association for Regional Cooperation (SAARC) Convention on Suppression of Terrorism, adopted 4 November 1987 (entered into force 22 August 1988)

South Pacific Nuclear Free Zone Treaty, opened for signature 6 August 1985, 1445 UNTS 177 (entered into force 11 December 1986)

Statute of the International Atomic Energy Agency, opened for signature 23 October 1956, 276 UNTS 3 (entered into force 29 July 1957) (as amended on 4 October 1961, 471 UNTS 334)

Treaty of Amity and Cooperation in Southeast Asia, adopted 24 February 1976, 1025 UNTS 319 (entered into force 15 July 1976)

Treaty on Cooperation among States Members of the Commonwealth of Independent States in Combating Terrorism, adopted 4 June 1999 (entered into force 4 June 1999)

Treaty on Mutual Legal Assistance in Criminal Matters, adopted 29 November 2004 (entered into force 28 April 2005 for Singapore, 25 October 2005 for Vietnam, 1 June 2005 for Malaysia, 15 February 2006 for Brunei Darussalam, 25 June 2007 for Lao PDR, 9 September 2008 for Indonesia, 12 December 2008 for the Philippines, 22 January 2009 for Myanmar, 8 April 2010 for Cambodia, 31 January 2013 for Thailand)

Treaty on the Southeast Asia Nuclear Weapon-Free Zone, adopted 15 December 1995, 1981 UNTS 129 (entered into force 25 March 1997)

UN Convention on the Law of the Sea, opened for signature 10 December 1982, 1833 UNTS 3 (entered into force 16 November 1994)

UN General Assembly Resolution 55/63, UN Doc A/RES/55/63 (4 December 2000) ('Combating the Criminal Misuse of Information Technologies')

UN Security Council Resolution 1373, UN Doc S/RES/1373 (28 September 2001)

UN Security Council Resolution 1540, UN Doc S/RES/1540 (28 April 2004)

UN Security Council Resolution 1624, UN Doc S/RES/1624 (14 September 2005)

Universal Declaration on the Eradication of Hunger and Malnutrition, adopted at the World Food Conference, Rome, Italy, 5–16 November 1974

Vienna Convention on the Law of Treaties, opened for signature 23 May 1969, 115 UNTS 331 (entered into force 27 January 1980)

ACCT	ASEAN Convention on Counter Terrorism
ACWC	ASEAN Commission on the Promotion and Protection of the Rights of Women and Children
ADMM	ASEAN Defence Ministers' Meeting
AERR	ASEAN Emergency Rice Reserve
AICHR	ASEAN Intergovernmental Commission on Human Rights
AIFS	ASEAN Integrated Food Security
APEC	Asia-Pacific Economic Cooperation
APTERR	ASEAN Plus Three Emergency Rice Reserve
ARF	ASEAN Regional Forum
ASEAN	Association of Southeast Asian Nations
ASEANTOM	ASEAN Network of Regulatory Bodies on Atomic Energy
CERT	Computer Emergency Response Team
COMMIT	Coordinated Mekong Ministerial Initiative against Trafficking
CSCE	Conference on Security and Co-operation in Europe
CTTC	Counter-Terrorism and Transnational Crime

CUES	Code for Unplanned Encounters at Sea
DOC	Declaration on the Conduct of Parties in the South China Sea
DPRK	Democratic People's Republic of Korea
EAS	East Asia Summit
EAERR	East Asia Emergency Rice Reserve
ETS	European Treaty Series
EU	European Union
FAO	Food and Agricultural Organization
IAEA	International Atomic Energy Agency
ICT	Information and Communications Technology
IMO	International Maritime Organization
Lao PDR	Lao People's Democratic Republic
LOSC	Law of the Sea Convention
MLAT	Mutual Legal Assistance Treaty
NEC-SSN	Nuclear Energy Cooperation Sub-Sector Network
OECD	Organisation for Economic Co-operation and Development
OSCE	Organization on Security and Co-operation in Europe
PRC	People's Republic of China
ReCAAP	Regional Cooperation Agreement on Combating Piracy and Armed Robbery against Ships in Asia
SAARC	South Asian Association for Regional Cooperation
SOM	Senior Officials Meeting

SOMTC	Senior Officials Meeting on Transnational Crime
SPA-FS	Strategic Plan of Action on Food Security
SUA	Suppression of Unlawful Acts against the Safety of Maritime Navigation
TAC	Treaty of Amity and Cooperation in Southeast Asia
TIP	Trafficking in Persons
UK	United Kingdom
UN	United Nations
UNCTAD	UN Conference on Trade and Development
UNTS	UN Treaty Series
US	United States of America
ZOPFAN	Zone of Peace, Freedom and Neutrality

Introduction

The security landscape of Southeast Asia is rapidly changing. While many Southeast Asian nations remain steadfast in maintaining their political regime stability against external interference, the region's contemporary security landscape has diversified with the emergence of various non-traditional security issues.[1] Transnational security challenges such as terrorism, piracy, cyber-attacks, human trafficking and people smuggling require concerted or collective responses. The rise of the People's Republic of China (PRC) as a regional great power is adding complexity to the regional security dynamics, which is illustrated by the increased tensions in the South China Sea involving multiple parties over territorial and maritime disputes. These dynamic changes to the region's security landscape pose challenges to the ability of Southeast Asian nations to steer through multilateral processes for regional integration.

The Association of Southeast Asian Nations (ASEAN) has achieved deeper regional market integration to lay a socio-economic foundation for the development of a regional community, yet interstate trust is by no means assured as Southeast

---

[1] Mely Caballero-Anthony and Alistair D. B. Cook (eds.), *Non-Traditional Security in Asia: Issues, Challenges and Framework for Action* (Singapore: Institute of Southeast Asian Studies, 2013); Mely Caballero-Anthony, Ralf Emmers and Amitav Acharya (eds.), *Non-Traditional Security in Asia: Dilemmas in Securitization* (Aldershot: Ashgate, 2006).

1

Asian nations remain jealously observant of the vested interests of their state security apparatus.[2] The notion of state sovereignty is prominent as a means to guarantee security and stability in societies confronting cultural, ethnic and religious diversity. For these reasons, the region is generally known for its preference for a 'soft' form of international law – vague, informal and non-binding instruments and arrangements – as the mode of multilateral cooperation,[3] of which ASEAN has become the pivot.

United for fear of Communist expansion in Southeast Asia,[4] Indonesia, Malaysia, the Philippines, Singapore and Thailand established ASEAN on 8 August 1967 to promote regional peace and stability.[5] It was designed to provide a political platform with a dual function of collectively maintaining the political stability of each member state and protecting regional security from external interference at the height of Cold War politics.[6]

---

[2] Jörg Friedrichs, 'East Asian Regional Security: What the ASEAN Family Can (Not) Do' (2012) 52(4) *Asian Survey* 754, 761.

[3] See Pablo Pareja-Alcaraz, 'International Law and East Asia's Regional Order: The Strengthening of a Fundamental Institution' in Matthew Happold (ed.), *International Law in a Multipolar World* (Abingdon: Routledge, 2012) 224, 239–40.

[4] Kishore Mahbubani and Jeffery Sng, *The ASEAN Miracle: A Catalyst for Peace* (Singapore: NUS Press, 2017) 51–9; Rodolfo C Severino, *ASEAN* (Singapore: Institute of Southeast Asian Studies, 2008) 5.

[5] Declaration Constituting an Agreement Establishing the Association of South-East Asian Nations, adopted 8 August 1967, 1331 UNTS 235 (entered into force 8 August 1967).

[6] For details, see e.g., Alice D. Ba, *(Re)Negotiating East and Southeast Asia: Region, Regionalism, and the Association of Southeast Asian Nations* (Stanford, CA: Stanford University Press, 2009) 42–100; Shaun Narine,

Its existence was threatened several times, for example, by the Sabah dispute between the Philippines and Malaysia, a decade-long struggle against Vietnam's occupation of Cambodia from 1978 to 1989, and the Asian financial crisis of 1997. ASEAN survived all these challenges and even thrived with the expansion of membership to include Brunei Darussalam in 1984, Vietnam in 1995, Lao People's Democratic Republic (Lao PDR) and Myanmar in 1997, and Cambodia in 1999. The political platform provided by ASEAN has further expanded with a wider geographical reach through ASEAN Plus Three, the ASEAN Regional Forum (ARF) and, most recently, the East Asia Summit (EAS), while maintaining 'ASEAN centrality' at the core of this regional order.

As a regional organisation to promote – rather than maintain or restore – peace and stability, ASEAN sets itself apart from the United Nations (UN) collective security system in that it does not have powers to maintain and restore international peace and security through centralised mechanisms to adopt and enforce mandatory decisions.[7] Although it may function as one of 'regional arrangements or agencies' for peaceful settlement of regional disputes,[8] its legal authority to

'ASEAN and the Management of Regional Security' (1998) 71(2) *Pacific Affairs* 195, 196–201; P Saipiroon, *ASEAN Governments' Attitudes towards Regional Security 1975–1979* (Bangkok: Institute of Asian Studies, 1982) 5–7.

[7] The literature on the UN collective security system is voluminous, but see especially, Nicholas Tsagourias and Nigel D. White, *Collective Security: Theory, Law and Practice* (Cambridge: Cambridge University Press, 2013).

[8] Charter of the United Nations, opened for signature 26 June 1945, 1 UNTS xvi (entered into force 24 October 1945) (hereinafter UN Charter) art. 52.

deal with regional conflicts is limited.[9] In lieu of a UN-like regional collective security organisation, ASEAN has arguably emerged as an alternative model of 'security institution' or as a 'security community-building institution'.[10] Rather than adopting or enforcing mandatory decisions, ASEAN manages intra-regional relations through a diplomatic convention known as the 'ASEAN Way' – intra-mural dialogues and consultations based on close working relationships between senior government officials.[11]

Due to these characteristics of the association's foundation and its mode of operation, ASEAN's role in and contribution to regional security has been extensively studied and debated.[12] These debates often proceed on the basis of a pre-determined

[9] Alexander Orakhelashvili, *Collective Security* (Oxford: Oxford University Press, 2011) 78. For detailed analysis, see Robert Beckman, Leonardo Bernard, Hao Duy Phan, TAN Hsien-Li and Ranyta Yusran, *Promoting Compliance: The Role of Dispute Settlement and Monitoring Mechanisms in ASEAN Instruments* (Cambridge: Cambridge University Press, 2016) ch 2.

[10] Amitav Acharya, *Constructing a Security Community in Southeast Asia: ASEAN and the Problem of Regional Order* (3rd edn, Abingdon: Routledge, 2014) 19. For debates about the characterisation of ASEAN, see Chapter 1.2.

[11] For historical development of the 'ASEAN Way', see e.g., Jürgen Haacke, *ASEAN's Diplomatic and Security Culture: Origins, Development and Prospects* (Abingdon: Routledge, 2003).

[12] See e.g., Acharya, above n. 10; Alan Collins, *Building a People-Oriented Security Community in the ASEAN Way* (Abingdon: Routledge, 2013); Christopher B. Roberts, *ASEAN Regionalism: Cooperation, Values and Institutionalisation* (Abingdon: Routledge, 2012); Mely Caballero-Anthony, *Regional Security in Southeast Asia: Beyond the ASEAN Way* (Singapore: Institute of Southeast Asian Studies, Singapore, 2005); See Seng Tan, *The Making of the Asia Pacific: Knowledge Brokers and the*

paradigm of what a security institution ought to be doing in making an assessment of ASEAN's various activities, or the lack thereof, under the prevailing political and diplomatic circumstances of the region.[13] There has been little reflection upon how these disparate activities help us understand the legal nature and form of ASEAN's authority that has become clearer over the course of its development.

In contrast to the extensive debate and study of security institution-building in Southeast Asia by political scientists, little attention has been given to the legal analysis of ASEAN's authority to address contemporary regional security issues. The absence of a legal perspective in this debate means that the legal nature and form of ASEAN's authority, and the corresponding legal relationship with its member states, in dealing with various regional security issues remains unclear. This leaves a critical gap in understanding ASEAN's commitment to the building of a 'rules-based' community.[14]

Following the adoption of the ASEAN Charter in 2007,[15] only a handful of legal commentaries have emerged. They have tended to critique the ASEAN Charter's legal regime – rather misleadingly – by comparing it with

---

Politics of Representation (Amsterdam: Amsterdam University Press, 2013).

[13] See Chapter 1.2.

[14] ASEAN Political-Security Community Blueprint 2025, in Kuala Lumpur Declaration on ASEAN 2025: Forging Ahead Together, adopted at the 27th ASEAN Summit, Kuala Lumpur, Malaysia, 2 November 2015, Section A.

[15] Charter of the Association of Southeast Asian Nations, adopted 20 November 2007, 2624 UNTS 223 (entered into force 15 December 2008).

supranational, constitutionalised bodies such as the European Union (EU) and identifying the lack of enforcement mechanisms as a weakness.[16] Instead, the legal debate about ASEAN's role in regional security must proceed on the premise that ASEAN is neither equipped nor designed to operate as a collective security institution with a delegation of enforcement powers (the first model of security institution as represented by the UN and African Union),[17] or as an integrated regional institution directed towards a centralised common defence and security mechanism (the second model of security institution as represented by the EU).[18]

ASEAN, on the other hand, is built upon alternative security approaches such as cooperative security and comprehensive security, which acknowledges the multidimensional nature of security that spans across political, economic and

[16] See e.g., Diane A. Desierto, 'ASEAN's Constitutionalization of International Law: Challenges to Evolution under the New ASEAN Charter' (2011) 49 *Columbia Journal of Transnational Law* 268, 295–305; LIN Chun Hung, 'ASEAN Charter: Deeper Regional Integration under International Law?' (2010) 9 *Chinese Journal of International Law* 821, 829–36.

[17] See generally, Tsagourias and White, above n. 7; Orakhelashvili, above n. 9; Ademola Abass, *Regional Organisations and the Development of Collective Security: Beyond Chapter VIII of the UN Charter* (Oxford and Portland, OR: Hart Publishing, 2004); Dan Sarooshi, *The United Nations and the Development of Collective Security: The Delegation by the UN Security Council of its Chapter VII Powers* (Oxford: Oxford University Press, 1999).

[18] See generally, Panos Koutrakos, *The EU Common Security and Defence Policy* (Oxford: Oxford University Press, 2013); Martin Trybus and Nigel D. White (eds.), *European Security Law* (Oxford: Oxford University Press, 2008).

social realms. These alternative approaches provide the conceptual and normative foundation upon which ASEAN is to form concerted or collective responses to contemporary security issues through more decentralised, dynamic processes of decision-making and implementation.[19]

Free from preconceptions of collective security or regional integration models, this study examines the legal nature and form of ASEAN's authority as the basis for a distinct model of security institution, built on mutually constitutive interactions between ASEAN and its member states in dealing with diverse regional security issues. By looking beyond the veneer of diplomacy and prevailing political circumstances, this study identifies the ways in which ASEAN can exercise its legal authority through detailed examination of its engagement with select security challenges in Southeast Asia. The 'legal authority' of ASEAN in the context of this study encompasses, in a broad meaning of the term, ASEAN's institutional ability to engage in normative processes, which has been nurtured through its engagement and interactions with its member states in response to shared security threats in practice.

To that end, the study engages in both a textual and contextual examination of relevant ASEAN instruments, guided by the governing principles of non-interference, comprehensive security, the 'ASEAN Way', and shared commitment and

---

[19] For these alternative security approaches, see especially, Hitoshi Nasu, 'The Expanded Conception of Security and International Law: Challenges to the UN Collective Security System' (2011) 3(3) *Amsterdam Law Forum* 15, 30–2.

collective responsibility. This is done through a careful examination of ASEAN instruments and the corresponding practice of
its member states, with a particular focus on the ways in which
ASEAN contributes to the development, localisation and internalisation of relevant norms and rules of international law in
dealing with contemporary security challenges confronting the
region.

For the purpose of this book, ASEAN instruments
consist of ASEAN treaties, declarations, communiqués and
other documents that are adopted at an ASEAN official
forum. These instruments, as well as their internalisation into
domestic law and policy, inform the contextual analysis of
ASEAN's legal authority. The term 'norm development' refers
to ASEAN's adoption of its own legal response to a regional
security issue in the form of an ASEAN instrument, whereas
'norm localisation' means adaptation of international norms
and rules as they are applied within ASEAN's legal contexts.[20]
The term 'norm internalisation' is distinguished from the mere
domestic implementation of international law; instead, it
encompasses the process of incorporating global or regional
norms and rules as collectively interpreted and translated into a
set of concrete actions for domestic implementation.

The primary regional focus of this study consists of
ASEAN and its member states: Brunei, Cambodia, Indonesia,
Lao PDR, Malaysia, Myanmar, the Philippines, Singapore,
Thailand and Vietnam. However, the analysis also encompasses

---

[20] See Amitav Acharya, 'How Ideas Spread: Whose Norms Matter? Norm
Localization and Institutional Change in Asian Regionalism' (2004) 58
International Organization 239, 245–53.

a wider geographical reach through ASEAN's external relations in various related forums with other countries in the Asia-Pacific and influential extra-regional powers such as Australia, the PRC, the United States (US) and the United Kingdom (UK),[21] to the extent that activities in these forums inform the legal nature and form of ASEAN's authority in addressing regional security challenges.

The following regional security issues are selected for examination: nuclear security (Chapter 2), counter-terrorism (Chapter 3), maritime security (Chapter 4), cyber security (Chapter 5), human trafficking and people smuggling (Chapter 6) and food security (Chapter 7). These issues are representative – but by no means a comprehensive list – of a range of traditional and non-traditional security challenges across different spatial domains where significant regional attention has been drawn.[22]

There are other areas that are not necessarily characterised as regional security issues, in which ASEAN has facilitated regional cooperation: for example, environmental problems such as haze;[23] public health threats such as the

[21] For ASEAN's external relations in general, see Marise Cremona et al., *ASEAN's External Agreements: Law, Practice and the Quest for Collective Action* (Cambridge: Cambridge University Press, 2015). See also, ZOU Keyuan, *China-ASEAN Relations and International Law* (Oxford: Chandos Publishing, 2009).

[22] Energy and resource security will be dealt with in the context of nuclear security (Chapter 2) and also in comparison with ASEAN's approach to food security (Chapter 7).

[23] ASEAN Agreement on Transboundary Haze Pollution, adopted 11 June 2002 (entered into force 25 November 2003).

spread of Avian Influenza in 2004;[24] and disaster management and emergency relief,[25] as highlighted with the critical role that ASEAN played in facilitating humanitarian relief to Myanmar after Cyclone Nargis struck the southern part of the country on 2 May 2008.[26] While regional cooperation in these areas may raise similar legal issues such as the interpretation and application of the principle of non-interference, the inquiry made in this book is essentially distinct in that it focuses on how the commonly shared interest to address a regional security issue has informed the way in which ASEAN establishes and exercises its legal authority within the parameters set by the governing principles.

Chapter 1 discusses the legal context in which ASEAN has established itself as a regional 'security institution'. It assesses the various views expressed by commentators as to how ASEAN's role in regional security can appropriately be characterised, a debate which, this chapter argues, often proceeds on the basis of prevailing geopolitical conditions in the region, rather than what the member states have committed themselves to in legal terms. It then introduces the legal, normative and institutional framework underpinning ASEAN's legal authority

---

[24] ASEAN established a task force to address the threat of Avian Influenza: see Chairman's Statement of the 11th ASEAN Summit, Kuala Lumpur, Malaysia, 12 December 2005, para. 17.

[25] ASEAN Agreement on Disaster Management and Emergency Response, adopted 26 July 2005 (entered into force 24 December 2009).

[26] For details, see e.g., Collins, above n. 12, 137–46; Karin Loevy, 'The Legal Politics of Jurisdiction: Understanding ASEAN's Role in Myanmar's Disaster, Cyclone Nargis' (2015) 5 *Asian Journal of International Law* 55; Jürgen Haacke, 'Myanmar, the Responsibility to Protect, and the Need for Practical Assistance' (2009) 1 *Global Responsibility to Protect* 156.

to address regional security issues, as the groundwork for contextual analysis undertaken in the remainder of the book.

Chapter 2 addresses the first common security issue that Southeast Asian nations collectively decided to pursue: nuclear security. ASEAN member states engaged in nuclear security cooperation initially through the creation of the Southeast Asian Nuclear Weapon-Free Zone, which has subsequently been developed to deal with nuclear non-proliferation and nuclear energy regulation. After reviewing ASEAN's engagement with nuclear security, this chapter examines the current state of nuclear power regulation among ASEAN member states and the role of ASEAN in developing institutional responses to the regulatory challenge of nuclear security in Southeast Asia.

Chapter 3 surveys and assesses the various ASEAN instruments that ASEAN and its wider regional arrangements, in particular the ARF, have adopted to combat terrorism which, in the pre-9/11 era, was treated as a subset of transnational organised crime. It identifies discrepancies between the promises rendered in those ASEAN instruments, on the one hand, and what ASEAN member states have collectively accomplished against terrorism on the other. This analysis reveals ASEAN's normative contribution in shaping the regional approach to counter-terrorism and in facilitating the construction and implementation of national counter-terrorism law and policy by member states.

Chapter 4 examines how ASEAN's legal and policy responses to maritime security threats such as piracy and maritime terrorism have developed and interacted with the global legal framework. After reviewing the historical developments and maritime security measures adopted, it examines ASEAN's legal authority to deal with non-traditional security issues such as piracy, and contrasts it with the limited role that ASEAN has played in relation to the South China Sea dispute.

The tension between traditional and non-traditional security concerns is further explored in Chapter 5 with another spatial dimension: cyberspace. As Information and Communications Technology (ICT) dependence continues to permeate Southeast Asian societies, the significance of securing cyberspace has increasingly been recognised by regional authorities. After reviewing the cyber security law and policy developed by ASEAN, this chapter discusses how the exercise of ASEAN's legal authority complements international initiatives to extend the application of international law to cyberspace, while taking account of the unique geopolitical and socio-economic conditions that prevail in Southeast Asia. This discussion reveals how ASEAN has filled the gap in the international initiatives on cyber security by focusing attention upon the particular needs of Southeast Asian nations.

Chapters 6 and 7 shift the focus to non-traditional security issues. The notion of non-traditional security is integral to the principle of comprehensive security espoused by ASEAN and the ARF. After introducing the distinct issues of human trafficking and people smuggling in the region, Chapter 6 discusses the extent to which ASEAN has contributed to the development, localisation and internalisation of international norms and rules that are relevant to the association's handling of these issues. It reveals the significant role that various multilateral processes have played in negotiating the legal and institutional constraints on ASEAN that stem from the principle of non-interference, in order to facilitate legislative responses and law enforcement capacity-building in ASEAN member states.

In contrast, Chapter 7 shows that ASEAN member states have maintained nationalistic food security laws and policies, despite the fact that ASEAN has developed and promoted a cooperative food security framework to address long-term and short-term food security issues. It reviews the history of ASEAN's food security efforts with particular focus on the regional action adopted in the aftermath of the 2007–2008 food crisis, and compares this with the approach adopted by the Asia-Pacific Economic Cooperation (APEC) forum. It then examines the extent to which domestic food security laws and policies in ASEAN member states are aligned with the regional legal and policy framework developed by ASEAN.

This book concludes by defining ASEAN's legal authority that has emerged from the examination of the processes of norm development, localisation and internalisation in the previous chapters. Consideration will also be given to future challenges to ASEAN's legal authority, sketching out those areas where ASEAN will be required to revisit the legal nature and form of its authority in order to maintain its status as the central security institution in Southeast Asia.

Chapter 1

ASEAN as a Security Institution: Its Legal, Normative and Institutional Framework

1.1 Defining ASEAN as a 'Security Institution'

There is no question that ASEAN is in legal terms classified as an 'international organisation', at least in accordance with the definition provisionally adopted by the UN International Law Commission as 'an organization established by a treaty or other instrument governed by international law and possessing its own international legal personality'.[1] While this legal qualification is important in ascertaining ASEAN's legal capacity on the international plane – for example, the power to conclude an international agreement or to assume international responsibility for an internationally wrongful act – it does not explain ASEAN's legal characteristics such as the legal nature and form of its authority to address regional security issues and the corresponding legal relationship with its member states. Therefore, the term 'security institution' is instead used to characterise ASEAN for its role in dealing with regional security issues.

Drawing on the definition of international institution proposed by Robert O. Keohane,[2] the term 'security institution' is

[1] International Law Commission, 'Draft Articles on the Responsibility of International Organizations' (2011) *Yearbook of International Law* vol. II, Part 2, art. 2(a).
[2] Robert O. Keohane, *International Institutions and State Power* (Boulder, CO: Westview Press, 1989) 3.

designed to capture a wide range of 'persistent and connected sets of rules, formal and informal, that prescribe behavioural roles, constrain activity, and shape expectations', with an impact on the action of their members towards continuing cooperation in the provision of security.[3] As will be discussed below, this definition allows us to avoid assessment of ASEAN according to any pre-determined paradigm of a security institution and, instead, to discuss its institutional ability to perform normative functions in dealing with regional security issues by examining the formal and informal rules that prescribe behavioural roles, constrain activity and shape expectations.

After reviewing the debates regarding the characterisation of ASEAN's role in regional security, this chapter provides ASEAN's legal, normative and institutional framework as the foundation upon which the legal nature and form of its authority for regional security is to be explored in subsequent chapters.

1.2 Characterising ASEAN's Role in Regional Security

Commentators have variously expressed their views as to how ASEAN's role in regional security can be characterised, often according to their pre-determined paradigms of a security institution. Writing in 1987, Michael Leifer considered ASEAN to be an 'embryonic security community' practising cooperative

---

[3] For discussion of the definitions of security institution, see Hitoshi Nasu and Kim Rubenstein, 'Introduction: The Expanded Conception of Security and Institutions' in Hitoshi Nasu and Kim Rubenstein (eds.), *Legal Perspectives on Security Institutions* (Cambridge: Cambridge University Press, 2015) 1, 3–9.

security as both a complement, and an alternative, to balance-of-power politics.[4] Likewise, Amitav Acharya argues that ASEAN may be considered as a 'security community-building institution', with an emphasis on ASEAN's less tangible role in dispute settlement through its norm development and processes of interaction, which in his view may be more desirable than the establishment of a formal, legalistic inter-governmental authority.[5]

David Martin Jones and Michael L. R. Smith, on the other hand, have adopted a more conservative view, observing that ASEAN 'remains an essentially intergovernmental [organisation] ... rather than [an organisation] that possesses the institutional infrastructure to develop into a "mature" security community'.[6] Alan Collins has argued that ASEAN can more appropriately be characterised as a 'security regime' – the concept that Robert Jervis suggested to explain systems that constrain state behaviour based on reciprocity[7] – rather than as

---

[4] Michael Leifer, 'ASEAN's Search for Regional Order' in Chin Kin Wah and Leo Suryadinata (eds.), *Michael Leifer: Selected Works on Southeast Asia* (Singapore: Institute of Southeast Asian Studies, 2005) 98, 100. See also, Michael Leifer, 'The ASEAN Peace Process: A Category Mistake' (1999) 12 *The Pacific Review* 25, 27–8.

[5] Amitav Acharya, *Constructing a Security Community in Southeast Asia: ASEAN and the Problem of Regional Order* (3rd edn, Abingdon: Routledge, 2014) 19–21.

[6] David Martin Jones and Michael L. R. Smith, 'Making Process, Not Progress: ASEAN and the Evolving East Asia Regional Order' (2007) 32 *International Security* 148, 184. See also, Nicholas Khoo, 'The ASEAN Security Community: A Misplaced Consensus' (2015) 2 *Journal of Asian Security and International Affairs* 180, 186–9; Sheldon Simon, 'ASEAN and Multilateralism: The Long Bumpy Road to Community' (2008) 30 *Contemporary Southeast Asia* 264, 288.

[7] Robert Jervis, 'Security Regimes' (1982) 36 *International Organization* 357.

a 'security community', in the absence of civil society organisations playing a prominent role.[8]

Similarly, diverse views have been expressed with
regard to the ARF and its role in regional security. Mark
Beeson describes it as a 'genuine region-wide grouping unam-
biguously dedicated to facilitating a "security dialogue" and
enhancing regional stability'.[9] While acknowledging that confidence-building measures directed by the ARF may decrease
the risk of escalating security dilemmas, John Ikenberry and
Jitsuo Tsuchiyama consider that it is unlikely to have deter-
rence and defence functions when a crisis erupts.[10] Indeed, the
ARF is based on the idea of cooperative security – an
approach or mechanism that promotes security through confidence-building and transparency measures with the primary
objective of reducing tensions and conflicts within a group of
states – rather than institutionalising the balance of power to
regional order.[11] From this perspective John Garofano

---

[8] Alan Collins, 'Forming a Security Community: Lessons from ASEAN'
(2007) 7 *International Relations of the Asia-Pacific* 203.

[9] Mark Beeson, *Institutions of the Asia Pacific: ASEAN, APEC and Beyond*
(Abingdon: Routledge, 2009) 56.

[10] John G. Ikenberry and Jitsuo Tsuchiyama, 'Between Balance of Power and
Community: The Future of Multilateral Security Co-operation in the Asia-
Pacific' (2002) 2 *International Relations of the Asia-Pacific* 69, 86.

[11] See generally, Hiro Katsumata, *ASEAN's Cooperative Security Enterprise:
Norms and Interests in the ASEAN Regional Forum* (Basingstoke: Palgrave
Macmillan, 2009); Amitav Acharya, 'Regional Institutions and Security in the
Asia-Pacific: Evolution, Adaptation, and Prospects for Transformation' in
Amitav Acharya and Evelyn Goh (eds.), *Reassessing Security Cooperation in
the Asia-Pacific: Competition, Congruence, and Transformation* (Cambridge,
MA: The MIT Press, 2007) 1, 23–7; Michael Leifer, *The ASEAN Regional
Forum* (Adelphi Paper No. 302, London: International Institute for Strategic

considers that there are 'insurmountable barriers on the road to a possible security community'.[12]

On the other hand, those who consider increasingly 'softer' roles in maintaining regional security, rather than materialist conceptions of power and politics, have found a greater potential in the ARF as a 'security institution'. Dominik Heller characterises the ARF as a 'security institution' that provides an important channel of communication on a wide range of security issues and facilitates common perceptions and understanding among regional and extra-regional actors.[13] Alastair Iain Johnston recognises the ARF's socialising role in encouraging Chinese leaders to identify concerns through consultation, rather than to act unilaterally, to facilitate its incorporation into a peaceful and stable region.[14] Hiro Katsumata characterises the ARF as a forum for the development and practice of regional norms that shape regional security relations.[15]

Studies, 1996) 55. Cf. Ralf Emmers, *Cooperative Security and the Balance of Power in ASEAN and the ARF* (Abingdon: RoutledgeCurzon, 2003).

[12] John Garofano, 'Power, Institutions, and the ASEAN Regional Forum' (2002) 42(3) *Asian Survey* 502, 520.

[13] Dominik Heller, 'The Relevance of the ASEAN Regional Forum (ARF) for Regional Security in the Asia-Pacific' (2005) 27 *Contemporary Southeast Asia* 123, 133–7.

[14] Alastair Iain Johnston, 'The Myth of the ASEAN Way? Explaining the Evolution of the ASEAN Regional Forum' in Helga Haftendorn, Robert Keohane and Celeste Wallander (eds.), *Imperfect Unions* (Oxford: Oxford University Press, 1999) 287. But see Mark Beeson, 'ASEAN's Ways: Still Fit for Purpose?' (2009) 22 *Cambridge Review of International Affairs* 333, 337.

[15] Hiro Katsumata, 'Establishment of the ASEAN Regional Forum: Constructing a "Talking Shop" or a "Norm Brewery"?' (2006) 19 *The Pacific Review* 181.

A variety of views discussed above focus primarily on what ASEAN and the ARF currently do or are likely to do, rather than what they are competent or authorised to do. Some of these commentators then express their assessment according to their pre-determined paradigm of what a 'security community' or a 'security institution' ought to be doing to be characterised as such.[16] There appears to be a critical omission in the existing literature in that it has neglected to examine ASEAN's normative role in facilitating the formation and development of 'persistent and connected sets of rules, formal and informal, that prescribe behavioral roles, constrain activity, and shape expectations',[17] in dealing with regional security issues.

This omission is critical for two related reasons. First, as Acharya observes, ASEAN's institutional rationale lies in seeking to reduce power asymmetries through institutional commitment,[18] rather than institutionalising power asymmetries through a collective security mechanism like the UN.[19] ASEAN is designed to collectively provide political stability for all member states in ways that increase the cost of unilateral action and induce them to voluntarily adopt more peaceful strategies towards their

[16] See Amitav Acharya, 'Arguing about ASEAN: What Do We Disagree about?' (2009) 22 *Cambridge Review of International Affairs* 493, 495-7.

[17] Keohane, above n. 2, 3.

[18] Amitav Acharya, 'Regional Institutions and Asian Security Order: Norms, Power, and Prospects for Peaceful Change' in Muthiah Alagappa (ed.), *Asian Security Order: Instrumental and Normative Features* (Stanford, CA: Stanford University Press, 2003) 210, 221.

[19] Cf. G. John Ikenberry, *After Victory: Institutions, Strategic Restraint, and the Rebuilding of Order After Major Wars* (Princeton, NJ: Princeton University Press, 2001) 9.

neighbours. Second, ASEAN, particularly through the ARF, has to engage in 'soft balancing' with extra-regional powers in an attempt to protect its own interests and stability in the strategically uncertain environment created by those external actors. For example, ASEAN welcomes the PRC's rise to protect ASEAN member states from Western liberal pressure whilst being wary of its self-interested assertive acts, and at the same time, welcomes the US 're-balancing' policy to restrain the PRC's growing assertiveness whilst wary of the uncertainty of its commitment and the forceful imposition of Western liberal values.[20]

These two geopolitical factors that characterise Southeast Asia render the traditional, power-based collective security model untenable, instead prompting ASEAN member states to build broad norm-based, flexible institutions with a view to institutionalising cooperation.[21] As explained in the Introduction, ASEAN may function as a regional arrangement or agency within the meaning of Article 52 of the UN Charter,[22]

[20] See generally, T. J. Pempel, 'Soft Balancing, Hedging, and Institutional Darwinism: The Economic-Security Nexus and East Asian Regionalism' (2010) 10 *Journal of East Asian Studies* 209, 221–8; Evelyn Goh, 'Great Powers and Hierarchical Order in Southeast Asia: Analyzing Regional Security Strategies' (2008) 32(3) *International Security* 113; Yuen Foong Khong, 'Coping with Strategic Uncertainty: The Role of Institutions and Soft Balancing in Southeast Asia's Post-Cold War Strategy' in J. J. Suh, Peter J. Katzenstein and Allen Carlson (eds.), *Rethinking Security in East Asia: Identity, Power, and Efficiency* (Stanford, CA: Stanford University Press, 2004) 172.

[21] See Pempel, above n. 20, 231–2; Nikolas Busse, 'Constructivism and Southeast Asian Security' (1999) 12 *The Pacific Review* 39.

[22] Charter of the United Nations, opened for signature 26 June 1945, 1 UNTS xvi (entered into force 24 October 1945) (hereinafter UN Charter) art. 52.

but its legal authority in dealing with regional conflicts is limited and its institutional role is premised upon alternative security approaches such as cooperative security and comprehensive security.[23] These two designations – 'regional arrangement or agency' and 'security institution' – are not mutually exclusive; neither is there any normative relationship between them. The designation of ASEAN as a 'security institution' is descriptive of its characteristics in regional cooperation for the provision of security, rather than its legal qualification within the broader UN collective security system. It is thus submitted that the examination of the actual legal framework, norms and institutional machinery that prescribe behavioural roles, constrain activity and shape expectations is key to understanding ASEAN's legal authority as a security institution in dealing with regional security challenges.

1.3 ASEAN's Legal Framework for Regional Security

ASEAN emerged as a political forum for regional cooperation among Southeast Asian nations, with the adoption of the 1967 Bangkok Declaration.[24] Established against the backdrop of the 1955 Bandung Conference and the

---

[23] See above n. 11 and accompanying text, and below Section 1.4.2.

[24] Declaration Constituting an Agreement Establishing the Association of South-East Asian Nations, adopted 8 August 1967, 1331 UNTS 235 (entered into force 8 August 1967) (hereinafter Bangkok Declaration). Its original membership was comprised of Indonesia, Malaysia, Thailand, Singapore and the Philippines, but was left open for participation to all Southeast Asian nations: Bangkok Declaration, para. 4.

subsequently formed Non-Aligned Movement,[25] ASEAN embodied the rejection of military alliances and its member states' determination to 'ensure their stability and security from external interference in any form or manifestation in order to preserve their national identities in accordance with the ideals and aspirations of their peoples'.[26] As Acharya has observed, the security arrangement thus put in place was as much for the stability of the entire region from external interference as for the protection of the national polity of each member state.[27]

This institutional rationale is also reflected in the 1971 Declaration on the Zone of Peace, Freedom and Neutrality (ZOPFAN), whereby the original member states committed themselves to regional efforts 'to secure the recognition of, and respect for, South East Asia as a Zone of Peace, Freedom and Neutrality, free from any form or manner of interference by outside Powers'.[28] Proposed originally by Malaysia in an attempt to limit the PRC's influence in the region, the idea of ZOPFAN embodied the aspirations for regional security autonomy, yet caused tension due to the continued dependence of some members on external powers for military

---

[25] See generally, Amitav Acharya and See Seng Tan, *Bandung Revisited: The Legacy of the 1955 Asian-African Conference for International Order* (Singapore: NUS Press, 2008).

[26] Bangkok Declaration, above n. 24, preamble para. 4. For the drafting background of the Bangkok Declaration and analysis of this particular paragraph, see Acharya, above n. 5, 44–6.

[27] Acharya, above n. 5, 49–52.

[28] Declaration on the Zone of Peace, Freedom and Neutrality, adopted at the Special ASEAN Foreign Ministers' Meeting, Kuala Lumpur, 27 November 1971, para. 1.

assistance.[29] Despite significant disagreement over the means to achieve ZOPFAN, the debate on this issue fostered the normative foundation for institutionalising ASEAN in the political-security field.[30]

The most foundational legal instrument underpinning the legal framework of ASEAN remains the 1976 Treaty of Amity and Cooperation in Southeast Asia (TAC).[31] Article 1 of the TAC enshrines the promotion of 'perpetual peace [and] everlasting amity' as one of the purposes of ASEAN. More specifically, Article 11 requires the High Contracting Parties to 'endeavour to strengthen their respective national resilience in . . . security fields'. The TAC has subsequently been acceded to by many non-ASEAN states such as Australia, Japan, the PRC, Russia, the UK, the US and the EU.[32] Accession by external powers reinforces this regional security framework by insisting that non-ASEAN states comply with the legal principles and rules that are applied in ASEAN when they are dealing with its member states, though those principles and rules may be understood differently.[33]

---

[29] Acharya, above n. 5, 52–6.

[30] For detailed analysis, see Kei Koga, *Reinventing Regional Security Institutions in Asia and Africa: Power Shifts, Ideas, and Institutional Change* (Abingdon: Routledge, 2017) 28–50; Kei Koga, 'Institutional Transformation of ASEAN: ZOPFAN, TAC, and the Bali Concord I in 1968–1976' (2014) 27 *The Pacific Review* 729.

[31] Adopted 24 February 1976, 1025 UNTS 319 (entered into force 15 July 1976).

[32] The status of accession to TAC is available at http://agreement.asean.org/agreement/detail/60.html.

[33] For analysis, see Daniel Seah, 'The Treaty of Amity and Cooperation in Southeast Asia: The Issue of Non-Intervention and Its Accession by Australia and the USA' (2012) 11 *Chinese Journal of International Law* 785;

ASEAN's legal framework has been buttressed with the adoption of the 2007 ASEAN Charter,[34] which sets out the maintenance and enhancement of regional security as one of its mandates. The Charter is designed to 'codify all ASEAN norms, rules, and values', with all previously concluded ASEAN agreements continuing to apply and be legally binding.[35] With the aim 'to enhance regional resilience by promoting greater political, security . . . cooperation' and 'to respond effectively, in accordance with the principle of comprehensive security, to all forms of threats, transnational crimes and transboundary challenges',[36] the ASEAN Charter sets out the principle of 'shared commitment and collective responsibility in enhancing regional peace, security and prosperity'.[37] In many respects, the ASEAN Charter has retained and formalised the existing ASEAN norms, structure and arrangements, but has also initiated changes that have the potential to facilitate deeper regional integration.[38]

Michael Bliss, 'Amity, Cooperation and Understanding(s): Negotiating Australia's Entry into the East Asia Summit' (2007) 26 *Australian Year Book of International Law* 63, 81–5.

[34] Charter of the Association of Southeast Asian Nations, adopted 20 November 2007, 2624 UNTS 223 (entered into force 15 December 2008) (hereinafter ASEAN Charter). See also, Walter Woon, *The ASEAN Charter: A Commentary* (Singapore: NUS Press, 2016); Daniel Seah, 'The ASEAN Charter' (2009) 58 *International and Comparative Law Quarterly* 197.

[35] Kuala Lumpur Declaration on the Establishment of the ASEAN Charter, Kuala Lumpur, Philippines, 12 December 2005, para. 3.

[36] ASEAN Charter, above n. 34, arts. 1(2) and 1(8) respectively.

[37] Ibid., art. 2(2)(b).

[38] See Simon S. C. Tay, 'The ASEAN Charter: Between National Sovereignty and the Region's Constitutional Moment' (2008) 12 *Singapore Year Book of International Law* 151, 169–70.

There are also issue-specific treaties that ASEAN member states have adopted to address particular regional security issues such as nuclear security, counter-terrorism, food security and human trafficking.[39] In addition to these treaty instruments, there are numerous ASEAN non-treaty instruments, some of which are relevant to the formation of ASEAN as a 'security institution'. Of particular significance are the Bali Concord II,[40] the ASEAN Political-Security Community Blueprint,[41] and the Bali Concord III,[42] which collectively provide a roadmap for the establishment of the ASEAN Political-Security Community as an independent goal of ASEAN cooperation.[43] Although those instruments are not legally binding per se, they may be considered as

[39] Treaty on the Southeast Asia Nuclear Weapon-Free Zone, adopted 15 December 1995, 1981 UNTS 129 (entered into force 25 March 1997); ASEAN Convention on Counter Terrorism, adopted 13 January 2007 (entered into force 27 May 2011); ASEAN Plus Three Emergency Rice Reserve Agreement, adopted 7 October 2011; ASEAN Convention against Trafficking in Persons, Especially Women and Children, adopted 21 November 2015 (entered into force 8 March 2017).

[40] Declaration of ASEAN Concord II (Bali Concord II), Bali, Indonesia, 7 October 2003.

[41] ASEAN Political-Security Community Blueprint 2025, in Kuala Lumpur Declaration on ASEAN 2025: Forging Ahead Together, adopted at the 27th ASEAN Summit, Kuala Lumpur, Malaysia, 2 November 2015; ASEAN Political-Security Community Blueprint, adopted at the 14th ASEAN Summit, Cha-am Hua Hin, Thailand, 1 March 2009.

[42] Bali Declaration on ASEAN Community in a Global Community of Nations (Bali Concord III), adopted at the 19th ASEAN Summit, Bali, Indonesia, 17 November 2011.

[43] See Lee Leviter, 'The ASEAN Charter: ASEAN Failure or Member Failure?' (2010) 43 *New York University Journal of International Law and Politics* 159, 187–8.

subsequent agreements or subsequent practice for the purposes of interpreting the text of the aforementioned treaties,[44] and contributing to their internalisation, as will be discussed in detail in subsequent chapters.

1.4 ASEAN's Normative Framework for Regional Security

The fundamental principles of ASEAN are set out in Article 2 of the TAC and Articles 1 and 2 of the ASEAN Charter, and include respect for the independence, sovereignty, equality, territorial integrity and national identity of its member states; renunciation of the threat or use of force, aggression or other actions in any manner inconsistent with international law; peaceful settlement of disputes; non-interference in their internal affairs; and the principle of comprehensive security to respond to all forms of threats, transnational crime and transboundary challenges.[45] Of these, renunciation of the threat or use of force and peaceful settlement of disputes are nothing more than the adoption of general international security law principles.[46] Unique to the ASEAN security regime are the four governing principles that are designed to guide the institution in dealing with regional security issues: non-interference; comprehensive security; the

---

[44] Vienna Convention on the Law of Treaties, opened for signature 23 May 1969, 115 UNTS 331 (entered into force 27 January 1980) arts. 31(3)(a) and (b).

[45] TAC, above n. 31, arts. 2(a) and (b), (e), (d), (c); ASEAN Charter, above n. 34, arts. 2(2)(a), (c), (d), (e), art. 1(8) respectively.

[46] See e.g., UN Charter, above n. 22, arts. 2(3) and 2(4).

'ASEAN Way'; and shared commitment and collective responsibility in enhancing regional peace, security and prosperity.

1.4.1 The Principle of Non-Interference

The ASEAN principle of non-interference is a concept that is often confused with, but clearly distinct from, the principle of non-intervention under general international law. While the exact content of the principle of non-intervention (particularly non-forcible forms of intervention such as political interference and economic coercion) remains the subject of ongoing debate,[47] it is nonetheless well established as a structural principle of international law that protects sovereign states from 'coercive' interference by other states under customary international law,[48] or by UN bodies under Article 2 (7) of the UN Charter.

The ASEAN principle of non-interference, on the other hand, is a regional norm that has been developed within ASEAN. It prohibits otherwise lawful forms of interference that would not constitute an 'intervention' (or 'coercive' interference) under general international law – such as criticising another government's actions in dealing with their

---

[47] See e.g., Maziar Jamnejad and Michael Wood, 'The Principle of Non-Intervention' (2009) 22 *Leiden Journal of International Law* 345, 367–77; Lori Fisler Damrosch, 'Politics Across Borders: Nonintervention and Nonforcible Influence over Domestic Affairs' (1989) 83 *American Journal of International Law* 1.

[48] *Case Concerning Military and Paramilitary Activities in and against Nicaragua (Nicaragua v. United States)* [1986] ICJ Rep 14, 108 para. 205.

domestic political affairs or providing assistance for political campaigns in another state.[49] Article 2(2)(e) of the ASEAN Charter refers to 'non-interference in the internal affairs of ASEAN Member States', while subparagraph (f) reaffirms 'respect for the right of every Member State to lead its national existence free from external interference, subversion and coercion'.

At the core of this regional norm is a shared concern about the preservation of national identities and the destabilisation of political regimes within ASEAN member states through external interference, even in the absence of coercion.[50] This was originally expressed in the 1963 Manila Accord, in which Indonesia, the Federation of Malaya and the Philippines (as part of their plan to establish 'Mapilindo') acknowledged their shared interest in protecting the region 'from subversion in any form or manifestation in order to preserve their respective national identities'.[51] These countries also agreed that 'foreign bases – temporary in nature – should not be allowed to be used directly or indirectly to subvert the

---

[49] See e.g., Hitoshi Nasu, 'Revisiting the Principle of Non-Intervention: A Structural Principle of International Law or a Political Obstacle to Regional Security in Asia?' (2013) 3 *Asian Journal of International Law* 25, 36–7; Acharya, above n. 5, 56–9; Amitav Acharya, *Regionalism and Multilateralism: Essays on the Cooperative Security in the Asia-Pacific* (Singapore: Eastern Universities Press, 2003) 227–30.

[50] See Pablo Pareja-Alcaraz, 'International Law and East Asia's Regional Order: The Strengthening of a Fundamental Institution' in Matthew Happold (ed.), *International Law in a Multipolar World* (Abingdon: Routledge, 2012) 224, 232.

[51] Manila Accord, signed 31 July 1963, 550 UNTS 344 (entered into force 31 July 1963) para. 3.

national independence of any of the three countries'.[52] These agreements were then incorporated, albeit differently worded, into the preamble of the 1967 Bangkok Declaration.[53] The ASEAN Charter specifically addresses concerns about external interference in Article 2(2)(k), calling for 'abstention from participation in any policy or activity, including the use of its territory, pursued by any ASEAN Member State or non-ASEAN State or any non-State actor, which threatens the sovereignty, territorial integrity or political and economic stability of ASEAN Member States'.

Although it is firmly established as a regional norm, the principle of non-interference has not necessarily been consistently applied or practised within ASEAN. Commentators have observed instances of political interference by various ASEAN member states, such as those in Cambodia during its transitional period until it was finally admitted to the Association on 30 April 1999, and in Myanmar under the policies of 'constructive engagement' and 'flexible engagement' with a view to promoting political change.[54]

Attempted policy shifts towards 'constructive engagement' and 'flexible engagement' in the 1990s, although

---

[52] Joint Statement by the Philippines, the Federation of Malaya and Indonesia, signed 5 August 1963, 550 UNTS 356 (entered into force 5 August 1963) para. 11.

[53] For analysis, see Acharya, above n. 5, 44–6.

[54] See e.g., Lee Jones, *ASEAN, Sovereignty and Intervention in Southeast Asia* (Basingstoke: Palgrave Macmillan, 2012) 135–48, 180–210; John Funston, *ASEAN and the Principle of Non-Intervention – Practice and Prospects* (Singapore: Institute of Southeast Asian Studies, 2000) 5–8.

largely unsuccessful,[55] indicate ASEAN's struggle to reconcile the principle of non-interference with the need to meet the contemporary challenges posed by ever-deepening economic interdependence and the influence of globalisation.[56] As Lee Jones observes, while it is generally accepted that ASEAN needs to maintain its coherence and relevance, there has only been a limited degree of consensus about what this means in practice; not least due to the different levels of recognition that the regional interest in the protection of political regimes is interdependent in nature between the original and the newer member states.[57]

This challenge to the coherent application of the principle of non-interference has loomed large as an increasingly greater range of regional security issues confront ASEAN, particularly since the dawn of the new millennium. Under the ASEAN Charter, ASEAN member states also commit themselves to 'enhanced consultation' on matters seriously affecting the common interest,[58] which according to Walter Woon, 'may plausibly cover domestic problems that

---

[55] See e.g., Hiro Katsumata, 'Why is ASEAN Diplomacy Changing? From "Non-Interference" to "Open and Frank Discussions"' (2004) 44 *Asian Survey* 237; Robin Ramcharan, 'ASEAN and Non-Interference: A Principle Maintained' (2000) 22(1) *Contemporary Southeast Asia* 60; Carlyle A Thayer, 'Reinventing ASEAN: From Constructive Engagement to Flexible Intervention' (1999) 3 *Harvard Asia Pacific Review* 67; Jürgen Haacke, 'The Concept of Flexible Engagement and the Practice of Enhanced Interaction: Intramural Challenges to the "ASEAN Way"' (1999) 12 *The Pacific Review* 581.

[56] Nasu, above n. 49, 39. [57] Jones, above n. 54, 214–15.

[58] ASEAN Charter, above n. 34, art. 2(2)(g).

spill over borders or imperil ASEAN cooperation with external partners'.[59]

Tension thus arises, as will be discussed below, between the traditional norm of non-interference, purported to protect the security of a political regime from external interference, and the contemporary norm of shared commitment and collective responsibility, purported to protect region-wide security interests. How the principle of non-interference is interpreted or applied to accommodate the competing security interests can only be ascertained through a careful examination of the practice of ASEAN and its member states.

1.4.2 The Principle of Comprehensive Security

While ASEAN bodies, particularly the ARF, are built upon the idea of cooperative security,[60] there has been a gradual redefinition of their role in regional security as transnational security challenges started confronting the region. The 2003 Bali Concord II, for example, refers to various security issues such as environmental security, maritime security and military defence as areas for regional cooperation. It then envisages the establishment of the ASEAN Security Community, which subscribes to the 'principle of comprehensive security'.[61]

This principle has been incorporated into Article 1 (8) of the ASEAN Charter, which calls upon its member

---

[59] Woon, above n. 34, 61.   [60] See above n. 11 and accompanying text.
[61] Bali Concord II, above n. 40, Section A, para. 2.

states to 'respond effectively, in accordance with the principle of comprehensive security, to all forms of threats, transnational crimes and transboundary challenges'.[62] The ASEAN Political-Security Community Blueprint, originally adopted in 2009 and revised in 2015, refers to a cohesive, peaceful, stable and resilient region with 'shared responsibility for comprehensive security'.[63] This principle is also reiterated in the 2011 Bali Concord III.[64] It is thus arguable that the principle of comprehensive security has been established as a governing norm, guiding ASEAN's normative development, decision-making and implementation for regional security.

The notion of comprehensive security acknowledges the multidimensional nature of security, encompassing both non-military and military concerns, and tends to focus on process rather than substance. As such, it is closely aligned with the security perspectives adopted internally by each ASEAN member state,[65] and is congruent with ASEAN's rejection of collective defence as its raison d'être (even though some of its member states are involved in military alliances and security partnerships with external powers). Therefore, it

[62] ASEAN Charter, above n. 34, art. 1(8).
[63] ASEAN Political-Security Community Blueprint 2025, above n. 41, para. 5.2; ASEAN Political-Security Community Blueprint 2009, above n. 41, Section B.
[64] Bali Concord III, above n. 42, Section A, para. 1(g).
[65] For details, see Muthiah Alagappa, 'Comprehensive Security: Interpretations in ASEAN Countries' in Robert A. Scalapino, Seizaburo Sato, Jusuf Wanandi and Sung-Joo Han (eds.), *Asian Security Issues: Regional and Global* (Berkeley, CA: Institute of East Asian Studies, University of California Press, 1988) 50.

must be clearly distinguished from the UN-like collective security system.

Unlike human security, the principle of comprehensive security is a prescriptive norm guiding how security threats should be addressed, rather than whose security threats are to be addressed.[66] As Acharya observes, '[t]he concept of human security, which stresses the security of people rather than states or governments, is more of a challenge to the national security concept in Asia, but precisely for that reason, it has yet to gain genuine acceptance from the region's governments'.[67] Indeed, there is no consensus among ASEAN member states as to how the international doctrine of the responsibility to protect – which is rooted in the notion of human security – might operate in the region.[68] This reluctance arguably informs the way in which ASEAN member states have interpreted ASEAN's role in dealing with essentially human security issues such

[66] Hitoshi Nasu, 'The Expanded Conception of Security and International Law: Challenges to the UN Collective Security System' (2011) 3(3) *Amsterdam Law Forum* 15, 31–2. See also, Hitoshi Nasu, 'The Place of Human Security in Collective Security' (2013) 18 *Journal of Conflict and Security Law* 95.

[67] Amitav Acharya, 'Securitization in Asia: Functional and Normative Implication' in Mely Caballero-Anthony, Ralf Emmers, and Amitav Acharya (eds.), *Non-Traditional Security in Asia: Dilemmas in Securitization* (Aldershot: Ashgate, 2006) 247, 249.

[68] See e.g., Sriprapha Petcharamesree, 'ASEAN Human Rights Regime and Mainstreaming the Responsibility to Protect: Challenges and Prospects' (2016) 8 *Global Responsibility to Protect* 133; Rizal Sukma, 'The ASEAN Political and Security Community (APSC): Opportunities and Constraints for the R2P in Southeast Asia' (2012) 25 *The Pacific Review* 135.

as human trafficking and people smuggling, as will be discussed in Chapter 6.

ASEAN member states officially acknowledged the importance of intra-regional security cooperation in 1992 and embarked on the establishment of a political-security community in 2003. Yet, they have invested their cooperative efforts only in select areas of non-traditional security.[69] The precise understanding of the principle in terms of what 'comprehensive' means may vary depending on the context in which it is formulated. For example, comprehensive security, as defined by the Organization on Security and Co-operation in Europe (OSCE), encompasses politico-military, economic/ecological, and human dimensions including human rights.[70] In a study report commissioned by former Japanese Prime Minister Masayoshi Ohira, comprehensive security was envisaged as the balancing of three complementary (but possibly contradictory) approaches to national security: (1) self-help; (2) efforts to make the entire international political environment more favourable to Japan's national security; and (3) efforts to make part of the international political environment more favourable to Japan's national security through coordination with other states that share the same ideals and interests.[71]

---

[69] See e.g., Vientiane Action Programme 2004–2010, adopted at the 10th ASEAN Summit, Vientiane, Lao PDR, 29 November 2004, Annex 1, Ref No. 1.2–1.5.

[70] Antonio Ortiz, 'Neither Fox Nor Hedgehog: NATO's Comprehensive Approach and the OSCE's Concept of Security' (2008) 4 *Security and Human Rights* 284, 284–5.

[71] Comprehensive Security Study Group, 'Sougou Anzenhoshou Kenkyuu Group Houkokusho [Comprehensive Security Study Group Report]' in

In the context of ASEAN, particularly drawing on similar concepts used in their domestic constituencies, commentators have observed that comprehensive security has been seen as an instrument of political regime legitimisation.[72] Comprehensive security emphasises the mutually constituted relationship between regime security and economic development, and places paramount importance on regime stability through economic development and cooperation. While the concept of comprehensive security is still at a nascent stage of development as a governing principle of ASEAN, there is a potential for further clarification of its meaning, role and relationship with other regional principles.

1.4.3 The 'ASEAN Way': The Institutional Decision-Making Principle

ASEAN has traditionally been making decisions on the basis of informality, expediency, consensus-building and non-

Ohira Souri no Seisaku Kenkyuukai Houkokusho [Policy Study Group Reports Commissioned by Prime Minister Ohira] (Tokyo: Liberal Democratic Party, 1980) 301, 309–13. For an English commentary on Japan's comprehensive security policy at that time, see J. W. M. Chapman, R. Drifte and I. T. M. Gow, Japan's Quest for Comprehensive Security: Defense – Diplomacy – Dependence (London: Frances Pinter, 1983).

[72] Mely Caballero-Anthony, 'Non-Traditional Security in Asia: The Many Faces of Securitisation' in Andrew F. Cooper, Christopher W. Hughes and Philippe de Lombaerde (eds.), Regionalism and Global Governance: The Taming of Globalisation (Abingdon: Routledge, 2008) 187, 193; Mely Caballero-Anthony, 'Revisioning Human Security in Southeast Asia' (2004) 28(3) Asian Perspective 155, 160–2; Acharya, above n. 67, 249; Alagappa, above n. 65, 56.

confrontational bargaining, which is often described as the 'ASEAN Way'.[73] Originally adopted as the working method of the 'Mapilindo',[74] the 'ASEAN Way' has evolved as a unique diplomatic convention to avoid and manage interstate conflicts in the region, with an emphasis on close consultation and consensus.[75] This approach to institutional decision-making has certain advantages, such as avoiding open disagreement and conflict, and providing scope for states to 'agree to disagree', rather than allowing disagreement to cloud and undermine the spirit of regionalism.[76] This traditional decision-making rule, originating from a particular style of decision-making in village societies in Southeast Asia,[77] has been codified in Article 20(1) of the ASEAN

[73] See e.g., Rodolfo C. Severino, *Southeast Asia in Search of an ASEAN Community: Insights from Former ASEAN Secretary-General* (Singapore: Institute of Southeast Asian Studies, 2006) 1–37.

[74] Joint Statement by the Philippines, the Federation of Malaya and Indonesia, above n. 52, para. 10.

[75] The 'ASEAN Way' can also be understood more broadly in conjunction with other ASEAN norms such as the principle of non-interference: see generally, Jürgen Haacke, *ASEAN's Diplomatic and Security Culture: Origins, Development and Prospects* (Abingdon: Routledge, 2003); Beverly Loke, 'The "ASEAN Way": Towards Regional Order and Security Cooperation?' (2005) 30 *Melbourne Journal of Politics* 8; Hiro Katsumata, 'Reconstruction of Diplomatic Norms in Southeast Asia: The Case of Strict Adherence to the "ASEAN Way"' (2003) 25 *Contemporary Southeast Asia* 104; Gillian Goh, 'The "ASEAN Way": Non-Intervention and ASEAN's Role in Conflict Management' (2003) 3(1) *Stanford Journal of East Asian Affairs* 113.

[76] Amitav Acharya, 'Culture, Security, Multilateralism: The "ASEAN Way" and Regional Order' (1998) 19(1) *Contemporary Security Policy* 55, 63.

[77] Ibid., 62; Miles Kahler, 'Legalization as Strategy: The Asia-Pacific Case' (2000) 54 *International Organization* 549, 552.

Charter as the fundamental principle of 'consultation and consensus' in decision-making.

Critical to the decision-making capacity of ASEAN bodies is how the term 'consensus' is defined to give a legal effect to decisions. The definition of 'consensus' does not appear in the ASEAN Charter, which raises many questions. For example, when one of the member states is neither ready to accept nor openly object to a decision, could the affirmative position of the rest be considered as achieving a 'consensus' for the purpose of Article 20(1) of the ASEAN Charter?[78] Could the failure to adopt a decision to take action be understood as achieving a 'consensus' to condone the existing situation?[79]

Within ASEAN, consensus has traditionally been seen as an attempt to create a common understanding to move forward without formal voting for unanimity even if there are misgivings from one or more member states (the 'ASEAN minus X' or '2 plus X' formula), as long as their

---

[78] Notably, the Government of Malaysia dissociated itself from the Chairman's Statement on the Humanitarian Situation in the Rakhine State of Myanmar and denied that the Statement was based on consensus: 'Malaysia Calls ASEAN Chairman's Statement on Rakhine a "Misrepresentation of the Reality"', *New Straits Times*, 24 September 2017, available at www.nst.com.my/news/nation/2017/09/283630/malay sia-calls-asean-chairmans-statement-rakhine-misrepresentation.

[79] Notably, ASEAN failed to adopt a joint communiqué for the first time in its history at the 45th ASEAN Ministerial Meeting in 2012 due to disagreement about a reference to the South China Sea dispute: for details, see Carlyle A. Thayer, 'ASEAN's Code of Conduct in the South China Sea: A Litmus Test for Community-Building' (2012) 10(34) *The Asia-Pacific Journal* No. 4.

interests are not damaged by non-participation or they are not excluded from future participation.[80] It remains to be seen whether the more formalised institutional decision-making process under the ASEAN Charter affects the meaning of 'consensus' in practice. However, too rigid an application of this decision-making rule could undermine the institutional legitimacy of ASEAN by depriving it of the benefits of flexible consensus that it has enjoyed to date.[81]

It is one thing to say that ASEAN bodies have the competence to make decisions by 'consensus' in accordance with Article 20 of the ASEAN Charter, and it is another to claim that ASEAN member states are legally bound by these decisions. Under Article 5 of the Charter, ASEAN member states are required to 'take all necessary measures, including the enactment of appropriate domestic legislation, to effectively implement the provisions of this Charter and to comply with all obligations of membership'. The Charter is silent on whether those 'obligations of membership' extend to declarations and communiqués adopted by ASEAN bodies.[82]

---

[80] See Acharya, above n. 76, 63–4; Woon, above n. 34, 157–9; Seah, above n. 34, 199.

[81] See Seng Tan, 'The Institutionalisation of Dispute Settlements in Southeast Asia: The Legitimacy of ASEAN in De-Securitising Trade and Territorial Disputes' in Hitoshi Nasu and Kim Rubenstein (eds.), *Legal Perspectives on Security Institutions* (Cambridge: Cambridge University Press, 2015) 248, 264–5.

[82] Robert Beckman, Leonardo Bernard, Hao Duy Phan, TAN Hsien-Li and Ranyta Yusran, *Promoting Compliance: The Role of Dispute Settlement and Monitoring Mechanisms in ASEAN Instruments* (Cambridge: Cambridge University Press, 2016) 135.

1.4.4 *The Principle of Shared Commitment and Collective Responsibility*

While the principle of non-interference remains the fundamental principle of ASEAN, it must be balanced against a new principle of 'shared commitment and collective responsibility in enhancing regional peace, security and prosperity'.[83] This principle is a codified expression of ASEAN member states' commitment to regional solidarity in recognition of common threats to shared security interests,[84] adding a normative layer to regional security cooperation. The reference to 'collective responsibility' is of particular significance given the background against which the ASEAN Charter was drafted – only two years after world leaders, including those from Southeast Asia, adopted the World Summit Outcome, in which the notion of the responsibility to protect was unanimously adopted.[85]

As the Report of the High-Level Advisory Panel on the Responsibility to Protect in Southeast Asia observes, '[c]ooperation to protect Southeast Asian peoples from genocide, war crimes, ethnic cleansing and crimes against humanity is a necessary corollary to the establishment of a caring and sharing ASEAN community'.[86] Indeed, on 19 December 2016,

---

[83] ASEAN Charter, above n. 34, art. 2(2)(b).

[84] On the notion of solidarity in security cooperation, see generally, Hanspeter Neuhold, 'Common Security: The Litmus Test of International Solidarity' in Rüdiger Wolfrum and Chie Kojima (eds.), *Solidarity: A Structural Principle of International Law* (Berlin and Heidelberg: Springer, 2010) 193–223.

[85] World Summit Outcome, UN Doc A/60/1 (2005) paras. 138–9.

[86] High-Level Advisory Panel on the Responsibility to Protect in Southeast Asia, 'Mainstreaming the Responsibility to Protect in

the ASEAN Foreign Ministers' Meeting was convened in Yangon to discuss the humanitarian crisis that developed as a result of the killing of Rohingyas, which the Malaysian Prime Minister labelled an act of 'genocide'.[87] The meeting led to Myanmar's agreement to grant 'necessary humanitarian access' to the Rakhine State, which marked a significant development in the practical application of the 'collective responsibility' of ASEAN member states.

Yet this principle, in conjunction with the principle of comprehensive security, creates tension, as it demands ASEAN member states accept that certain issues which threaten regional peace, security and prosperity are beyond the protection of the principle of non-interference, upon which any policy debate must otherwise be formed in ASEAN.[88] ASEAN's approach to the Rohingya crisis in August 2017, triggered by the military offensive in the Rakhine State of Myanmar and the mass influx of refugees produced as a result, illustrated difficulties in reconciling such commitment with the principle of non-interference. The ASEAN Chairman's Statement on this issue, adopted at the sidelines of the UN General Assembly meeting on 23 September 2017, avoided direct reference to Rohingyas and the action of

Southeast Asia: Pathway Towards a Caring ASEAN Community' (Report, 9 September 2014) 3–4, available at https://r2pasiapacific.org/files/382/mainstreaming-r2p-hlap-report-sep-2014.pdf.

[87] Liam Cochrane, 'ASEAN Meeting on Rohingya "Genocide" Ends with Humanitarian Access Promise', ABC News, 20 December 2016, available at www.abc.net.au/news/2016–12-20/asean-meeting-on-rohingyas-secures-humanitarian-access-promise/8133666.

[88] Nasu, above n. 49, 45–50.

Myanmar's security forces against them, while condemning all acts of violence.[89]

It is only through a careful examination of ASEAN's practice that we can clarify the ways in which ASEAN's shared commitment and collective responsibility interacts with more traditional norms, such as the principle of non-interference.[90] Such clarification involves an interpretation of these principles by reference to relevant ASEAN instruments and the corresponding practice of member states, without requiring any legally binding instrument or decision that makes a formal revision to the principles.[91] ASEAN instruments and the

---

[89] ASEAN Chairman's Statement on the Humanitarian Situation in Rakhine State, New York, US, 23 September 2017.

[90] See Alex J. Bellamy and Catherine Drummond, 'The Responsibility to Protect in Southeast Asia: Between Non-Interference and Sovereignty As Responsibility' (2011) 24 *The Pacific Review* 179.

[91] Vienna Convention on the Law of Treaties, above n. 44, arts. 31(3)(a) and 31(3)(b). The subsequent agreements for this purpose does not have to be adopted in a treaty form but are rather based on the fact of agreement or shared understanding formed by a 'common single act': see e.g., Second Report on Subsequent Agreements and Subsequent Practice in relation to the Interpretation of Treaties: Georg Nolte, UN Doc A/CN.4/671 (26 March 2014) 26–9 paras. 54–60. Likewise, although the evidence of subsequent practice can take a variety of forms including the practice of the regional organisation itself, it must reflect a common understanding of the parties regarding the interpretation of a treaty provision: First Report on Subsequent Agreements and Subsequent Practice in relation to Treaty Interpretation: Georg Nolte, UN Doc A/CN.4/660 (19 March 2013) 36–43 paras. 91–110. For detailed analyses, see Richard Gardiner, *Treaty Interpretation* (2nd edn, Oxford: Oxford University Press, 2016) 242–50 and 253–87; Jean-Marc Sorel and Velérie Boré Eveno, '1969 Vienna Convention: Article 31 General Rule of Interpretation' in Olivier Corten and Pierre Klein (eds.), *The Vienna Conventions on the Law of*

corresponding practice of member states will also inform how regional security concerns might be translated into shared commitment and collective responsibility through the process of norm development, localisation and internalisation within ASEAN.

1.5 ASEAN's Institutional Framework for Regional Security

Through its external relations powers, ASEAN has become the focal point of overlapping, multiple regional institutions that address shared security issues within a greater region including, most relevantly, ASEAN Plus Three (namely, Japan, the Republic of Korea and the PRC), the ARF and the EAS. This institutional proliferation is a reflection of the complex strategic interests and options that states are keen to maintain due to political uncertainties and instabilities in the region.[92] This complexity makes it difficult to build an overarching, coherent regional security architecture at least in the immediate future.[93] Nevertheless, the fact that ASEAN, through the conscious efforts to maintain 'ASEAN

Treaties: A Commentary (Oxford: Oxford University Press, 2011) 804, 825–9.

[92] See Tsutomu Kikuchi, 'Asia Taiheiyo ni okeru Chiikiseido no Keisei to Doutai: Chiikiseido wo tsuujiteno Hedge Senryaku to Seido wo meguru Bargaining [The Formation and Dynamics of Regional Institutions in the Asia-Pacific: The Hedge Strategy through Regional Institutions and the Institutional Bargaining]' (2011) 84 *Aoyama Journal of International Politics and Economics* 171.

[93] Cf. William T. Tow and Brendan Taylor, 'What is Asian Security Architecture?' (2010) 36 *Review of International Studies* 95.

centrality',[94] remains as the institutional bedrock for the operation of these family institutions, means that their legal authority, decision-making and the legal effects of their decisions are all derivative of the ASEAN legal framework.

While the institutional framework in the region is evolving with a view to the development of the ASEAN Political-Security Community,[95] the following analysis focuses on the current institutional structure for regional security, which essentially centres upon the ASEAN structure including its extended bodies, particularly the ARF and the EAS. The ASEAN Plus Three is a process that facilitates a multilateral approach to economic cooperation in East Asia more widely, without an institutional structure based on a constituent instrument.[96] Given that ASEAN provides the institutional framework for its operation this process is not explored in detail below; however, it should be noted that the

---

[94] For details, see e.g., Alice D. Ba, 'The Institutionalization of Southeast Asia: ASEAN and ASEAN Centrality' in Alice D. Ba, Cheng-Chwee Kuik and Sueo Sudo (eds.), *Institiutionalizing East Asia: Mapping and Reconfiguring Regional Cooperation* (Abingdon: Routledge, 2016) 11, 22–4; Alice D. Ba, 'ASEAN Centrality Imperiled? ASEAN Institutionalism and Challenges of Major Power Institutionalisation' in Ralf Emmers (ed.), *ASEAN and Institutionalization of East Asia* (Abingdon: Routledge, 2011) 114.

[95] On the emergence and development of the idea, see especially, Acharya, above n. 5, 226–32.

[96] For details, see e.g., Chu Shulong, 'The ASEAN Plus Three Process and East Asian Security Cooperation' in Amitav Acharya and Evelyn Goh (eds.), *Reassessing Security Cooperation in the Asia-Pacific: Competition, Congruence, and Transformation* (Cambridge, MA: The MIT Press, 2007) 155; Richard Stubbs, 'ASEAN Plus Three: Emerging East Asian Regionalism?' (2002) 42(3) *Asian Survey* 440.

ASEAN Plus Three is a process that ASEAN has indeed employed in addressing food security, as will be discussed in Chapter 7.

As an international organisation possessing international legal personality,[97] ASEAN is required to exercise powers that are expressly provided for by its constituent instrument.[98] While ASEAN initially emerged as a political forum, its institutional structure has been clarified with the adoption of the ASEAN Charter in 2007. Under the Charter, the ASEAN Summit is authorised as the primary decision-making body to 'deliberate, provide policy guidance and take decisions' on any issues relating to the wide range of objectives of ASEAN,[99] including the maintenance and enhancement of peace, security and stability in the region.[100]

Of particular relevance is the power conferred upon the ASEAN Summit to 'address emergency situations affecting ASEAN by taking appropriate actions'.[101] Thus, the ASEAN Summit is the primary decision-making body with the general competence to make decisions on the maintenance and enhancement of peace, security and stability in the region, and to take actions to address 'emergency

---

[97] ASEAN Charter, above n. 34, art. 3. See also, Hao Duy Phan, 'The Association of Southeast Asian Nations: International Legal Personality and Its Treaty-Making Power' (2016) 13 *International Organizations Law Review* 273.

[98] *Jurisdiction of the European Commission of the Danube between Galatz and Braila (Advisory Opinion)* [1927] PCIJ Reports (Series B) No. 14, 64, para. 179.

[99] ASEAN Charter, above n. 34, art. 7. For details, see Woon, above n. 34, 85–93.

[100] ASEAN Charter, above n. 34, art. 1(1).   [101] Ibid., art. 7(2)(d).

situations'. Yet, it remains to be seen what 'action' the ASEAN Summit is competent to take and how the ASEAN Summit may exercise its legal authority for the maintenance and enhancement of regional security.

The Charter also establishes the ASEAN Coordinating Council as its subsidiary body, and ASEAN Community Councils to implement the ASEAN Summit's decisions under their respective purview.[102] However, the Charter more or less preserves the pre-existing institutional structure. Thus, ASEAN Sectoral Ministerial Bodies – such as the ASEAN Ministerial Meeting, established in 1968 as 'the principal organ responsible for overall policy direction of ASEAN',[103] and the ASEAN Defence Ministers' Meeting (ADMM), established in 2006 in order to 'promote regional peace and stability through dialogue and cooperation in defence and security'[104] – continue to play a critical role. These forums are supported by respective ASEAN Senior Officials Meetings (SOMs), which comprise permanent secretaries and officials from the relevant ministries of member states.

The ARF, on the other hand, is specifically designated in the 2003 Bali Concord II as 'the primary forum in enhancing political and security cooperation in the Asia-Pacific

---

[102] Ibid., arts. 8–9. For details, see Woon, above n. 34, 93–9.

[103] Joint Communiqué of the 9th ASEAN Ministerial Meeting, Manila, Philippines, 24–26 June 1976, para. 22. For details of its role and history, see Woon, above n. 34, 102–4.

[104] Concept Paper for the Establishment of the ASEAN Defence Ministers' Meeting, adopted at the 1st ASEAN Defence Ministers' Meeting, Kuala Lumpur, Malaysia, 9 May 2006, para. 6(a).

region'.[105] Although the ARF was not founded by any constituent instrument, the 1995 Concept Paper provides the rationale for its establishment and the parameters of its activities.[106] The lack of a clear institutional basis may well be due to the resistance of member states against a legalised form of security institution.[107] The rationale for the creation of the ARF was 'the need to develop a more predictable and constructive pattern of relations for the Asia-Pacific region', as agreed upon by the participants of the first ARF Ministerial Meeting, held in Bangkok in July 1994.[108]

With a gradual evolutionary approach, the ARF's role was to expand in three stages: (1) promotion of confidence-building measures; (2) development of preventive diplomacy mechanisms; and (3) development of conflict resolution mechanisms.[109] Yet, the ARF's actual activities have spanned across a broad range of issues, from nuclear security to arms control, maritime security, the Asian financial crisis, the impact of globalisation on regional security, and counter-terrorism and transnational crimes, particularly after the

[105] Bali Concord II, above n. 40, para. 6.
[106] The ASEAN Regional Forum: A Concept Paper, adopted at the 2nd ARF Meeting, Bandar Seri Begawan, Brunei Darussalam, 1 August 1995 (hereinafter ARF Concept Paper).
[107] See Noel M. Morada, 'The ASEAN Regional Forum: Origins and Evolution' in Jürgen Haacke and Noel M. Morada (eds.), *Cooperative Security in the Asia-Pacific: The ASEAN Regional Forum* (Abingdon: Routledge, 2010) 13, 15; Alice Ba, 'The ASEAN Regional Forum: Maintaining the Regional Idea in Southeast Asia' (1997) 52 *International Journal* 635, 644–6.
[108] ARF Concept Paper, above n. 106, para. 7.   [109] Ibid., para. 6.

terrorist attacks in New York on 11 September 2001 and in Bali on 12 October 2002.[110]

The ARF's institutional structure also has unique features. First, its institutional decision-making is housed in ASEAN, with its primary decision-making forum, the ARF Ministerial Meetings, held annually in an ASEAN capital following the ASEAN Ministerial Meeting and chaired by the ASEAN member state that hosts the ASEAN Ministerial Meeting.[111] The rules of procedure are also based on ASEAN norms and practices, with all decisions made by consensus after careful and extensive consultations.[112] ASEAN's central role in the ARF reflects ASEAN member states' shared concerns about the region's vulnerability to manipulation by external powers.[113] Second, as a form of compromise with non-ASEAN states, the ARF Inter-Sessional Meetings and the Inter-Sessional Support Group meetings were set up, which were to be co-chaired with a non-ASEAN state and were to assist the chair of the ARF Senior Officials' Meetings in making recommendations to the Forum.[114] While initially designed to deal with cooperative security activities such as peacekeeping and maritime search-and-rescue operations,[115]

---

[110] For a comprehensive list of security issues that the ARF dealt with between 1994 and 2008, see Morada, above n. 107, 21–3. See also, Jürgen Haacke, 'The ASEAN Regional Forum: From Dialogue to Practical Cooperation' (2009) 22 *Cambridge Review of International Affairs* 427.

[111] ARF Concept Paper, above n. 106, para. 16.   [112] Ibid., para. 20.

[113] Ba, above n. 107, 644–6; Alice D. Ba, *(Re)Negotiating East and Southeast Asia: Region, Regionalism, and the Association of Southeast Asian Nations* (Stanford, CA: Stanford University Press, 2009) ch 6.

[114] Morada, above n. 107, 19.   [115] Leifer, above n. 11, 42.

the Inter-Sessional Meetings came to play a more prominent role in dealing with nuclear non-proliferation, terrorism and transnational crimes after the terrorist attacks in New York and in Bali.[116] Third, the ARF formally incorporates 'Track Two' activities, creating a closer link between the inter-governmental activities and civil society groups.

The 2005 Kuala Lumpur Declaration on the East Asia Summit established the EAS as 'a forum for dialogue on broad strategic, political and economic issues of common interest'.[117] The focus of its activities is 'fostering strategic dialogue and promoting cooperation in political and security issues'.[118] While being characterised as 'an integral part of the overall evolving regional architecture', it has a distinct role as a 'leaders-led Summit for strategic discussions on key issues affecting the region', leaving responsibility for follow-up action and implementation with the ASEAN Secretariat.[119] The EAS has been considered by some as the 'most important hub for multilateral regional security cooperation' in the region,[120] because of the wide coverage of its membership including the ASEAN member states, Australia, India, Japan, New Zealand, the PRC, the Republic of Korea, Russia and the US. The constituent instrument of the EAS is a non-

---

[116] See Chapters 2.2 and 3.2.
[117] Adopted at the 1st East Asia Summit, Kuala Lumpur, Malaysia, 14 December 2005.
[118] Ibid.
[119] Chairman's Statement of the First East Asia Summit, Kuala Lumpur, Malaysia, 14 December 2005, paras. 10, 12 and 13.
[120] Jörg Friedrichs, 'East Asian Regional Security: What the ASEAN Family Can (Not) Do' (2012) 52(4) *Asian Survey* 754, 757.

legally binding document, but, as has been the case with the Conference on Security and Co-operation in Europe (CSCE) founded by the 1975 Helsinki Accord, this does not prevent EAS from being characterised as an institution.

The EAS has been particularly active in the field of non-traditional security. Established in the wake of the 2004 Avian Influenza epidemic, the EAS commenced its operation with the adoption of the 2005 East Asia Summit Declaration on Avian Influenza Prevention, Control and Response, whereby the participating countries pledged to enhance national, regional and international capacities to deal with the epidemic.[121] In 2007, the EAS adopted the Cebu Declaration on East Asian Energy Security[122] and the Singapore Declaration on Climate Change, Energy and the Environment,[123] both of which similarly set out various policy goals and measures for achieving more efficient, cleaner and cost-effective energy supply.

Following a very successful coordination mission led by ASEAN in response to Cyclone Nargis in Myanmar, the EAS adopted the Cha-am Hua Hin Statement on EAS Disaster Management in 2009, for greater cooperation in different aspects of disaster risk reduction and preparedness and for supporting the efforts of ASEAN in enhancing humanitarian coordination.[124] More recently, the EAS adopted the 2012 Declaration on Regional Responses to Malaria Control

[121] Adopted at the 1st East Asia Summit, Kuala Lumpur, Malaysia, 14 December 2005.
[122] Adopted at the 2nd East Asia Summit, Cebu, Philippines, 15 January 2007.
[123] Adopted at the 3rd East Asia Summit, Singapore, 21 November 2007.
[124] Adopted at the 4th East Asia Summit, Cha-am Hua Hin, Thailand, 25 October 2009.

and Addressing Resistance to Antimalarial Medicines,[125] in response to growing concerns about an emerging public health threat posed by widespread parasitic resistance to antimalarial medicines. Further, in 2013 the EAS adopted the Declaration on Food Security,[126] following the 2012 Phnom Penh Declaration on the East Asia Summit Development Initiative, which encouraged EAS countries to cooperate in promoting food security.[127]

This brief account of EAS activities since its inception in 2005 clearly illustrates three characteristics of the institution. First, while promoting cooperation in political and security issues, no direct action or measure is contemplated as its function. Second, the strategic dialogue has exclusively focused on non-traditional security issues such as health security, energy security, environmental security, food security and disaster management. Third, notwithstanding its aspirational objective of fostering strategic dialogue and discussions, its actual activities tend to be reactive and supportive of existing initiatives and measures.

Together with the Shangri-La Dialogue – a global forum of defence and military leaders held annually in Singapore since 2002[128] – the ARF and other ASEAN-based

---

[125] Adopted at the 7th East Asia Summit, Phnom Penh, Cambodia, 20 November 2012.

[126] Adopted at the 8th East Asia Summit, Bandar Seri Begawan, Brunei Darussalam, 10 October 2013.

[127] Adopted at the 7th East Asia Summit, Phnom Penh, Cambodia, 20 November 2012, para. 9.

[128] For details of its origin and development, see David Capie and Brendan Taylor, 'The Shangri-La Dialogue and the Institutionalization of Defence Diplomacy in Asia' (2010) 23 The Pacific Review 359.

multilateral consultative mechanisms such as the EAS are emblematic of ASEAN's emphasis on 'open' and 'inclusive' regionalism.[129] Of these, the ARF and the Shangri-La Dialogue arguably paved the way towards ASEAN's formation of the ADMM-Plus with eight dialogue partners.[130] Regular interaction among ASEAN defence leaders within those older region-wide arrangements presumably enhanced their mutual confidence and raised their comfort levels sufficiently to develop their own defence ministerial forum. This is not to imply that ASEAN regionalism necessarily follows any sequential logic. Indeed, as will be discussed in subsequent chapters, ASEAN member states have often relied on extra-regional powers and global institutions, rather than their own regional association and its mechanisms, to meet their own security needs, not least because of underlying distrust among member states.[131]

[129] ASEAN Defence Ministers' Meeting-Plus (ADMM-Plus): Concept Paper, adopted at the 2nd ASEAN Defence Ministers' Meeting, Singapore, 13–15 November 2007, para. 7(c). See also, See Seng Tan, *Multilateral Asian Security Architecture: Non-ASEAN Stakeholders* (Abingdon: Routledge, 2015) 22–4.

[130] Namely Australia, India, Japan, New Zealand, PRC, Republic of Korea, Russia and the US. For details, see See Seng Tan, 'From Talkshop to Workshop: ASEAN's Quest for Practical Security Cooperation through the ADMM and ADMM-Plus Processes' in Bhubhindar Singh and See Seng Tan (eds.), *From 'Boots' to 'Brogues': The Rise of Defence Diplomacy in Southeast Asia* (Singapore: S. Rajaratnam School of International Studies, 2011) 28, 35–40; See Seng Tan, '"Talking Their Walk"? The Evolution of Defence Regionalism in Southeast Asia' (2012) 8(3) *Asian Security* 232.

[131] Bilahari Kausikan, 'The Roots of Strategic Distrust: The US, China, Japan and Asean in East Asia', *The Straits Times*, 18 November

1.6 The Legal Parameters of ASEAN's Authority as a 'Security Institution'

Examined in light of general rules of international law, ASEAN has prima facie legal authority to adopt findings, recommendations or decisions with regard to any regional security issues by 'consultation and consensus'. This entails certain legal significance in facilitating norm development, localisation and internalisation, even if these do not have a legally binding effect on ASEAN member states. No matter how ASEAN is to be characterised, the preliminary analysis above suggests that its legal and institutional infrastructure potentially provides a 'persistent and connected sets of rules, formal and informal, that prescribe behavioral roles, constrain activity, and shape expectations',[132] in which ASEAN's legal authority can be located at the centre of regional efforts to address shared security issues.

Built upon this legal and institutional infrastructure, the legal parameters of ASEAN's legal authority are set by the four fundamental principles governing the association, namely: non-interference; comprehensive security; decision-making by consultation and consensus; and shared commitment and collective responsibility in enhancing regional peace, security and prosperity. Questions nonetheless remain about the legal nature and form of this authority that has been nurtured within these parameters in relation to contemporary

2014, available at www.straitstimes.com/opinion/the-roots-of-strate gic-distrust-the-us-china-japan-and-asean-in-east-asia.

[132] Keohane, above n. 2, 3.

security challenges in Southeast Asia. How can we define and conceptualise ASEAN's legal authority, in its relationship with member states, to address regional security issues beyond the level of regional security cooperation? How do these governing principles formulate or constrain the ways in which ASEAN may exercise its legal authority in dealing with regional security issues? To what extent can ASEAN use its legal authority to deal with regional security issues involving the significant interests of extra-regional powers such as Australia, the PRC and the US? All of these questions can only be answered through careful observation of actual institutional practice with respect to specific common security concerns shared within ASEAN.

Chapter 2

Nuclear Security

2.1 Introduction

The common security concern shared within ASEAN of external interference and internal subversive activities was reflective of the reality that faced many of its member states during the Cold War when threats of communist insurgency dominated regional politics.[1] ASEAN's role as a security institution diversified following the end of the Cold War due to the perceived need to adapt to the new global security environment,[2] with the rise of new and evolving transnational security issues such as terrorism and cyber-attacks. Nuclear security is the first specific security agenda that Southeast Asian nations collectively decided to pursue, which culminated in the adoption of the Treaty on the Southeast Asia Nuclear Weapon-Free Zone (Bangkok Treaty) in 1995.[3]

The region's engagement with nuclear security has since then expanded, and its focus has shifted from the traditional military threat or use of nuclear weapons to the proliferation of

---

[1] For details, see Lee Jones, *ASEAN, Sovereignty and Intervention in Southeast Asia* (Basingstoke: Palgrave Macmillan, 2012) 39–91.

[2] Leszek Buszynski, 'Southeast Asia in the Post-Cold War Era: Regionalism and Security' (1992) 32(9) *Asian Survey* 830, 846–7.

[3] Adopted 15 December 1995, 1981 UNTS 130 (entered into force 27 March 1997).

nuclear materials and technology – particularly in the context of transnational terrorism – and further to nuclear energy regulation.[4] Despite very limited nuclear capability in Southeast Asia,[5] nuclear security has been high on the agenda for ASEAN due to concerns about its nexus with global power politics and the globalised nature of terrorist networks. An additional dimension has emerged with the increased interest, among Southeast Asian nations, in nuclear energy as an option for satisfying the growing energy demands necessary to maintain rapid economic growth and also for reducing dependence on oil and gas imports to combat climate change.[6]

This chapter begins with an overview of ASEAN's legal framework of nuclear security and its development,

---

[4] Therefore, for the purpose of this chapter, the concept of nuclear security is understood to be broader than the oft-cited definition of nuclear security adopted by the International Atomic Energy Agency (IAEA), which is 'the prevention of, detection of, and response to, criminal or intentional unauthorized acts involving or directed at nuclear material, other radioactive material, associated facilities, or associated activities': IAEA, *Objective and Essential Elements of a State's Nuclear Security Regime: Nuclear Security Fundamentals* (Vienna: IAEA Nuclear Security Series No. 20, 2013) para. 1.1.

[5] There are research nuclear reactors operating in Indonesia, Malaysia, Thailand and Vietnam: James Martin Center for Nonproliferation Studies, Center for Energy and Security Studies, and Vienna Center for Disarmament and Non-Proliferation, 'Prospects for Nuclear Security Partnership in Southeast Asia' (May 2012) 4, available at www.nonpro liferation.org/wp-content/uploads/2014/01/120515_prospects_nuclear_ security_partnership_southeast_asia.pdf.

[6] Ibid., 4–7; Prashanth Parameswaran, 'Southeast Asia's Nuclear Energy Future: Promises and Perils' (Project 2049 Institute, 2009) 1–2, available at https://project2049.net/documents/southeast_asia_nuclear_energy_ future.pdf.

including an introduction to the Southeast Asian Nuclear Weapon-Free Zone and subsequent ASEAN nuclear security initiatives. This is followed by an assessment of the current state of nuclear regulation among ASEAN member states with a view to understanding the normative functions that ASEAN has performed in developing, localising and internalising institutional responses to nuclear security as a regulatory challenge in the region.

2.2 ASEAN's Engagement with Nuclear Security

Since 1997, Southeast Asia has been designated as a nuclear weapon-free zone and has strongly supported and promoted nuclear non-proliferation.[7] The idea to establish a nuclear weapon-free zone emerged as part of the broader agenda for creating ZOPFAN after the ASEAN-SOM decided to focus on the denuclearisation aspect of the ZOPFAN Conceptual Framework.[8] The linkage between the two agendas, which emerged against the political background that prevailed in the 1980s, is articulated in the following remarks made by the then

[7] Art. 1(3) of the ASEAN Charter provides that one of its purposes is '[t]o preserve Southeast Asia as a Nuclear Weapon-Free Zone and free of all other weapons of mass destruction'.

[8] This is a report of the Working Group established by the ASEAN-SOM and was adopted by the First ASEAN Summit in 1976. For the political background, see Amitav Acharya, *Constructing a Security Community in Southeast Asia: ASEAN and the Problem of Regional Order* (3rd edn, Abingdon: Routledge, 2014) 55–56; M. C. Abad Jr., 'A Nuclear Weapon-Free Southeast Asia and its Continuing Strategic Significance' (2005) 27 *Contemporary Southeast Asia* 165, 167–71.

Malaysian Foreign Minister, Tengku Ahmad Rithauddeen, in his opening address at the inaugural meeting of the ASEAN Standing Committee on 10 September 1984:

> We have together agreed in Jakarta to initiate measures in the implementation of Zopfan in our region beginning with the declaration of a nuclear-weapons-free zone in Southeast Asia. The concept of a nuclear-weapons-free zone, of course, is inherent in the Zopfan concept and would constitute one of the attributes or prerequisites of a Zone of Peace, Freedom and Neutrality in Southeast Asia. While the Kampuchea issues has [sic] hampered our efforts towards the realisation of Zopfan, I think it would be a serious setback to the Zopfan concept if we were to await the final resolution of the Kampuchean problem before we begin to exert the necessary steps towards the realisation of the concept.[9]

As with ZOPFAN, the creation of a nuclear weapon-free zone in Southeast Asia also presented challenges, given its potential strategic impacts on the power balance that was maintained through support of external nuclear powers such as the PRC, Soviet Union and the US.[10] It was the end of the Cold War and

---

[9] Remarks made by Tengku Ahmad Rithauddeen, Foreign Minister of Malaysia, at the first meeting of ASEAN Standing Committee, Kuala Lumpur, Malaysia, 10 September 1984, reproduced in J. Soedjati Djiwandono, *Southeast Asia as a Nuclear-Weapons-Free Zone* (Kuala Lumpur: Institute of Strategic and International Studies, 1986) 2.

[10] For details, see Carolina G. Hernandez, 'Southeast Asia – The Treaty of Bangkok' in Ramesh Thakur (ed.), *Nuclear Weapons-Free Zones* (Basingstoke: Palgrave Macmillan, 1998) 81, 84–5; Muthiah Alagappa, *Towards a Nuclear-Weapons-Free Zone in Southeast Asia* (Kuala Lumpur: Institute of Strategic and International Studies, 1987) 6–7.

the stabilisation of Cambodia, with the adoption of the 1991 Paris Accord,[11] that accelerated the process towards the conclusion of the Bangkok Treaty.[12]

The zone is defined to include all the territories, continental shelves and exclusive economic zones of the states parties.[13] While preserving the right of member states 'to use nuclear energy, in particular for their economic development and social progress',[14] the Bangkok Treaty imposes upon the states parties a comprehensive ban on the development, manufacturing, acquisition, possession, transfer, test or use of nuclear weapons inside or outside the zone.[15] It also requires each member state to conclude an agreement with the International Atomic Energy Agency (IAEA) 'for the application of full scope safeguards to its peaceful nuclear activities', and to subject their nuclear programme to 'rigorous nuclear safety assessment conforming to guidelines and standards recommended by the IAEA'.[16]

[11] Final Act of the Paris Conference on Cambodia, UN Doc S/23177/Annex (30 October 1991).

[12] Hernandez, above n. 10, 86.

[13] Bangkok Treaty, above n. 3, arts. 1(a) and 2(1). Compare with the different approach adopted by the South Pacific Nuclear Free Zone Treaty, opened for signature 6 August 1985, 1445 UNTS 177 (entered into force 11 December 1986) (hereinafter Treaty of Rarotonga).

[14] Bangkok Treaty, above n. 3, art. 4(1).

[15] Ibid., art. 3. However, each state party retains the right to decide for itself whether or not to allow the entry or passage of foreign nuclear-armed vessels and aircraft through its territorial sea or archipelagic waters: ibid., art. 7.

[16] Ibid., arts. 4(2)(b) and 5. The IAEA is empowered to administer safeguards over nuclear materials placed under its supervision by the safeguards agreement with a state: Statute of the International Atomic Energy Agency, opened for signature 23 October 1956, 276 UNTS 3

Although all ASEAN member states are party to the Bangkok Treaty, non-ASEAN states which acceded to the TAC are not automatically subject to any additional obligations created therein. Indeed, the Treaty has a Protocol that is open for signature by five nuclear weapon states – namely, the PRC, France, Russia, the UK and the US. However, none of the nuclear weapon states have thus far signed the Protocol due to concern that the inclusion of continental shelves and exclusive economic zones might impose unwarranted restrictions upon military operations. The potential restrictions upon the passage of nuclear-armed navy vessels and aircraft through the zone are of particular concern,[17] especially in the South China Sea where the continental shelves and exclusive economic zones of respective parties are not clearly settled.[18]

As an essential component of ZOPFAN, ASEAN has facilitated the implementation of the Bangkok Treaty, especially through the adoption of the Plan of Action in 2007.[19]

(entered into force 29 July 1957) (as amended on 4 October 1961, 471 UNTS 334) art. III(A).

[17] Art. 3(2) of the Bangkok Treaty requires each state party to undertake not to allow any other state to (a) develop, manufacture or otherwise acquire, possess or have control over nuclear weapons; (b) station nuclear weapons; or (c) test or use nuclear weapons, while acknowledging the freedom of navigation on the high seas in art. 2(2).

[18] Abad Jr., above n. 8, 180–2; Hernandez, above n. 10, 90. By contrast, Protocols to the Treaty of Rarotonga (above n. 13) have largely been ratified by nuclear weapon states. The status of the Treaty and the Protocols are available at http://disarmament.un.org/treaties/t/rarotonga.

[19] Joint Statement on the Commission for the Treaty on the Southeast Asia Nuclear Weapon-Free Zone, Manila, Philippines, 30 July 2007. A new Plan of Action was adopted on 30 June 2013.

The ASEAN Charter enshrines, as one of its purposes, the preservation of Southeast Asia as a nuclear weapon-free zone and a region free of all other weapons of mass destruction.[20] The ASEAN Political-Security Community Blueprint pledges to ensure compliance with the Bangkok Treaty and the Plan of Action.[21] More recently, the Chairman's Statement of the 25th ASEAN Summit, issued on 12 November 2014, acknowledges the importance of the Bangkok Treaty 'as an instrument to ensure regional peace, security and stability'.[22]

ASEAN's engagement with nuclear security has also expanded to include nuclear non-proliferation. The ARF issued its first statement on non-proliferation in 2004 which, pursuant to UN Security Council Resolution 1540,[23] encouraged participants to comply with their respective non-proliferation commitments and to adopt new measures such as effective export control laws and regulations.[24] On 1–3 July 2009, the ARF held its first Inter-Sessional Meeting on Non-Proliferation and Disarmament, in which delegations shared national and regional experiences and discussed

---

[20] Charter of the Association of Southeast Asian Nations, adopted 20 November 2007, 2624 UNTS 223 (entered into force 15 December 2008) art. 1(3).

[21] ASEAN Political-Security Community Blueprint, adopted at the 14th ASEAN Summit, Cha-am Hua Hin, Thailand, 1 March 2009, Section A para. 2.4.

[22] Chairman's Statement of the 25th ASEAN Summit: 'Moving Forward in Unity to a Peaceful and Prosperous Community', Nay Pyi Taw, Myanmar, 12 November 2014, para. 9.

[23] UN Doc S/RES/1540 (28 April 2004).

[24] ASEAN Regional Forum Statement on Non-Proliferation, adopted at the 11th ARF Meeting, Jakarta, Indonesia, 2 July 2004, paras. 2(H), 3 and 4.

challenges to implementing their obligations under Resolution 1540.[25] In 2012, the ARF adopted its Work Plan on Non-Proliferation and Disarmament, which provided a set of measures to promote non-proliferation, disarmament efforts and the peaceful use of nuclear energy.[26]

At the same time, political support for the Southeast Asia Nuclear Weapon-Free Zone appeared to have been re-energised in the context of nuclear non-proliferation. In his speech on 12 February 2013, the ASEAN Secretary-General, Le Luong Minh, characterised the Bangkok Treaty as 'the most important regional treaty on non-proliferation in Southeast Asia – a strategic instrument for peace and security in the region, and a key contribution to the global disarmament and non-proliferation regime'.[27]

The nuclear security agenda in Southeast Asia has also merged with ASEAN's cooperative energy security programmes such as cross-border electricity transmission supply and the creation of a common electricity market.[28] The EAS endorsed regional cooperation for the development and use

[25] Co-Chair's Summary Report of the First ASEAN Regional Forum Inter-Sessional Meeting on Non-Proliferation and Disarmament, Beijing, PRC, 1–3 July 2009, paras. 14–15.

[26] Chairman's Statement of the 19th ASEAN Regional Forum, Phnom Penh, Cambodia, 12 July 2012, para. 14 and Annex 2.

[27] Speech by Le Luong Minh, Secretary General of ASEAN, delivered at the Regional Seminar: Maintaining a Southeast Asia Region Free of Nuclear Weapons, Jakarta, Indonesia, 12 February 2013, para. 7, available at www.asean.org/storage/images/2013/resources/speech/SG%20speech_Regional%20Seminar_Indonesia%20MFA_Feb%202013.pdf.

[28] Andrew Symon, 'Southeast Asia's Nuclear Power Thrust: Putting ASEAN's Effectiveness to the Test?' (2008) 30(1) *Contemporary Southeast*

of civilian nuclear power in the 2007 Singapore Declaration on Climate Change, Energy and the Environment.[29] As Southeast Asian nations start building their nuclear capabilities, pressure has mounted on ASEAN to address nuclear regulatory issues and the potential cross-border impact of a nuclear incident. Indeed, Le Luong Minh acknowledged the fact that 'while several ASEAN Member States have either decided on or are considering the option of going nuclear to meet their energy needs, they are also facing the challenge of ensuring nuclear safety and security'.[30]

Concerns about a nuclear incident as a potential security issue were heightened in the aftermath of the Fukushima nuclear disaster in March 2011, which immediately prompted ASEAN member states to agree 'to develop a coordinated ASEAN approach that would contribute to global undertakings to improve nuclear safety'.[31] In 2012, the Joint Ministerial Statement of the 30th ASEAN Ministers of Energy Meeting expressed an intention to 'develop a coordinated ASEAN approach that would contribute to the global undertaking to improve nuclear safety . . . as well as to promote and uphold the IAEA standards of safety and security in the development of

---

Asia 118, 130–3. See also, Cebu Declaration on East Asian Energy Security, adopted at the 2nd East Asia Summit, Cebu, Philippines, 15 January 2007.

[29] Singapore Declaration on Climate Change, Energy and the Environment, adopted at the 3rd East Asia Summit, Singapore, 21 November 2007, para. 8(e).

[30] Speech by Le Luong Minh, above n. 27, para. 13.

[31] Chair's Statement of the 18th ASEAN Summit: 'ASEAN Community in a Global Community of Nations', Jakarta, Indonesia, 7–8 May 2011, para. 24.

nuclear energy'.[32] The new Plan of Action to Strengthen the Implementation of the Treaty on the Southeast Asia Nuclear Weapon-Free Zone (2013–2017) has consequently incorporated the nuclear safety agenda as part of continuing institutional development.[33]

The focus of the nuclear security agenda in Southeast Asia has thus expanded beyond its original remit – protecting the region from the threat of nuclear weapons – to include cooperation for nuclear non-proliferation and, in the wake of the 2011 Fukushima nuclear disaster, nuclear energy regulation. In each of these different phases, ASEAN has provided a regional platform to coordinate efforts to address nuclear security issues as they emerge. The Bangkok Treaty regime has been reinvigorated as the legal framework through which ASEAN exercises its legal authority to facilitate the development of the regulatory infrastructure that its member states require in order to meet their international obligations and build their own nuclear capabilities.

2.3 Nuclear Security Law and Policy in ASEAN Member States

As anticipated in the Bangkok Treaty, the region's status as a net importer of oil and gas for energy has routinely enlivened consideration of alternative energy sources, including nuclear

---

[32] Joint Ministerial Statement of the 30th ASEAN Ministers of Energy Meeting (AMEM), Phnom Penh, Cambodia, 12 September 2012, para. 11.
[33] Plan of Action to Strengthen the Implementation of the Treaty on the South East Asia Nuclear Weapon-Free Zone (2013–2017), adopted 30 June 2013 (hereinafter 2013 Plan of Action).

energy.[34] National outlooks on nuclear energy are quite disparate,[35] and many ASEAN member states have been delaying or suspending nuclear power development plans for political, financial or safety reasons.[36] Nevertheless, ASEAN member states have taken steps, to a varying degree, to develop regulatory frameworks for nuclear activities. They have ratified or acceded to major nuclear treaties such as the Convention on Early Notification of a Nuclear Incident,[37] the Convention on Nuclear Safety,[38] the Comprehensive Nuclear Test Ban Treaty,[39] and the Additional Protocol to the IAEA Safeguards Agreement,[40] in accordance with their commitments made in the Plans of Action under the Bangkok Treaty (see Table 2.1).

[34] For details, see Catharin Dalpino and Timothy Westmyer, 'Southeast Asia: A Measured Nuclear Policy' in Mike M. Mochizuki and Deepa M. Ollapally (eds.), *Nuclear Debates in Asia: The Role of Geopolitics and Domestic Processes* (Lanham, MD: Rowman & Littlefield, 2016) 185, 186–95; Rajesh Basrur, Koh Swee Lean Collin and Kalyan M. Kemburi, 'Nuclear Energy and Energy Security in Asia: Through the Human Security Lens' in Rajesh M. Basrur and Koh Swee Lean Collin (eds.), *Nuclear Power and Energy Security in Asia* (Abingdon: Routledge, 2012) 1, 12–14.

[35] Parameswaran, above n. 6, 2–3; Symon, above n. 28, 125–8.

[36] For details, see Viet Phuong Nguyen, 'Nuclear Energy in Southeast Asia: A Bridge too Far?', *The Diplomat*, 9 November 2016, available at http://thediplomat.com/2016/11/nuclear-energy-in-southeast-asia-a-bridge-too-far/.

[37] Adopted 26 September 1986, 1457 UNTS 133 (entered into force 27 October 1986).

[38] Adopted 17 June 1994, 1963 UNTS 293 (entered into force 24 October 1996).

[39] Adopted 10 September 1996, 35 ILM 1439 (1996) (not in force).

[40] See Model Protocol Additional to the Agreements between State(s) and the International Atomic Energy Agency for the Application of Nuclear Safeguards, IAEA Doc INFCIRC/540 (Corrected) (1 September 1997) (hereinafter INFCIRC/540). The Additional Protocol strengthens

Table 2.1 *Status of Nuclear Security-Related Treaties and Legislation*

CENNI: Convention on Early Notification of a Nuclear Incident
CNS: Convention on Nuclear Safety
CTBT: Comprehensive Test Ban Treaty
AP: Additional Protocol to the IAEA Safeguards Agreement
a: accession   s: signature   r: ratification   eif: entry into force

	CENNI	CNS	CTBT	AP	Primary Legislative Instruments
Brunei					
Cambodia	a (5 Apr. 2012) eif (5 May 2012)	a (5 Apr. 2012) eif (4 Jul. 2012)	s (26 Sep. 1996) r (10 Nov. 2000)	s (3 Feb. 2015) eif (24 Apr. 2015)	Law on the Prohibition of Chemical, Nuclear, Biological and Radiological Weapons 2009
Indonesia	s (26 Sep. 1986) r (12 Nov. 1993) eif (13 Dec. 1993)	s (20 Sep. 1994) r (12 Apr. 2002) eif (11 Jul. 2002)	s (24 Sep. 1996) r (6 Feb. 2012)	s/eif (29 Sep. 1999)	Law on Nuclear Energy 1997
Lao PDR	a (10 May 2013) eif (9 June 2013)		s (30 Jul. 1997) r (5 Oct. 2000)	s (5 Nov. 2014)	Law on Electricity 2008
Malaysia	s (1 Sep. 1987) eif (2 Oct. 1987)		s (23 Jul. 1998) r (17 Jan. 2008)	s (22 Nov. 2005)	Atomic Energy Licensing Act 1984
Myanmar	a (18 Dec. 1997) eif (18 Jan. 1998)	a (6 Dec. 2016) eif (6 Mar. 2017)	s (25 Nov. 1996)	s (17 Sep. 2013)	Atomic Energy Law 1998

Table 2.1 (cont.)

	CENNI	CNS	CTBT	AP	Primary Legislative Instruments
Philippines	a (5 May 1997) eif (5 Jun. 1997)	s (14 Oct. 1994)	s (24 Sep. 1996) r (23 Feb. 2001)	s (30 Sep. 1997) eif (26 Feb. 2010)	Atomic Energy Regulatory and Liability Act 1968
Singapore	a (15 Dec. 1997) eif (15 Jan. 1998)	a (15 Dec. 1997) eif (15 Mar. 1998)	s (14 Jan. 1999) r (10 Nov. 2001)	s (22 Sep. 2005) eif (31 Mar. 2008)	Radiation Protection Act 2007 (amended in 2014)
Thailand	s (25 Sep. 1987) r (21 Mar. 1989) eif (21 Apr. 1989)		s (12 Nov. 1996)	s (22 Sep. 2005)	Atomic Energy for Peace Act 1961, 2016
Vietnam	a (29 Sep. 1987) eif (30 Oct. 1987)	a (16 Apr. 2010) eif (15 Jul. 2010)	s (24 Sep. 1996) r (10 Mar. 2006)	s (10 Aug. 2007) eif (17 Sep. 2012)	Law on Atomic Energy 2008; Ordinance on Radiation Safety and Control 1996

The construction of new nuclear power plants has been envisaged in the national power development plans in Indonesia, Thailand and Vietnam, which all rely heavily on imported fossil fuels for their domestic energy needs.[41] The Fukushima nuclear disaster in March 2011 in Japan sparked deep concerns about nuclear safety around the world, and has delayed national nuclear development plans, especially in Indonesia and the Philippines due to their geographic location in a volcanic region.[42] Nevertheless, within the framework established by Law No. 10/1997 on Nuclear Energy, Indonesia has revitalised its nuclear energy planning by signing a memorandum of understanding with Rusatom Overseas – a Rusatom subsidiary that promotes Russian nuclear technology globally and the developer of Rusatom's foreign nuclear technology projects.[43]

With a view to supporting the plan to build nuclear power plants, Thailand signed the Additional Protocol to the IAEA Safeguards Agreement on 22 September 2005 and made

inspection powers and reporting requirements under the comprehensive safeguards agreement with each state party. For details, see e.g., Kalman A. Robertson, 'The Evolution of the Nuclear Non-Proliferation Regime: The International Atomic Energy Agency and Its Legitimacy' in Hitoshi Nasu and Kim Rubenstein (eds.), *Legal Perspectives on Security Institutions* (Cambridge: Cambridge University Press, 2015) 205.

[41] National Long-Term Development Plan 2005–2025 (Indonesia); Power Development Plan 2010–2030 (Thailand); Master Plan for Nuclear Power Infrastructure Development 2014 (Vietnam).

[42] Vlado Vivoda, 'After Fukushima: The Future of Nuclear Power in Asia', *East Asia Forum*, 16 March 2013, available at www.eastasiaforum.org/2013/03/16/after-fukushima-the-future-of-nuclear-power-in-asia/.

[43] 'RI Revives Nuclear Power Plants Vision', *The Jakarta Post*, 21 September 2015, available at www.thejakartapost.com/news/2015/09/21/ri-revives-nuclear-power-plants-vision.html.

amendments to the Atomic Energy for Peace Act 1961 (Thailand) designed to strengthen Thailand's regulatory framework for nuclear activities.[44] In Vietnam, on the other hand, although the Law on Atomic Energy 2008 (Vietnam) was enacted, development of the regulatory framework and capacity-building is lagging behind.[45] Vietnam relies heavily on external assistance from Japan, Russia, the US and the IAEA for the development of nuclear facilities, the enhancement of nuclear safety, as well as for the physical protection of nuclear and radiological materials. It acceded to the Convention on Nuclear Safety in 2010 and ratified the Additional Protocol to the IAEA Safeguards Agreement, which came into force for Vietnam in 2012.[46]

The Malaysian government signed the Additional Protocol on 22 November 2005 and, with a Cabinet Decision

[44] Tan Hui Yee, 'Cambodia, Thailand Edging Closer to Nuclear Power', *The Jakarta Post*, 30 May 2016, available at www.thejakartapost.com/seasia/2016/05/30/cambodia-thailand-edging-closer-to-nuclear-power.html. For details, see Jarunee Kraikaew, 'Implementation of Nuclear Materials Regulation in Thailand' (2015) 4(2) *International Nuclear Safety Journal* 13.

[45] Norimitsu Onishi, 'Vietnam's Nuclear Dreams Blossom Despite Doubts', *New York Times*, 1 March 2012, available at www.nytimes.com/2012/03/02/world/asia/vietnams-nuclear-dreams-blossom-despite-doubts.html?_r=0.

[46] See e.g., Government of Vietnam, 'National Progress Report: Vietnam', delivered at the Nuclear Security Summit, Washington DC, 31 March 2016, available at www.nss2016.org/document-center-docs/2016/3/31/national-progress-report-vietnam; 'Russia Signs Framework Agreement for Vietnam's Ninh Thuan 1', *World Nuclear News*, 3 August 2015, available at www.world-nuclear-news.org/NN-Russia-signs-framework-agreement-for-Vietnams-Ninh-Thuan-1-03081501.html; US Department of State, 'U.S.-Vietnam Cooperation on Civil Nuclear Power and Nuclear Security' (Press Release, 30 March 2010), available at www.state.gov/r/pa/prs/ps/2010/03/139255.htm.

on 26 June 2009, formally indicated that it would consider nuclear energy as an energy source option for electricity generation from 2020. The Atomic Energy Licensing Act 1984 (Malaysia) regulates and controls the development and use of atomic energy, allowing exploratory studies with foreign partners. The Act has been reviewed by reference to the IAEA regulatory standards.[47] Similarly, Lao PDR acceded to the Convention on Early Notification of a Nuclear Incident in 2013 and signed the Additional Protocol in 2014. While excluding nuclear energy from the scope of the Law on Electricity 2008,[48] it has been engaging in exploratory studies with foreign partners with a view to facilitating familiarity with the design, construction and operation of nuclear power plants and research reactors.[49]

By contrast, the Philippines remains reluctant to reopen the Bataan Nuclear Power Plant, which was constructed in the 1980s and subsequently closed due to safety concerns in the wake of the 1986 Chernobyl nuclear incident.[50] The Philippine

---

[47] IAEA, 'IAEA Completes Nuclear Security Review Mission in Malaysia' (Press Release, 22 April 2016), available at www.iaea.org/newscenter/press releases/iaea-completes-nuclear-security-review-mission-in-malaysia; 'Malaysia's Nuke Dream is "Overly Ambitious": Analyst', *Nuclear Forum Asia*, 4 January 2016, available at http://nuclearforum.asia/policy-infra structure/malaysias-nuke-dream-overly-ambitious-analyst.

[48] Law on Electricity 2008 (Lao PDR) art. 7.

[49] 'Russia and Laos Plan Nuclear Cooperation', *World Nuclear News*, 15 April 2016, available at www.world-nuclear-news.org/NP-Russia-and-Laos-plan-nuclear-cooperation-1504164.html.

[50] 'Philippines May Open Mothballed Marcos-era Nuclear Power Plant', *Reuters*, 30 August 2016, available at http://in.reuters.com/article/philippines-energy-nuclear-idINKCN1150NW.

Government explored plans to revise the Bataan Plant in the 1980s and 1990s, when it became a party to a number of nuclear safety treaties. The debate has been re-ignited under the Duterte Administration, with his Energy Secretary Alfonso Cusi advocating for restarting the Bataan Plant.[51]

In the past, Myanmar was suspected of pursuing a nuclear weapons development programme, because of possible links with the Democratic People's Republic of Korea in relation to nuclear proliferation.[52] However, Myanmar signed the Additional Protocol on 17 September 2013 and announced that it was 'actively pursuing nuclear disarmament and nonproliferation'.[53] This improved the international community's confidence in Myanmar's peaceful intentions regarding its nuclear activities.[54] In 2015, Myanmar confirmed that it had re-commenced cooperation with Rusatom, primarily with a view to taking 'concrete steps aimed at creating favourable conditions for cooperation in the use of advanced nuclear technology, including

---

[51] 'Duterte Okays Nuclear Power', *Executive Intelligence Review*, 21 November 2016, available at www.larouchepub.com/pr/2016/161121_duterte_nuke_ok.html.

[52] Julian Borger, 'Burma Suspected of Forming Nuclear Link with North Korea', *The Guardian*, 22 July 2009, available at www.theguardian.com/world/2009/jul/21/burma-north-korea-nuclear-clinton.

[53] Kelsey Davenport, 'Myanmar Signs Agreement with IAEA', *Arms Control Today*, 2 October 2013, available at www.armscontrol.org/act/2013_10/Myanmar-Signs-Agreement-With-IAEA.

[54] US Department of State, 'Adherence to and Compliance with Arms Control, Non-Proliferation, and Disarmament Agreements and Commitments' (July 2014) 21, available at www.state.gov/documents/organization/230108.pdf.

strengthening the legal framework for cooperation and training'.[55]

Even other ASEAN member states that have no current plans to develop nuclear power capabilities have followed suit in developing a regulatory framework for nuclear security through international treaty mechanisms, in accordance with the Plans of Action under the Bangkok Treaty. Cambodia, for example, acceded to the Convention on Nuclear Safety and the Convention on Early Notification of a Nuclear Incident in 2012, and in 2015 ratified the Additional Protocol to the IAEA Safeguards Agreement, despite the fact that it has focused on investing in other forms of renewable energy, such as hydro-power.[56]

Singapore ratified the Additional Protocol on 22 September 2005 and re-enacted the Radiation Protection Act in 2007, which was further amended in 2014. For Singapore, the lack of space to keep the required safety

---

[55] 'Russia, Myanmar Reaffirm Nuclear Cooperation', *World Nuclear News*, 26 March 2015, available at www.world-nuclear-news.org/NN-Russia-Myanmar-agree-to-cooperate-26031501.html.

[56] Arno Maierbrugger, 'No Nuclear Plant in Cambodia: PM', *Investvine*, 15 January 2014, available at http://investvine.com/no-nuclear-plant-in-cambodia-pm/. However, more recent reports suggest that Cambodia is pursuing an arrangement with Russia in support of a nuclear energy development agenda: 'Russia to Help Cambodia Build Capacity for Nuclear Power', *Reuters*, 26 November 2015, available at www.reuters.com/article/us-cambodia-russia-nuclear-id USKBN0TF0W220151126; Kuch Naren, 'Prime Minister Says Cambodia's Nuclear Plans Purely Peaceful', *The Cambodia Daily*, 19 May 2016, available at www.cambodiadaily.com/news/prime-minister-says-cambodias-nuclear-plans-purely-peaceful-112785/.

stand-off range of a nuclear site from urban areas has led to the conclusion that 'the safety risks are too high and current technology is not advanced enough to embark on the use of nuclear power technology'.[57] Brunei is not a party to any of the nuclear treaties with the exception of the IAEA Safeguards Agreement, but has been engaging with the IAEA on nuclear technology development for limited purposes, for example, 'in agriculture for accelerated crop development as well as in medicine for cancer diagnosis and treatment'.[58]

Thus, the ASEAN member states collectively and individually evidence a clear – but relatively sedate – progression towards the development of nuclear energy production capabilities, together with the necessary regulatory infrastructure. The lack of technical expertise and institutional experience within ASEAN regarding nuclear regulation has meant that its role must be limited to facilitating its member states' access to the global nuclear safeguards and assurance regime as reliable mechanisms for ensuring nuclear security in the region. Contrary to the observation made in 2008,[59] the regional uptake of the relevant nuclear security instruments

---

[57] Barry Desker, 'Energy Security: Southeast Asia Revives Nuclear Power Plans' (Commentary No. 226/2013, S Rajaratnam School of International Studies, 11 December 2013) 1, available at www.rsis.edu. sg/wp-content/uploads/2014/07/CO13226.pdf.

[58] Danial Norjidi, 'IAEA Ready to Work with Brunei to Develop Nuclear Technology', *Borneo Bulletin*, 30 January 2015, available at http://borneo bulletin.com.bn/iaea-ready-work-brunei-develop-nuclear-technology/.

[59] Michael S. Malley, 'Bypassing Regionalism? Domestic Politics and Nuclear Energy Security' in Donald K. Emmerson (ed.), *Hard Choices: Security, Democracy and Regionalism in Southeast Asia* (Stanford, CA: Shorenstein Asia-Pacific Research Center, 2008) 241, 256.

has significantly improved since the adoption of the 2007 Plan of Action. This is despite the fact that to the extent that nuclear activities are zealously pursued as national development programmes, the principle of non-interference necessarily restricts ASEAN's legal authority in developing its own regional norm for nuclear regulation.

2.4 ASEAN's Institutional Evolution for Nuclear Energy Regulation

As an increasing number of Southeast Asian nations started seriously pursuing their nuclear energy programmes since the millennium, the mutual assurances that they made one another became all the more important,[60] prompting ASEAN senior government officials to engage in serious discussions on nuclear regulation. Concerned about the possibility and impact of fallout from planned nuclear reactors in its neighbourhood, Singapore proposed the establishment of an ASEAN Nuclear Energy Safety Sub-Sector Network (NES-SSN), which was agreed at the annual meeting of ASEAN Energy Ministers in August 2007.[61] However, the role of this network was exploratory only in relation to nuclear safety issues and made no meaningful progress towards a firm institutional arrangement.[62]

---

[60] Rodolfo Severino, 'Look Past the Headlines to What Matters', *The Straits Times*, 23 July 2007, 16, cited in Malley, above n. 59, 253.

[61] Joint Ministerial Statement of the 25th ASEAN Ministers on Energy Meeting: 'Energising ASEAN to Power a Dynamic Asia', Singapore, 23 August 2007.

[62] James Martin Center for Nonproliferation Studies et al., above n. 5, 42.

The aspiration of developing a regional nuclear regulatory regime remains on ASEAN's agenda as one of the key initiatives adopted by the 2013 Plan of Action to Strengthen the Implementation of the Treaty on the Southeast Asia Nuclear Weapon-Free Zone. This initiative is to:

> Strengthen the existing and prospective mechanisms within ASEAN such as the Nuclear Energy Cooperation Sub-Sector Network (NEC-SSN) and the ASEAN Network of Regulatory Bodies on Atomic Energy (ASEANTOM) to contribute to the eventual development of a regional nuclear safety regime to regulate and oversee the safety assessment requirements for those States Parties which have embarked on peaceful nuclear energy programmes, in accordance with Article 4 of the [Southeast Asia Nuclear Weapon-Free Zone] Treaty . . .[63]

At its inaugural meeting, the ASEAN Network of Regulatory Bodies on Atomic Energy (ASEANTOM) presented its revised terms of reference for adoption by the ASEAN-SOM. This network provides an institutional framework for cooperation amongst nuclear regulatory bodies or relevant authorities within ASEAN through, for example, information exchange and the sharing of best practices with a view to enhancing regional nuclear safety, security and safeguards.[64] ASEANTOM is envisaged to be associated with, but separate

---

[63] 2013 Plan of Action, above n. 33, para. 1(i).

[64] Summary of 1st Meeting of ASEAN Network of Regulatory Bodies on Atomic Energy (ASEANTOM), Phuket, 3–4 September 2013, Appendix 3, available at www.iaea.org/inis/collection/NCLCollectionStore/_Public/45/075/45075439.pdf.

from, the Southeast Asia Nuclear Weapon-Free Zone and its institutional arrangements, together forming part of the ASEAN Political-Security Community.[65]

While still in its infancy, ASEANTOM presents significant potential as ASEAN's institutional response to the challenge of developing an improved architecture for nuclear technical and regulatory cooperation. As distinct from political forums, such technical and regulatory cooperation is vital to enhanced nuclear security outcomes for the region. For example, ASEANTOM could provide an institutional platform to build a centralised nuclear fuel processing capability for distribution of nuclear fuel to ASEAN member states even without their own technical expertise and capacity to enrich uranium.[66]

ASEANTOM is fundamentally different to the European Atomic Energy Community in terms of its institutional rationale and approach. This is because, as articulated during discussions at the Council for Security Cooperation in the Asia Pacific Nuclear Energy Experts Group Meeting, 'it is a network rather than a treaty-based governance mechanism'.[67] However, even in the EU, nuclear safety is primarily regulated by the national regulatory authorities within the legal framework of the Community, posing challenges to the legitimacy and effectiveness of any regulatory measure that

---

[65] Ibid., 3.   [66] Symon, above n. 28, 133–5.

[67] David Santoro and Carl Baker, 'Institutionalizing Nuclear Governance in the Asia Pacific: A Conference Report of the Council for Security Cooperation in the Asia Pacific Nuclear Energy Experts Group Meeting' (2013) 13(16) *Issues and Insights* online, 11, available at www.files.ethz.ch/isn/176496/issuesinsights_vol13no16.pdf.

may be imposed, such as conditionality attached to technical or financial assistance.[68] These challenges will be further compounded in ASEAN due to the strong emphasis on state sovereignty and the principle of non-interference.

2.5 Concluding Observations

In Southeast Asia, the nuclear security agenda is a by-product of Cold War politics, emerging originally as an aspiration to remove the region from the dictates of power balance played by nuclear weapon states. The idea was consonant with the region's greater objective of establishing ZOPFAN and also with the principle of non-interference as it emerged in the context of ASEAN. The focus of global nuclear security concerns has since then shifted to nuclear proliferation and nuclear disasters, while the region witnesses the rudimentary development of a nuclear power industry. As a result, ASEAN has become more entangled in complex regulatory challenges involving highly technical monitoring and safeguards of nuclear materials and technologies.

While assuming a more central role in facilitating the development of regulatory frameworks, ASEAN has relied on

---

[68] For analysis of these issues in the European context, see Kalin Ivanov, 'Legitimate Conditionality? The European Union and Nuclear Power Safety in Central and Eastern Europe' (2008) 45 *International Politics* 146. For the subsequent legal development, see e.g., European Atomic Energy Community, 'Report on the Implementation of the Obligations under the Convention on Nuclear Safety' (presented by the European Commission at the 7th Review Meeting of the Contracting Parties to the Convention on Nuclear Safety, Vienna, 27 March–7 April 2017), available at https://www-ns.iaea.org/downloads/ni/safety_convention/7th-review-meeting/euratom_nr-7th-rm.pdf.

the Bangkok Treaty as the regional legal framework within which it has prompted member states to internalise the relevant rules of international law with direct access to the global nuclear security safeguards and assurance regime. This may well be due to the lack of technical expertise required to build safeguard mechanisms and implement verification activities. However, at the heart of the challenge facing ASEAN is the tension between nuclear aspirational states, whose national development agenda drives their own nuclear power programmes in accordance with global nuclear security standards and mechanisms, and those that are concerned about nuclear fallout and its potential cross-border impact, and therefore have an interest in pursuing a region-wide nuclear security regime.

ASEAN's ability to develop a region-wide nuclear security regime is necessarily constrained by the principle of non-interference, to the extent that nuclear activities are zealously pursued as national development programmes. Nevertheless, as national nuclear power programmes mature in the region, they may become unwitting sources of nuclear security risk. A greater awareness of such risk, when coupled with the clear regional attitude towards nuclear weapons and proliferation concerns, could strengthen the shared view that nuclear regulation is a common security issue in the region. Thus, there is a scope for ASEAN to become more engaged with nuclear security regulation, for example, in localising international norms and rules concerning nuclear security through further development of technical and regulatory mechanisms such as ASEANTOM.

Chapter 3

Counter-Terrorism

3.1 Introduction

Following the Bali Bombings on 12 October 2002, ASEAN member states have made a joint commitment to counter-terrorism, particularly through the ARF Inter-Sessional Meeting on Counter-Terrorism and Transnational Crime. Central to the joint commitment to counter-terrorism is the ASEAN Convention on Counter Terrorism (ACCT),[1] adopted in January 2007 as a framework for regional cooperation to counter, prevent and suppress terrorism in all its forms and to deepen cooperation among law enforcement agencies and other relevant authorities within ASEAN member states.

ASEAN's relatively slow pace to adopt a regional treaty on counter-terrorism stands in marked contrast to other regions such as Africa, the Americas, Arab, Europe and South Asia, whose respective treaties were established prior to the 9/11 terrorist attacks.[2] Indeed, the ACCT only achieved full ratification

---

[1] Adopted 13 January 2007 (entered into force 27 May 2011) (hereinafter ACCT).

[2] For example, Organization of American States Convention to Prevent and Punish Acts of Terrorism Taking the Form of Crimes against Persons and Related Extortion that are of International Significance, adopted 2 February 1971, 1438 UNTS 191 (entered into force 16 October 1973); European Convention on the Suppression of Terrorism, adopted 27 January 1977, 1137

by all ASEAN member states in 2013 – six years after it was signed – although it came into force in 2011 upon ratification by the sixth member state.[3]

The legal instruments adopted hitherto by ASEAN are aimed at facilitating coordination of various counter-terrorism policies of each ASEAN member state and grant them region-wide endorsement. In this respect, ASEAN's efforts on counter-terrorism serve to complement national and sub-regional efforts,[4] arguably acting in conformity with the association's long-standing principle of non-interference.

UNTS 93 (entered into force 4 August 1978); South Asian Association for Regional Cooperation (SAARC) Convention on Suppression of Terrorism, adopted 4 November 1987 (entered into force 22 August 1988); Arab Convention on the Suppression of Terrorism, adopted 22 April 1998 (entered into force 7 May 1999); Treaty on Cooperation among States Members of the Commonwealth of Independent States in Combating Terrorism, adopted 4 June 1999 (entered into force 4 June 1999); Convention of the Organization of the Islamic Conference on Combating International Terrorism, adopted 1 July 1999 (entered into force 7 November 2002); Organization of African Union Convention on the Prevention and Combating of Terrorism, adopted 14 July 1999, 2219 UNTS 179 (entered into force 6 December 2002).

[3] ACCT, above n. 1, art. XXI.

[4] For detailed studies on each state's counter-terrorism measures, see e.g., Arabinda Acharya, *Whither Southeast Asia Terrorism?* (London: Imperial College Press, 2015) ch 5; Victor V. Ramraj, Michael Hor, Kent Roach and George Williams (eds.), *Global Anti-Terrorism Law and Policy* (2nd edn, Cambridge: Cambridge University Press, 2012) chs. 11 (Singapore), 12 (Indonesia) and 13 (Philippines); Ralf Emmers, 'Comprehensive Security and Resilience in Southeast Asia: ASEAN's Approach to Terrorism' (2009) 22 *The Pacific Review* 159; Victor V. Ramraj, Michael Hor and Kent Roach (eds.), *Global Anti-Terrorism Law and Policy* (Cambridge: Cambridge University Press, 2005) chs. 13 (Singapore and Malaysia), 14 (Indonesia) and 15 (Philippines).

However, commentators have been sceptical of the value of such regional efforts in counter-terrorism cooperation. Writing before the ACCT's entry into force, Andrew Chau observed that while there was a rhetorical commitment to counter-terrorism amongst ASEAN leaders, 'their declarations, meetings, and process of extensive consultation and consensus-building have resulted in little that is concrete'.[5] Other critics similarly argue that ASEAN counter-terrorism cooperation on the whole has been ill-conceived, half-hearted and weak.[6]

Furthermore, potentially complicating, if not compromising, ASEAN-based efforts is the perception that the sources of militancy and terrorism stem from neighbouring territories.[7]

---

[5] Andrew Chau, 'Security Community and Southeast Asia: Australia, the US, and ASEAN's Counter-Terror Strategy' (2008) 48(4) *Asian Survey* 626, 648.

[6] See e.g., Greg Fealy and Carlyle A. Thayer, 'Problematizing "Linkages" between Southeast Asia and International Terrorism' in William T. Tow (ed.), *Security Politics in the Asia-Pacific: A Regional-Global Nexus?* (Cambridge: Cambridge University Press, 2009) 211; Alfred Gerstl, 'The Depoliticisation and "ASEANisation" of Counter-Terrorism Policies in South-East Asia: A Weak Trigger for a Fragmented Version of Human Security' (2010) 3 *Austrian Journal of South-East Asian Studies* 48; Natasha Hamilton-Hart, 'Terrorism in Southeast Asia: Expert Analysis, Myopia and Fantasy' (2005) 18 *The Pacific Review* 303; David Martin Jones, Michael L. R. Smith and Mark Weeding, 'Looking for the Pattern: *Al Qaeda* in Southeast Asia – The Genealogy of a Terror Network' (2003) 26 *Studies in Conflict and Terrorism* 443.

[7] See generally, Jonathan T. Chow, 'ASEAN Counterterrorism Cooperation since 9/11' (2005) 45 *Asian Survey* 302; Neal Imperial, *Securitisation and the Challenge of ASEAN Counter-Terrorism Cooperation* (Hong Kong: Centre of Asian Studies, The University of Hong Kong, 2005). Also see Vincent-Joël Proulx, *Transnational Terrorism and State Accountability: A New Theory of Prevention* (London: Bloomsbury, 2012).

David Leheny considers this to be 'emblematic of the problems that a seemingly uncontroversial goal – such as a world without terrorism – has when it confronts other domestic and regional priorities for Asia-Pacific governments'.[8]

This chapter unravels the dynamic interactions of counter-terrorism law and policy in Southeast Asia, with a view to understanding ASEAN's normative role in shaping the regional approach to counter-terrorism, and in the process of localising and internalising it, in response to the development of international law in this field.

3.2 ASEAN's Engagement with Counter-Terrorism

ASEAN has evolved in its response towards terrorism. Before 9/11, 'transnational crime' was the broad category or rubric under which declarations on and regional responses to terrorism were included. This approach highlighted the traditional understanding of terrorism as a criminal act and internal subversion, best managed by law enforcement agencies. At the operational level, it was acknowledged that there were significant overlaps between terrorism and other areas of transnational criminal activity such as money laundering, the trafficking of drugs and people, and piracy.[9]

---

[8] David Leheny, 'The War on Terrorism in Asia and the Possibility of Secret Regionalism' in T. J. Pempel (ed.), *Remapping East Asia: The Construction of a Region* (Ithaca, NY: Cornell University Press, 2005) 236, 250.

[9] See generally, Arabinda Acharya, *Targeting Terrorist Financing: International Cooperation and New Regimes* (Abingdon: Routledge,

Crucially, the foregoing approach did not necessarily imply that ASEAN governments viewed terrorism as insignificant in comparison to other security problems. Rather, their shared reluctance to fully securitise transnational crime and non-military issues more broadly ensured that the counter-terrorism policies within ASEAN member states by and large precluded the use of armed forces as the exclusive means to combat terrorism, particularly on their respective domestic fronts. At the First Conference to Address Transnational Crimes held in Manila on 20 December 1997, then Philippine President Fidel Ramos urged ASEAN Interior and Home Affairs Ministers as follows:

> The concept of regional security should extend beyond the mere absence of armed conflict among and within nations. Enduring regional security continues to be assaulted by transnational crime and from time to time international terrorism, which threaten the attainment of our peoples' goals and aspirations. We cannot allow these criminals and terrorists to steal our future and that of our young people away from us.[10]

2009); Graham Gerard Ong-Webb (ed.), *Piracy, Maritime Terrorism and Securing the Malacca Straits* (Singapore: Institute of Southeast Asian Studies, 2006).

[10] Fidel V. Ramos, 'Speech of His Excellency President Fidel V Ramos at the Meeting of ASEAN Ministers of Interior/Home Affairs (AMIHA) and First Conference to Address Transnational Crimes', Manila, Philippines, 20 December 1997, cited in Ralf Emmers, 'The Securitization of Transnational Crime in ASEAN' (Working Paper No. 39, Institute of Defence and Strategic Studies, Nanyang Technological University, 2002) 10.

It was against this background that the ASEAN Declaration on Transnational Crime was signed in Manila on 20 December 1997. While the 1997 Declaration arguably underscored the collective commitment of ASEAN member states to cooperate against transnational criminal activity, it nonetheless adhered to the 'ASEAN Way' of decision-making by consultation and consensus and the reliance on non-binding rules.

The treatment of terrorism as a subset of transnational crime – or, from a conceptual perspective, a criminal justice approach to terrorism, rather than a military response – persisted at the regional level until the end of the 1990s, with the adoption of two addenda to the 1997 Declaration on Transnational Crime: the 1998 Manila Declaration on the Prevention and Control of Transnational Crime;[11] and the 1999 ASEAN Plan of Action to Combat Transnational Crime.[12] However, despite their collective acknowledgement of terrorism as a transnational phenomenon and problem, little concrete progress was made until the game-changing impact of the 9/11 events brought terrorism to the forefront of national and regional security agendas.

ASEAN's response to terrorism since then has tended to follow other multilateral initiatives such as APEC and the UN. The ASEAN Declaration on Joint Action to Counter Terrorism was adopted on 5 November 2001,[13] two weeks after the release of the APEC Leaders' Statement on Counter-Terrorism at their

[11] Adopted at the 1st Asia Regional Ministerial Meeting on Transnational Crime, Manila, Philippines, 25 March 1998.
[12] Adopted at the 2nd ASEAN Ministerial Meeting on Transnational Crime, Yangon, Myanmar, 23 June 1999.
[13] Adopted at the 7th ASEAN Summit, Bandar Seri Begawan, Brunei Darussalam, 5 November 2001.

Shanghai Summit. In the view of Tatik Hafidz, who once coordinated ASEAN cooperation on combating transnational crime
including terrorism at the ASEAN Secretariat, three points in
the Declaration's preamble are especially noteworthy, not least
for their purported riposte to the US-led global 'War on
Terror'.[14] According to Hafidz:

> Whilst it may sound normative to ASEAN outsiders, the
> declaration's preamble signifies a Southeast Asian united
> front on the issue of terrorism. The first point is indeed a
> universal principle, but it also underscores concerns over
> what some Southeast Asian Muslims perceived to be a
> camouflaged war on Islam. The second recognises that
> despite the fact that [the] global war on terrorism is an
> American-led agenda, it is also a regional issue as it has
> significant ramifications for ASEAN. But the third clearly
> signifies a denunciation of the Bush Administration's
> unilateralism and its widely-criticised doctrine of pre-
> emptive strike. In this regard, ASEAN asserts that the fight
> against terrorism must be guided by [the] multilateralism
> principle as set forth in the United Nations (UN) Charter.
> This explains the centrality of the UN multilateral
> framework on counter-terrorism – known as the universal
> anti-terrorism instruments (UATIs) – as [a] primary

[14] The 2001 Declaration's preamble reads, inter alia: 'Reaffirming our
primary responsibility in ensuring the peaceful and progressive
development of our respective countries and our region'; 'Deeply
concerned over the formidable challenge posed by terrorism to regional
and international peace and stability as well as to economic
development'; and 'Underlining the importance of strengthening
regional and international cooperation in meeting the challenges
confronting us'.

reference for intra as well as extra-regional cooperation on counter terrorism.[15]

On that basis, ASEAN member states tasked themselves with undertaking practical measures including, most relevantly: reviewing and strengthening their national mechanisms to combat terrorism; studying relevant international conventions on terrorism with a view to integrating them with ASEAN mechanisms; enhancing intelligence sharing on terrorists and terrorist organisations; and developing regional capacity-building programmes.[16] The Joint Communiqué of the Third ASEAN Ministerial Meeting on Transnational Crime, issued on 11 October 2001, detailed efforts to eradicate regional security challenges such as terrorism. This was followed by a 'special' ASEAN Ministerial Meeting on 17 May 2002 dedicated specifically to terrorism, where the Work Programme to Implement the ASEAN Plan of Action to Combat Transnational Crime was adopted.[17] The Work Programme detailed a six-pronged strategy including the establishment of legal facilities and institutional capacities within the ASEAN member states.[18]

---

[15] Tatik S. Hafidz, 'A Long Row to Hoe: A Critical Assessment of ASEAN Cooperation on Counter-Terrorism' (2009) 11 *Kyoto Review of Southeast Asia* online, available at http://kyotoreview.org/issue-11/a-long-row-to-hoe-a-critical-assessment-of-asean-cooperation-on-counter-terrorism/.

[16] ASEAN Declaration on Joint Action to Counter Terrorism, above n. 13, paras. 1, 4, 5 and 7.

[17] Work Programme to Implement the ASEAN Plan of Action to Combat Transnational Crime, adopted at the Special Meeting of the ASEAN Ministerial Meeting on Transnational Crime, Kuala Lumpur, Malaysia, 17 May 2002. The Work Programme was originally signed in June 1999.

[18] Ibid., s. 6.

Following the Bali Bombings in October 2002, a standalone declaration on terrorism was released at the ASEAN Summit in Phnom Penh on 3 November 2002, a week after the APEC Leaders issued the Statement on Fighting Terrorism and Promoting Growth.[19] The 2002 ASEAN Declaration on Terrorism urged member countries 'to continue to intensify their cooperation in combating terrorism and, in particular, in expeditiously carrying out the Work Programme, raising the level of cooperation, coordination and the sharing of information in the fight against terrorism'.[20] APEC, on the other hand, has developed Counter Terrorism Action Plans providing a space where member economies can record their APEC commitments to various counter-terrorism measures, such as securing cargoes, protecting people in transit, international shipping and aviation, and promoting cyber security.[21]

ASEAN has since then signed a number of joint declarations with its external dialogue partners – the US, the EU, Australia, India, Russia, Japan, the Republic of Korea, New Zealand, Pakistan and Canada – before it adopted its own counter-terrorism treaty.[22] Although ASEAN has no

[19] Adopted at the 14th APEC Joint Ministerial Meeting, Los Cabos, Mexico, 26 October 2002.
[20] ASEAN Declaration on Terrorism, adopted at the 8th ASEAN Summit, Phnom Penh, Cambodia, 3 November 2002, para. 4.
[21] Each of the APEC member economies' reports is available via www.apec .org/Groups/SOM-Steering-Committee-on-Economic-and-Technical-Cooperation/Working-Groups/Counter-Terrorism/Counter-Terrorism-Action-Plans.aspx.
[22] The text of these joint declarations is reproduced in ASEAN Political-Security Department Security Cooperation Division, *ASEAN Documents*

3.2 ASEAN'S ENGAGEMENT WITH COUNTER-TERRORISM

joint declaration with the PRC on counter-terrorism as such, it forms part of a priority issue in the 2002 Joint Declaration on Cooperation of ASEAN and China in the Field of Non-Traditional Security Issues.[23] This Declaration is reinforced by the Strategic Partnership for Peace and Prosperity, established on 8 October 2003, as well as a memorandum of understanding on non-traditional security cooperation, signed on 10 January 2004.

All these efforts helped lay the groundwork for the adoption of the ACCT in 2007. The ACCT simply refers to a list of relevant international counter-terrorism treaties to define 'offence' for the purpose of the ACCT, while allowing variation for those member states that are not party to every treaty referenced.[24] The primary obligation imposed upon the member states under the ACCT is summarised in the General Provisions under Article XI(1), which provides:

on Combating Transnational Crime and Terrorism (Jakarta: ASEAN Secretariat, 2012) 27–60. For backgrounds, see Mushahid Ali and Kumar Ramakrishna, 'ASEAN-US Cooperation to Combat International Terrorism: A More Nuanced Approach Needed' (Commentary No. 10/2002, S Rajaratnam School of International Studies, 29 August 2002), available at https://dr.ntu.edu.sg/handle/10220/3955; Felix Heiduk, 'In It Together Yet Worlds Apart? EU–ASEAN Counter-Terrorism Cooperation After the Bali Bombings' (2014) 36 *Journal of European Integration* 697; Ted Osius and C. Raja Mohan, *Enhancing India-ASEAN Connectivity* (Lanham, MD: Rowman and Littlefield, 2013); Sarah Teo, Bhubhindar Singh and See Seng Tan, 'South Korea's Middle Power Engagement Initiatives: Perspectives from Southeast Asia' (2016) 56 *Asian Survey* 555.

[23] Adopted at the 6th ASEAN-China Summit, Phnom Penh, Cambodia, 4 November 2002.

[24] ACCT, above n. 1, art. II.

> The Parties shall adopt such measures as may be necessary,
> including, where appropriate, national legislation, to
> ensure that offences covered in Article II of this
> Convention, especially when it is intended to intimidate a
> population, or to compel a government or an international
> organisation to do or to abstain from doing any act, are
> under no circumstances justifiable by considerations of a
> political, philosophical, ideological, racial, ethnic, religious
> or other similar nature.

The legal significance of this provision is twofold. First, it introduces an element of intention as commonly found in the definition of terrorism adopted in many countries,[25] although whether states are required to include it in domestic counter-terrorism legislation is subject to interpretation. Second, it establishes a shared understanding that the nature of the motive behind the act, such as a political, religious or ideological motivation on the part of terrorists, should be excluded from criminalisation of terrorism within the region.[26] The latter aspect is particularly important given the political, religious, racial, ethnic and

---

[25] See e.g., Christian Walter, 'Defining Terrorist in National and International Law' in Christian Walter, Silja Vöneky, Volker Röben and Frank Schorkopf (eds.), *Terrorism as a Challenge for National and International Law: Security versus Liberty?* (Berlin: Springer, 2004) 23, 28–30.

[26] For controversies on the inclusion of motives in the definition of terrorism, see especially, Ben Saul, 'The Curious Element of Motive in Definitions of Terrorism: Essential Ingredient or Criminalising Thought' in Andrew Lynch, Edwina MacDonald and George Williams (eds.), *Law and Liberty in the War on Terror* (Sydney: The Federation Press, 2007) 28; Ben Saul, *Defining Terrorism in International Law* (Oxford: Oxford University Press, 2006) 40–5.

ideological diversity in Southeast Asia where criminal investigations and trials can easily be politicised on those grounds.

Other provisions of the ACCT are largely facilitative in nature, rather than prescriptive of new obligations, clarifying obligations under the relevant counter-terrorism treaties for national implementation,[27] and identifying areas of cooperation 'in conformity with their respective domestic laws'.[28] Nevertheless, as a legally binding instrument,[29] the ACCT has been described as 'a significant milestone in ASEAN counter-terrorism cooperation with much potential in the areas of information-sharing and capacity-building'.[30] In a statement released a few days following the tenth and final ratification by Malaysia on 11 January 2013, the ASEAN Secretariat noted that '[t]he ACCT is a significant achievement for ASEAN's counterterrorism efforts as it serves as a framework for regional cooperation to counter, prevent, and suppress terrorism and deepen counter-terrorism cooperation'.[31]

---

[27] ACCT, above n. 1, arts. VII, X, XIII–XIV.   [28] ACCT, arts. VI, XII.

[29] Ong Keng Yong, 'ASEAN's Contribution to Regional Efforts in Counter-Terrorism', delivered at the National Security Australia Conference, Sydney, Australia, 21 February 2005, available at http:// asean.org/?static_post=asean-s-contribution-to-regional-efforts-in-cou nter-terrorism.

[30] As acknowledged by the Senior Minister of State for Home Affairs and Foreign Affairs of Singapore, Masagos Zulkifli, in a speech delivered at the 2nd ASEAN Counter-Terrorism Workshop on Joint Incident Management, Singapore, 15 July 2014, para. 13, available at www.nas.gov .sg/archivesonline/data/pdfdoc/20140722001/goh_speech_for_asean_ct_ workshop_on_joint_incident_management.pdf.

[31] ASEAN, 'ASEAN Convention on Counter-Terrorism Completes Ratification Process' (22 January 2013), available at http://asean.org/ asean-convention-on-counter-terrorism-completes-ratification-process.

The adoption of this Convention was soon followed by the development of the 2009 ASEAN Comprehensive Plan of Action on Counter Terrorism.[32] For the purpose of internalising the ACCT rules, the comprehensive action plan detailed measures 'to counter, prevent and suppress terrorism, terrorist organisations and their associations, to disrupt their support networks and impede their plan of terror acts, and to bring them to justice'.[33] This was to be accomplished through, among others: adherence to relevant UN Security Council Resolutions and international counter-terrorism instruments;[34] the implementation of the relevant existing regional legal frameworks, instruments and agreements; and the establishment of institutionalised mechanisms for the exchange of information and intelligence for surveillance, tracking and interdiction of suspected terrorist groups and their activities, while addressing the root causes of terrorism through various societal changes.[35]

[32] ASEAN Comprehensive Plan of Action on Counter Terrorism, Nay Pyi Taw, Myanmar, 30 June 2009, reproduced in *ASEAN Documents on Combating Transnational Crime and Terrorism*, above n. 22, 69.

[33] Ibid., s. 1.1.

[34] The Comprehensive Plan of Action does not refer to any specific Security Council Resolution or counter-terrorism instrument, but the state practice as examined below in Section 3 suggests that it encompasses key Security Council Resolutions such as UN Doc S/RES/1373 (28 September 2001) and UN Doc S/RES/1624 (14 September 2005), as well as the applicable counter-terrorism treaties as identified in ACCT, above n. 1, art. II.

[35] ASEAN Comprehensive Plan of Action on Counter Terrorism, above n. 32, ss. 3–5, 10. There is no change to this basic approach in the updated ASEAN Comprehensive Plan of Action on Counter Terrorism, adopted at the 11th ASEAN Ministerial Meeting on Transnational Crime, Manila, Philippines, 20 September 2017.

These ASEAN initiatives have attempted to overcome the limits of national efforts against transnational threats posed by modern terrorist activities.[36] The regional counter-terrorism cooperation through ASEAN can thus be characterised as multilateral initiatives that complement respective national efforts, drawing on the traditional strategies and structures that remain as the legacies of their fight against communist insurgency and dissidence.

Another ASEAN agreement relevant to its counter-terrorism efforts is the 2004 Mutual Legal Assistance Treaty (MLAT).[37] The aim of the MLAT is to enhance the effectiveness of law enforcement agencies within ASEAN member states in the prevention, investigation and prosecution of offences through cooperation and mutual legal assistance in criminal matters. In 2015, the MLAT came under the spotlight when Indonesian authorities decided to execute eight convicted drug smugglers. An eleventh-hour reprieve was given to a Filipina woman, Mary Jane Veloso, which ostensibly came as a consequence of Philippines' appeal to Indonesia by way of the MLAT.[38]

---

[36] See Arabinda Acharya, above n. 9, 216–19.

[37] Treaty on Mutual Legal Assistance in Criminal Matters, adopted 29 November 2004 (entered into force 28 April 2005 for Singapore, 25 October 2005 for Vietnam, 1 June 2005 for Malaysia, 15 February 2006 for Brunei Darussalam, 25 June 2007 for Lao PDR, 9 September 2008 for Indonesia, 12 December 2008 for the Philippines, 22 January 2009 for Myanmar, 8 April 2010 for Cambodia, 31 January 2013 for Thailand).

[38] Mark Merueas, 'De Lima: ASEAN Mutual Legal Assistance Treaty saved Veloso', *GMA News*, 29 April 2015, available at www.gmanetwork.com/news/story/478474/news/nation/de-lima-asean-mutual-legal-assistance-treaty-saved-veloso.

Both the ACCT and MLAT constitute examples of the 'ASEAN minus X' and 'flexible consensus' principles, which guide intramural cooperation within ASEAN.[39] Past practice among ASEAN Economic Ministers allowed member states to agree on economic liberalisation with the flexible application of the 'ASEAN minus X' or the 'two plus X' formula.[40] This ensured that member states that wished to embark on cooperative initiatives at a faster pace than the rest could still proceed. Suggestions have been made that the ASEAN minus X formula should only be applied as a measure of last resort when it would not be possible for all ASEAN member states to ratify an agreement for its entry into force within a reasonable period, or that there should be a maximum or threshold number of ASEAN member states that would comprise the 'X' to which ASEAN treaties are to apply.[41] In providing for the entry into force of the ACCT after ratification by only six member states,[42] ASEAN clearly elected to avoid such alternatives in order to facilitate

---

[39] See Chapter 1.4.3.
[40] For details, see Paul J. Davidson, 'The Role of International Law in the Governance of International Economic Relations in ASEAN' (2008) 12 *Singapore Year Book of International Law* 213, 222; Thitapha Wattanapruttipaisan, 'A Brief on ASEAN Economic Integration' (Bureau for Economic Integration and Finance Studies Unit Paper No. 07/2006, ASEAN Secretariat, 2006) 8, available at www.asean.org/uploads/archive/STU_Paper_07-2006-Brief_on_ASEAN_Economic_Integration.pdf.
[41] Pieter Jan Kuijper, James H. Mathis, and Natalie Y. Morris-Sharma, *From Treaty-Making to Treaty-Breaking: Models for ASEAN External Trade Agreements* (Cambridge: Cambridge University Press, 2015) 114.
[42] ACCT, above n. 1, art. XXI.

legislative and policy responses to terrorism and encourage regional cooperation in areas such as information-sharing and capacity-building.

Much like ASEAN, counter-terrorism cooperation in the ARF proceeds on the assumption that transnational crime and terrorism are intimately linked. In the aftermath of the 9/11 attacks, the ARF issued a series of statements focusing on specific functional areas on which ARF participants (including the EU) agreed to collaborate, such as border security,[43] transport security,[44] and information sharing, intelligence exchange and document integrity.[45]

On 23 July 2009, the ARF issued a Vision Statement, which identified five key areas of practical cooperation for its participants: disaster relief; counter-terrorism and transnational crime; maritime security; non-proliferation and disarmament; and peacekeeping operations.[46] On the same day that the Vision Statement was released, the ARF adopted its Work Plan for Counter-Terrorism and Transnational Crime (CTTC Work

---

[43] ASEAN Regional Forum Statement on Cooperative Counter-Terrorist Action on Border Security, adopted at the 10th ARF Meeting, Phnom Penh, Cambodia, 18 June 2003.

[44] ASEAN Regional Forum Statement on Strengthening Transport Security against International Terrorism, adopted at the 11th ARF Meeting, Jakarta, Indonesia, 2 July 2004.

[45] ASEAN Regional Forum Statement on Information Sharing and Intelligence Exchange and Document Integrity and Security in Enhancing Cooperation to Combat Terrorism and Other Transnational Crimes, adopted at the 12th ARF Meeting, Vientiane, Lao PDR, 29 July 2005.

[46] ASEAN Regional Forum Vision Statement, adopted at the 16th ARF Meeting, Phuket, Thailand, 23 July 2009.

Plan). Stressing the need for 'concrete and practical cooperation' among ARF participants, the Work Plan advocates for a 'more focused and coordinated strategy' to deal with transnational security issues such as terrorism, piracy and cyber terrorism. The Hanoi Plan of Action to implement the ARF's Vision Statement emphasises the ARF's support for ASEAN's counter-terrorism instruments – the ACCT and the MLAT – as well as the relevant instruments and strategies of the UN.[47]

The ARF's CTTC Work Plan was conceived as a long-term strategy aimed at enhancing the ASEAN Comprehensive Plan of Action on Counter Terrorism (discussed earlier), which was issued less than a month earlier, in June 2009. A key part of the CTTC Work Plan strategy is to concentrate ARF efforts on concrete capacity-building measures, technical support and information exchange with a view to enhancing ARF participants' ability to combat terrorism. Interestingly, the Work Plan notes that the ARF should not be expected to 'do everything' in the vast field of counter-terrorism in the short term, but that it should aim to 'do some things very well' – namely, in priority areas such as cyber security, cyber terrorism and bio-terrorism, whereas nuclear terrorism and human trafficking are marked as future priority areas for the ARF.[48] A key cogwheel of the ARF counter-terrorism process is its Inter-Sessional Meetings on Counter Terrorism and Transnational Crime, whose aim is

[47] Hanoi Plan of Action to Implement the ASEAN Regional Forum Vision Statement, adopted at the 17th ARF Meeting, Hanoi, Vietnam, 23 July 2010, Section I-2.

[48] 'ARF to Adopt "More Focused" Counterterrorism Strategy', *Balita*, 22 July 2009, available at http://balita.ph/2009/07/22/arf-to-adopt-more-focused-counterterrorism-strategy/.

to coordinate the effective implementation of the Work Plan and make additional recommendations on strengthening the capacity of the Asia-Pacific to counter terrorism and transnational crime.

Practical measures in advancing regional cooperation in counter-terrorism have been further pursued through the ADMM-Plus.[49] At their inaugural forum in October 2010, ADMM-Plus Ministers agreed on five areas of practical cooperation that their mechanism would pursue: maritime security; humanitarian assistance and disaster management; peacekeeping operations; military medicine; and counter-terrorism. Cooperation in these areas was to be facilitated by respective Experts' Working Groups.[50] In September 2013, the ADMM-Plus conducted its first counter-terrorism exercise in Sentul, Indonesia, and since then the scale of such exercises has continued to expand.[51] It should be noted, however, that for some ASEAN and Asia-Pacific countries, their armed forces are not

---

[49] See Seng Tan, 'A Tale of Two Institutions: The ARF, ADMM-Plus and Security Regionalism in the Asia Pacific' (2017) 39 *Contemporary Southeast Asia* 259–64. For the role of ADMM-Plus in ASEAN, see Chapter 1.5.

[50] Since then, two additional areas for demining and cyber security have been added, each with its own Experts' Working Group.

[51] For details, see See Seng Tan, 'The ADMM-Plus: Regionalism That Works?' (2016) 22 *Asia Policy* 70, 73. At the 2017 Special ASEAN Defence Ministers' Meeting, there was agreement on the need for ASEAN to develop a 'stronger cooperative intelligence sharing platform to facilitate the flow of information, in particular on terrorists and terrorist organisations': Joint Statement of Special ASEAN Defence Ministers' Meeting on Countering Violent Extremism (CVE), Radicalization and Terrorism, Manila, Philippines, 23 October 2017, para. 2.

necessarily their lead agencies responsible for handling counter-terrorism, which is often tasked to domestic law enforcement and security services. This reinforces the importance which many ASEAN member states accord to the concept of comprehensive security and their consequent emphasis on comprehensive or holistic approaches to counter-terrorism.

3.3 Counter-Terrorism Law and Policy in ASEAN Member States

ASEAN member states have sought to deal with terrorism through varying combinations of measures: military action; socio-economic, ideological and educational policies; and the enactment and enforcement of counter-terrorism laws. ASEAN member states have also sought to enhance counter-terrorism cooperation among themselves and with external partners such as Australia and the US.[52] However, they have not handled terrorism in the same way. For example, Indonesia and Singapore have tended to adopt a non-militaristic, law enforcement approach to tackling the challenge posed by terrorism, whereas Malaysia and Thailand have relied on more coercive, militaristic responses. This remains the case despite the fact that ASEAN member states are more than ever united in counter-terrorism as 'the biggest security concern' and 'unprecedented emergency' presently confronting Southeast

---

[52] See the table of bilateral agreements and memorandums of understanding in Amitav Acharya, *Constructing a Security Community in Southeast Asia; ASEAN and the Problem of Regional Order* (3rd edn, Abingdon: Routledge, 2014) 215.

Asia,[53] with the rising prospect of the so-called 'Islamic State' fighters coming or returning to the region as their fight in the Middle East draws to a close.

History clearly plays a role in the strategic choice of these countries. Malaysia's experience in dealing with armed communist rebellions, and the manner in which Thailand has responded to the separatist insurgency in its southern Malay-Muslim provinces, have likely shaped their preferences for a militarised approach to their respective terrorism challenges.[54] On the other hand, with the end of the military's prominent role in Indonesian politics in 1998, internal threats of terrorism, communal violence and separatist activities became the primary responsibility of the Indonesian National Police. Dissatisfied with the ineffective response of the Indonesian National Police to terrorist attacks, the Indonesian military launched a new counter-terrorism squad known as the Joint Special Operations Command (*Koopsusgab*) in June 2015, which immediately re-ignited concerns about the military's role in the country's domestic affairs.[55]

---

[53] Expressions used by the Singaporean and Indonesian Defence Ministers respectively at the 2017 Shangri-La Dialogue, cited in David Tweed and Jason Koutsoukis, 'Southeast Asian Defence Chiefs Sound Alarm on Terror Threat', *Bloomberg*, 4 June 2017, available at www.bloomberg.com/news/a rticles/2017–06-04/southeast-asian-defense-chiefs-sound-alarm-on-terror ism-threat.

[54] See generally, Donald Mackay, *The Malayan Emergency 1948–60: The Domino That Stood* (London and Washington DC: Brassey's, 1997); Zachary Abuza, *Conspiracy of Silence: The Insurgency in Southern Thailand* (Washington DC: United States Institute of Peace,2009).

[55] Prashanth Parameswaran, 'The Trouble with Indonesia's New Counterterrorism Command', *The Diplomat*, 11 June 2015, available at

Critical for the purpose of this chapter, however, are the differences in legal approaches to counter-terrorism. The following analysis, therefore, focuses on legislative and policy measures that each ASEAN member state has adopted in order to implement relevant rules of international law – in particular, the 1997 Terrorist Bombing Convention,[56] 1999 Terrorist Financing Convention[57] and the ACCT (see also Table 3.1).

For Indonesia, the 2002 Bali and 2003 Jakarta bombings furnished ample reasons to establish a legislative scheme conducive to effective counter-terrorism, despite the fact that Jakarta had denied the existence of Jemaah Islamiyah within its territory until then.[58] Nevertheless, Indonesia's legislative response to terrorism has been slow due to, among other factors, public resistance to the introduction of a new anti-terrorism law. There is fear among the public of the use of draconian laws to suppress dissidents as previously applied under the Suharto regime.[59]

---

http://thediplomat.com/2015/06/the-trouble-with-indonesias-new-counterterrorism-command/.

[56] International Convention for the Suppression of Terrorist Bombings, adopted 15 December 1997, 2149 UNTS 256 (entered into force 23 May 2001).

[57] International Convention for the Suppression of the Financing of Terrorism, adopted 9 December 1999, 2178 UNTS 197 (entered into force 10 April 2002).

[58] The Indonesian government, 'which had continued to deny that there was a terrorist network in Indonesia, now had to openly admit its existence': Leo Suryadinata, 'Indonesia: Continuing Challenges and Fragile Stability' in Daljit Singh and Chin Kin Wah (eds.), *Southeast Asian Affairs 2004* (Singapore: Institute of Southeast Asian Studies, 2004) 89, 90.

[59] See Kent Roach, *The 9/11 Effect: Comparative Counter-Terrorism* (Cambridge: Cambridge University Press, 2011) 145–53.

Table 3.1 *Status of Counter-Terrorism Treaties and Legislation*

a: accession s: signature r: ratification

	Terrorist Bombing Convention	Terrorist Financing Convention	ACCT	Primary Legislative Instruments
Brunei	a (14 Mar. 2002)	a (4 Dec. 2002)	r (28 Apr. 2011)	Anti-Terrorism (Financial and Other Measures) Act 2002; Anti-Terrorism Order 2011; Anti-Terrorism (Terrorist Financing) Regulations 2013
Cambodia	a (31 Jul. 2006)	s (11 Nov. 2001) r (12 Dec. 2005)	r (14 Jun. 2010)	Law on Counter-Terrorism 2007; Law on Anti-Money Laundering and Combating the Financing of Terrorism 2007
Indonesia	a (29 Jun. 2006)	s (24 Sep. 2001) r (29 Jun. 2006)	r (14 May 2012)	Law concerning the Crime of Money Laundering 2002 (amended in 2010); Law on Combating Criminal Acts of Terrorism 2002; Law on Prevention and Eradication of Crimes of Financing of Terrorism 2013
Lao PDR	a (22 Aug. 2002)	a (29 Sep. 2008)	r (12 Nov. 2012)	Law on Anti-Money Laundering and Counter-Financing of Terrorism 2015
Malaysia	a (24 Sep. 2003)	a (29 May 2007)	r (1 Nov. 2012)	Anti-Money Laundering, Anti-Terrorist Financing and Proceeds of Unlawful Activities Act 2001; Penal Code (Amendment) Act 2003; Security Offences (Special Measures) Act 2012; Prevention of Terrorism Act 2015; Special Measures against Terrorism in Foreign Countries Act 2015

Table 3.1 (*cont.*)

	Terrorist Bombing Convention	Terrorist Financing Convention	ACCT	Primary Legislative Instruments
Myanmar	a (12 Nov. 2001)	s (12 Nov. 2001) r (16 Aug. 2006)	r (18 Jan. 2012)	The Control of Money Laundering Law 2002; Mutual Legal Assistance in Criminal Matters Law 2004
Philippines	s (23 Sep. 1998) r (7 Jan. 2004)	s (16 Nov. 2001) r (7 Jan. 2004)	r (24 Mar. 2010)	Anti-Money Laundering Act 2001; Human Security Act 2007; Terrorism Financing Prevention and Suppression Act 2012
Singapore	a (31 Dec. 2007)	s (18 Dec. 2001) r (30 Dec. 2002)	r (31 Oct. 2007)	United Nations (Anti-Terrorism Measures) Regulations 2001; Terrorism (Suppression of Financing) Act 2002; Terrorism (Suppression of Bombings) Act 2007
Thailand	a (12 Jun. 2007)	s (18 Dec. 2001) r (29 Sep. 2004)	r (21 Feb. 2008)	Anti-Money Laundering Act 1999, (No. 2) 2008, (No. 3) 2009; Internal Security Act 2008; Counter-Terrorist Financing Act 2013
Vietnam	a (9 Jan. 2014)	a (25 Sep. 2002)	r (30 Jan. 2011)	Decree No. 74/2005/ND-CP on Prevention and Combat of Money-Laundering; Decree No. 25/2007/CT-TTg on Countering Terrorism

Since 2003, Indonesia has been advocating for an ASEAN-wide extradition treaty 'that would help speed up the investigation process especially with terrorism', according to an official from the Indonesian foreign ministry.[60] From Indonesia's perspective, the problem standing in the way of establishing a region-wide extradition agreement is Singapore, which has sought to link its bilateral extradition treaty with Indonesia to a defence agreement the two countries had signed in 2007.[61] However, Indonesia has yet to ratify this defence agreement because of the perception, fair or otherwise, that Singapore is seeking to avoid the forced repatriation of Indonesians suspected of corruption who had allegedly fled to Singapore.[62] Indonesia ratified the ACCT on 20 March 2012 with the expectation that it would provide a foundation for mutual legal assistance and extradition in combating terrorism.[63]

---

[60] Gary Jusuf, Director of ASEAN Security Affairs in the Foreign Ministry of Indonesia, quoted in 'Indonesia Pushes ASEAN Extradition Agreement', *Manila Standard*, 23 January 2003, 5A.

[61] Defence Cooperation Agreement between Singapore and Indonesia, adopted 27 April 2007 (not in force).

[62] 'Singapore Refutes Accusations that It Refused to Cooperate with Indonesian Police on Graft Suspect's Extradition', *The Straits Times*, 2 April 2017, available at www.straitstimes.com/asia/se-asia/singapore-refutes-accusations-that-it-refused-to-cooperate-with-indonesian-police-on.

[63] Ministry of Foreign Affairs (Indonesia), 'The House of Representatives and Government of Indonesia Reached a Mutual Agreement on the Ratification of ASEAN Convention on Counter Terrorism' (Media Release, 8 March 2012), available at www.kemlu.go.id/en/berita/Pages/The-House-of-Representatives-and-Government-of-Indonesia-Reached-a-Mutual-Agreement-on-the-Ratificat.aspx.

Upon acceding to the Terrorist Bombing Convention in 2003, Malaysia amended its Penal Code to insert offences relating to terrorism, defining a terrorist act in a manner that closely mirrors the UK definition.[64] In July 2003, Malaysia established a Southeast Asia Regional Centre for Counterterrorism tasked with regional training, information sharing and public awareness campaigns. Even though Malaysia repealed its Internal Security Act 1960 in 2012 as part of a political campaign led by Prime Minister Datuk Seri Najib Tun Razak, the executive power to detain for an extended period without a court order remained in matters concerning terrorism, with the enactment of the Security Offences (Special Measures) Act 2012 (Malaysia), which was modelled upon counter-terrorism legislation in different Western countries.[65]

In 2003, Malaysia re-arrested Yazid Sufaat, a former Malaysian army captain who had been detained without trial for more than seven years under the Internal Security Act until his release in 2008 and was the first to be charged under the 2012 Act.[66] It was observed that '[t]he fact that [Yazid] has to be rearrested shows the learning process that the Malaysian police and courts have to go through under the new legal

---

[64] Penal Code 1936 (Malaysia) s. 130B, as inserted by Penal Code (Amendment) Act 2003 (Malaysia). See also, Kent Roach, 'Comparative Counter-Terrorism Law Comes of Age' in Kent Roach (ed.), *Comparative Counter-Terrorism Law* (Cambridge: Cambridge University Press, 2015) 1, 25.

[65] Roach, above n. 64, 27.

[66] See Mathilde Tarif, 'Malaysia Keeps Ruling under Controversial Security Laws in Secret', *Le Journal International*, 4 August 2013, available at www.lejournalinternational.fr/Malaysia-keeps-ruling-under-controversial-security-laws-in-secret_a1131.html.

regime'.[67] Malaysia continued its law reform efforts with the re-introduction of preventative detention through the 2013 amendments to the Prevention of Crime Act 1959 (Malaysia), the enactment of the Prevention of Terrorism Act 2015 (Malaysia) and the Special Measures against Terrorism in Foreign Countries Act 2015 (Malaysia) to confront the threat posed by the so-called 'Islamic State'.

The Philippines has seen its fair share of contemporary security challenges in the form of the New People's Army (the armed wing of the Community Party of the Philippines), the Abu Sayyaf Group and, most recently, the Islamic State-affiliated Maute Group. In the immediate aftermath of 9/11, then President Gloria Macapagal-Arroyo labelled the Abu Sayyaf Group as an international terrorist movement and accepted from the US a significant military aid package and direct military assistance to counter Abu Sayyaf Group fighters on Basilan Island.[68] In 2017, the Philippines declared a state of emergency in order to regain control of Marawi in Mindanao from the Abu Sayyaf Group and Maute Group insurgents, with military assistance from the neighbouring ASEAN member states such as Singapore out of concern

---

[67] Abhrajit Gangopadhyay and Celine Fernandez, 'Malaysian Police Re-Arrest High-Profile Terror Suspect', *The Wall Street Journal*, 28 May 2013, available at http://blogs.wsj.com/indonesiarealtime/2013/05/28/malaysian-police-re-arrest-high-profile-terror-suspect/.

[68] For details, see e.g., Larry Niksch, 'Abu Sayyaf: Target of Philippine-U.S Anti-Terrorism Cooperation' (Congress Research Service, US Congress, 24 January 2007), available at www.fas.org/sgp/crs/terror/RL31265.pdf.

that further deterioration of the situation 'would cause instability to the rest of ASEAN'.[69]

The focus on internal armed conflicts under the guise of a counter-terrorism agenda in the Philippines is clearly reflected in the broad definition of terrorism adopted in the Human Security Act 2007 (Philippines).[70] It encompasses 'sowing and creating a condition of widespread and extraordinary fear and panic among the populace, in order to coerce the government to give in to an unlawful demand'.[71] Similarly,

---

[69] 'Singapore Offers SAF Assistance to Help Philippines Fight Terrorism', *Channel News Asia*, 19 July 2017, available at www.channelnewsasia.com/news/singapore/singapore-offers-saf-assistance-to-help-philippines-fight-9044142.

[70] The broad definition of terrorism may be adopted for the purpose of domestic legislation without prejudice to the applicability of the law of armed conflict. For details, see e.g., Jelena Pejic, 'Armed Conflict and Terrorism: There Is A (Big) Difference' in Ana María Salinas de Frías, Katja L. H. Samuel and Nigel D. White (eds.), *Counter-Terrorism: International Law and Practice* (Oxford: Oxford University Press, 2012) 171.

[71] Human Security Act 2007 (Philippines) s. 3. Compare with the definition of terrorism adopted for the purpose of Terrorism Financing Prevention and Suppression Act 2012 (Philippines) s. 3(j)(1)(a) ('any act intended to cause death or serious bodily injury to a civilian, or to any other person not taking an active part in the hostilities in a situation of armed conflict, when the purpose of such act, by its nature or context, is to intimidate a population, or to compel a government or an international organization to do or to abstain from doing any act'). For critical analysis, see H. Harry L. Roque Jr., 'The Human Security Act and the IHL Law of the Philippines: Of Security and Insecurity' in Victor V. Ramraj, Michael Hor, Kent Roach and George Williams (eds.), *Global Anti-Terrorism Law and Policy* (2nd edn, Cambridge: Cambridge University Press, 2012) 310, 316–25.

Thailand's counter-terrorism approach was aimed at suppressing separatist movements in the southern Malay-Muslim provinces and has become more institutionalised with the enactment of the Internal Security Act 2008 (Thailand).[72]

The development of anti-terror security apparatuses and legal instruments has not been such a vital priority for newer member states as it was for the founding members of ASEAN. Cambodia has sought assistance from Australia and the US in developing its counter-terrorism capability, while maintaining the policy emphasis on transnational crime.[73] In 2003, Cambodia established the National Counter-Terrorism Committee, a policy-level decision-making body chaired by the Prime Minister, which directly addresses the government's domestic and international counter-terrorism responsibilities. This decision was made in light of grave concerns that a Jemaah Islamiyah leader Hambali had reportedly travelled freely through Cambodia.[74] After ratifying or acceding to all the major counter-terrorism treaties, Cambodia enacted the Law on Counter Terrorism 2007 (Cambodia) and the Law on Anti-Money Laundering and

---

[72] For details, see Peter Chalk, Angel Rabasa, William Rosenau and Leanne Piggott, *The Evolving Terrorist Threat to Southeast Asia: A Net Assessment* (Santa Monica, CA, Arlington, VA and Pittsburgh, PA: RAND Corporation, 2009) ch 6.

[73] Vannarith Chheang, 'Cambodian Security and Defence Policy' in *Security Outlook of the Asia Pacific Countries and Its Implications for the Defense Sector* (Tokyo: National Institute of Defense Studies, 2013) 3, 9–10.

[74] Julie Masis, 'Hearts, Minds and Tongues in Cambodia', *Asia Times*, 18 April 2012, available at www.atimes.com/atimes/Southeast_Asia/ND18 Ae01.html.

Combating the Financing of Terrorism 2007 (Cambodia) to provide mechanisms for domestic counter-terrorism measures and international legal cooperation in counter-terrorism. However, as noted in its 2006 Defence Policy, the real challenges in enhancing Cambodia's counter-terrorism capabilities have been the lack of communication infrastructure, equipment, specialised skills, training and resources.[75]

Many Southeast Asian states have attempted to address terrorism financing as part of their anti-money laundering policies, which is consistent with ASEAN's approach to regional cooperation against transnational crime. Malaysia enacted the Anti-Money Laundering, Anti-Terrorism Financing and Proceeds of Unlawful Activities Act 2001 (Malaysia), and Myanmar introduced the Control of Money Laundering Law 2002 (Myanmar),[76] with a view to implementing obligations under relevant UN Security Council Resolutions.

While maintaining the official position that its existing criminal law provides a comprehensive and effective legal framework to combat terrorism,[77] Vietnam also responded by promulgating the Decree on Prevention and Combat of

---

[75] Defense Policy of the Kingdom of Cambodia 2006: Security, Development and International Cooperation (Cambodia) 18, available at http://aseanregionalforum.asean.org/files/library/ARF%20Defense%20White%20Papers/Cambodia-2006.pdf.

[76] For an official explanation of its operation, see Letter dated 14 November 2006 from the Permanent Representative of Myanmar to the United Nations addressed to the Chairman of the Counter-Terrorism Committee, UN Doc S/2006/902/Annex (14 November 2006).

[77] Report submitted to the Counter-Terrorism Committee on Implementation by Viet Nam of Security Council Resolution 1624 (2005)

Money-Laundering in 2005. On the other hand, the anti-money laundering legislation in Indonesia, the Philippines and Thailand was deemed inadequate by the Financial Action Task Force – a Paris-based global standard-setting body for anti-money laundering and combating the financing of terrorism – and was replaced by new, specific counter-terrorist financing laws in 2012–2013 to avoid possible financial sanctions.[78]

Both Brunei and Singapore enacted legislation to combat the financing of terrorism upon their respective accession to and ratification of the Terrorism Financing Convention in 2002.[79] However, no further counter-terrorism measure was adopted until they ratified the ACCT in 2011 and 2007 respectively. Singapore acceded to the 1997 Terrorist Bombing Convention only in 2007 and in the same year

on Additional Measures to Combat Terrorism, UN Doc S/2007/425 (12 July 2007).

[78] Ben Otto, 'Indonesia Takes Aim at Financing of Terrorism', *Wall Street Journal*, 12 February 2013, available at www.wsj.com/articles/S B10001424127887323511804578299911897063222; 'FATF Upgrades Philippines for Move against Money Laundering, Terrorist Financing', *Global Times*, 23 June 2012, available at www.globaltimes.cn/content/71 6615.shtml; Ministry of Foreign Affairs of the Kingdom of Thailand, 'FATF Removes Thailand from Public Statement on Money Laundering/ Financing of Terrorism' (Press Release, 1 May 2013), available at www. mfa.go.th/main/en/media-center/14/34910-FATF-removes-Thailand-from-Public-Statement-on-Mon.html.

[79] Anti-Terrorism (Financial and Other Measures) Act 2002 (Brunei); Terrorism (Suppression of Financing) Act 2002 (Singapore). Earlier, Singapore enacted the United Nations (Anti-Terrorism Measures) Regulations 2001, following the adoption of UN Security Council Resolution 1373, UN Doc S/RES/1373 (28 September 2001).

enacted the Terrorism (Suppression of Bombings) Act 2007 (Singapore) in order to give effect to the 1997 Convention.[80] Brunei enacted its comprehensive counter-terrorism legislation on 1 August 2011 soon after its ratification of the ACCT on 28 April 2011,[81] even though it had acceded to the 1997 Convention much earlier, in 2002. In a similar vein, Vietnam commenced the process of developing programmes to implement the provisions of the ACCT upon ratification in 2010, including the enactment of counter-terrorism specific legislation.[82]

Although it has not had to deal with terrorism in any significant way, Lao PDR established a National Ad Hoc Committee for implementing UN Security Council Resolution 1373,[83] and amended its penal law in 2005 to criminalise various acts of terrorism.[84] Recently, the Law on

---

[80] For detailed analysis, see e.g., Michael Hor, 'Singapore's Anti-Terrorism Laws: Reality and Rhetoric' in Victor V. Ramraj, Michael Hor, Kent Roach and George Williams (eds.), *Global Anti-Terrorism Law and Policy* (2nd edn, Cambridge: Cambridge University Press, 2012) 271, 284–5.

[81] Anti-Terrorism Order 2011 (Brunei), which repealed the Anti-Terrorism (Financing and Other Measures) Act 2002 and replaced it with the Anti-Terrorism (Terrorist Financing) Regulations 2013.

[82] See Statement by Pham Vinh Quang Deputy Permanent Representative of the Socialist Republic of Viet Nam at the United Nations Secretary-General's Symposium on International Counter-Terrorism Cooperation, addressed in New York, US, 19 September 2011, available at http://www.un.org/en/terrorism/ctitf/pdfs/vietnam.pdf.

[83] UN Doc S/RES/1373 (28 September 2001).

[84] See Report of the Government of the Lao People's Democratic Republic to the Security Council on the Implementation of Resolution 1624 (2005), UN Doc S/2007/141 (13 March 2007).

Anti-Money Laundering and Counter-Financing of Terrorism 2015 (Lao PDR) was promulgated, defining terrorism broadly to include acts that 'affect lives, health, freedom, or [pose] physical and psychological intimidation'.[85] Likewise, Myanmar has been working with the International Monetary Fund and the UN Office on Drugs and Crime to draft counter-terrorism and anti-money laundering laws pursuant to UN Security Council Resolutions 1373 and 1624,[86] while seeking assistance from the US and international organisations for the capacity-building of its Financial Intelligence Unit that oversees terrorist financing issues.[87]

3.4 Concluding Observations

This chapter has provided a review of the evolving practice of ASEAN, the ARF, other ASEAN-based arrangements and ASEAN member states themselves with a view to identifying the ways in which ASEAN has engaged in normative processes concerning counter-terrorism in Southeast Asia. Challenges and constraints that have helped define ASEAN's legal authority as a security institution in general have equally

---

[85] Law on Anti-Money Laundering and Counter-Financing of Terrorism 2015 (Lao PDR) art. 7(2).
[86] UN Doc S/RES/1373 (28 September 2001); UN Doc S/RES/1624 (14 September 2005).
[87] Government of Myanmar, 'National Experience of Myanmar', presented at the Special Meeting of the Counter-Terrorism Committee on Preventing and Suppressing Terrorist Financing, New York, US, 20 November 2012, available at www.un.org/en/sc/ctc/specialmeetings/2012/docs/Myanmar_statement.pdf.

shaped the association's approach to counter-terrorism cooperation. This is reflected in the fact that the ACCT was established to localise international norms and rules on counter-terrorism only after a number of Southeast Asian nations, between 2002 and 2006, concluded agreements and memoranda of understanding on counter-terrorism cooperation among themselves. During the same period, ASEAN issued joint counter-terrorism declarations with no less than nine of its dialogue partners – Australia, EU, India, Japan, New Zealand, Pakistan, Russia, the Republic of Korea and the US – and a joint declaration on non-traditional security issues including counter-terrorism with a tenth dialogue partner, the PRC.

There is no denying that the political and legal constraints within each member state necessarily limit ASEAN's institutional ability to facilitate norm development in the area of counter-terrorism. The history of political struggles and armed violence that continues to confront many Southeast Asian nations has been causing ambivalence towards rigorous counter-terrorism measures in the region. ASEAN's counter-terrorism initiatives must be understood in this wider political context where national counter-terrorism efforts are enmeshed with each country's own political agenda of promoting national harmony and combating dissidents. Nevertheless, as this chapter has demonstrated, there is sufficient evidence to suggest that ASEAN's gradual development of a regional counter-terrorism framework has assisted its member states, particularly those with less experience in this area, in building their legal and institutional capacity to engage with international efforts to combat terrorism.

ASEAN legal instruments such as the ACCT and the cooperative arrangements established between ASEAN and its dialogue partners have furnished Southeast Asian nations with legitimacy and guidance in localising and internalising international norms and rules on counter-terrorism into their own counter-terrorism laws and policies.

Chapter 4

Maritime Security

4.1 Introduction

The first decade of the twenty-first century has seen a significant increase in focus upon maritime security. Maritime security has traditionally reflected concerns over piracy and freedom of navigation. The First and Second World Wars, the Cold War, the implications of nuclear conflict, as well as the operations of nuclear-armed and nuclear-powered US and Soviet warships dominated maritime security concerns in the twentieth century. However, in the first decade of the new century, non-traditional maritime security issues such as armed robbery at sea, trafficking in persons and maritime terrorism have gained precedence.[1]

Southeast Asia has been at the centre of many of those challenges. Piracy, in and around the Indonesian and Philippine archipelagos, was a major issue within the region in the 1990s and the early part of the 2000s. This had consequences for the internal maritime security of these archipelagic states, which during this period were also tackling local insurgencies

---

[1] See generally, Natalie Klein, 'Maritime Security' in Donald R. Rothwell, Alex G. Oude Elferink, Karen N. Scott and Tim Stephens (eds.), *The Oxford Handbook of the Law of the Sea* (Oxford: Oxford University Press, 2015) 582.

and the subversive activities of non-state actors.[2] Territorial and maritime disputes throughout the region, especially in the South China Sea, have also had consequences for regional maritime security. The long-standing US naval presence in the region has caused tensions, particularly following the rise of the PRC as a naval power, and there have been equally significant issues with respect to the freedom of navigation through the labyrinth of straits, sea lanes and archipelagos that dominate the region.[3]

The ADMM-Plus Maritime Security Expert Working Group has observed that these maritime security challenges arise from a combination of the following factors:

- Dependence on sea lines of communication, in which safe, free and lawful navigation through international sea lanes is considered vital for regional security and economic stability; and
- Constraints on cooperation and threats to good order at sea, which encompass piracy and armed robbery against ships, maritime terrorism, illicit trafficking in drugs and arms, people smuggling, illegal fishing, marine natural hazards and uncertain maritime domains.[4]

---

[2] See Chapter 3.3.
[3] See generally, Joshua H. Ho and Sam Bateman (eds.), *Maritime Challenges and Priorities in Asia: Implications for Regional Security* (Abingdon: Routledge, 2012); Kwa Chong Guan and John K. Skogan (eds.), *Maritime Security in Southeast Asia* (Abingdon: Routledge, 2007).
[4] ADMM-Plus Maritime Security Expert Working Group (EWG) Concept Paper, Yogyakarta, Indonesia, 28 April 2011, 1, available at http://amscip.

While maritime security in ASEAN is central to the economic success of the region, it is also critical to national and regional security. This has been reflected in the increasing attention given to maritime security as a collective interest of ASEAN member states.[5] ASEAN maritime security is also pivotal for a number of extra-regional states both within Asia, such as India, Japan, PRC and the Republic of Korea, and for countries such as Australia, New Zealand, Russia and the US as reflected in their membership of ADMM-Plus. However, as will be examined in this chapter, these extra-regional dimensions, as well as varying degrees of maritime security interests among ASEAN member states, have affected the extent to which ASEAN exercises its legal authority in developing, localising or internalising maritime security norms and rules.

4.2 ASEAN's Engagement with Maritime Security

Maritime security initially had a strong 'national' focus in the law of the sea, which primarily concentrated upon the security of the state such that territorial integrity was maintained and that maritime threats were capable of being thwarted at sea. A distinct body of law relating to naval warfare has developed in this regard.[6] Over time, however, maritime security has

org/wp-content/uploads/2012/11/3-ADMM-Plus-Paper-Maritime-Security-EWG-endorsed.pdf.

[5] See e.g., Chairman's Statement of the 3rd ASEAN Maritime Forum, Manila, Philippines, 9 October 2012, para. 2.

[6] The body of international law that emerged in response was the law of naval warfare, which developed through customary international law and

developed different and wider dimensions.[7] Ship security was one of the first additional dimensions, due to the increasing threat and occurrence of pirate attacks, and international law developed responses to piracy under both customary international law and treaty law.[8] In an age of international terrorism, the international law response to ship security has now expanded even further, through the adoption of instruments such as the 1988 Convention for the Suppression of Unlawful Acts against the Safety of Maritime Navigation (SUA Convention) and its Protocols.[9]

ASEAN's engagement with maritime security has evolved over time consistently with the development of the law of the sea,[10] particularly following the negotiation and conclusion of the 1982 United Nations Convention on the Law

treaties: see Louise Doswald-Beck (ed.), *San Remo Manual on International Law Applicable to Armed Conflicts at Sea* (Cambridge: Cambridge University Press, 1995).

[7] For discussion, see Natalie Klein, *Maritime Security and the Law of the Sea* (Oxford: Oxford University Press, 2011) 1–23.

[8] See e.g., Barry Hart Dubner, *The International Law of Sea Piracy* (The Hague: Martinus Nijhoff, 1980).

[9] Convention for the Suppression of Unlawful Acts against the Safety of Maritime Navigation, adopted 10 March 1988, 1678 UNTS 221 (entered into force 1 March 1992) as amended in 2005 (hereinafter SUA Convention); Protocol for the Suppression of Unlawful Acts against the Safety of Fixed Platforms on the Continental Shelf, adopted 10 March 1988, 1678 UNTS 304 (entered into force 1 March 1992) as amended in 2005.

[10] See generally, Tullio Treves, 'Historical Development of the Law of the Sea' in Donald R. Rothwell, Alex G. Oude Elferink, Karen N. Scott and Tim Stephens (eds.), *The Oxford Handbook of the Law of the Sea* (Oxford: Oxford University Press, 2015) 1.

of the Sea (LOSC).[11] Three aspects in particular can be highlighted. First, at the time of ASEAN's formation the new law
of the sea, as reflected in the LOSC, remained under negotiation.[12] Accordingly, the benefits to ASEAN member states of
the LOSC have been realised in more recent decades, at a time
when the maritime domain of Southeast Asia has also been
radically modified as a result of the emergence of recognised
archipelagic states and multiple new maritime claims.[13]
Second, maritime security challenges have also evolved during this period, including the rise and fall of piracy and
transnational crimes, and the emergence of terrorism and its
associated implications for shipping.[14] Third, as will be discussed below, the PRC has emerged as a significant regional

[11] UN Convention on the Law of the Sea, opened for signature 10 December
1982, 1833 UNTS 397 (entered into force 16 November 1994) (hereinafter
LOSC). On the significance of the LOSC, see Robin R. Churchill, 'The
1982 United Nations Convention on the Law of the Sea' in Donald R.
Rothwell, Alex G. Oude Elferink, Karen N. Scott and Tim Stephens (eds.),
The Oxford Handbook of the Law of the Sea (Oxford: Oxford University
Press, 2015) 24.

[12] Donald R. Rothwell and Natalie Klein, 'Maritime Security and the Law of
the Sea' in Natalie Klein, Joanna Mossop and Donald R. Rothwell (eds.),
Maritime Security: International Law and Policy Perspectives from
Australia and New Zealand (Abingdon: Routledge, 2010) 22, 23–4.

[13] These developments for the region are reviewed in Victor Prescott and
Clive Schofield, Maritime Political Boundaries of the World (2nd edn,
Leiden: Martinus Nijhoff, 2005) 429–59; Tommy T. B. Koh, 'The
Territorial Sea, Contiguous Zone, Straits and Archipelagoes under the
1982 Convention on the Law of the Sea' (1987) 29 Malaya Law Review 163.

[14] See generally, José Luis Jesus, 'Protection of Foreign Ships against Piracy
and Terrorism at Sea: Legal Aspects' (2003) 18 International Journal of
Marine and Coastal Law 363.

actor in Southeast Asian maritime affairs, especially as a result of its assertive position with respect to South China Sea territorial and maritime claims.

Against this backdrop, ASEAN's focus on maritime security has significantly increased post-9/11, driven by the threats posed by non-state actors with respect to terrorism and piracy, especially within the enclosed waters of the Straits of Malacca and Singapore.[15] While there is some evidence that these issues were attracting ASEAN's attention before 2001,[16] the 2003 Bali Concord II represented a turning point in ASEAN's focus on maritime security. This was not only because of the recognition in the instrument that '[m]aritime issues and concerns are transboundary in nature', but also through the acknowledgement that 'maritime cooperation between and among ASEAN member countries shall contribute to the evolution of the ASEAN Security Community'.[17] Nevertheless, doubts remain over the capacity of ASEAN to take a strong lead in combating piracy in the Straits of Malacca, because of sovereignty sensitivities.[18]

---

[15] This has especially been the case with respect to piracy: see Karsten von Hoesslin, 'Piracy and Armed Robbery against Ships in the ASEAN Region: Incidents and Trends' in Robert C. Beckman and J. Ashley Roach (eds.), *Piracy and International Maritime Crimes in ASEAN: Prospects for Cooperation* (Cheltenham: Edward Elgar, 2012) 119.

[16] See e.g., ASEAN Declaration on Transnational Crime, Manila, Philippines, 20 December 1997, para. 8; Hanoi Declaration of 1998, Hanoi, Vietnam, 16 December 1998, para. 26.

[17] Declaration of ASEAN Concord II (Bali Concord II), Bali, Indonesia, 7 October 2003, Section A, para. 5.

[18] Laura Southgate, 'Piracy in the Malacca Strait: Can ASEAN Respond?', *The Diplomat*, 8 July 2015, available at http://thediplomat.com/2015/07/piracy-in-the-malacca-strait-can-asean-respond/.

Regional initiatives began to take further shape in the 2009 ASEAN Political-Security Blueprint, which promoted the establishment of an ASEAN Maritime Forum.[19] However, since it was convened for the first time in 2010 in Surabaya, Indonesia, the ASEAN Maritime Forum has focused on 'soft' maritime security issues such as linkages within maritime transport, and providing assistance to persons in distress at sea.[20] More traditional maritime security issues have been addressed through the ADMM, which introduced support for promoting ASEAN maritime security cooperation in its 2007 Three Year Work Programme.[21] ASEAN maritime security cooperation has continued in the work of the ADMM and, since 2010, the expanded ADMM-Plus. In 2013, for example, the ADMM-Plus encouraged the establishment of 'practical measures that reduce vulnerability to miscalculations, and avoid misunderstanding and undesirable incidents at sea'.[22] In 2016, the ADMM restated support

[19] ASEAN Political-Security Community Blueprint, adopted at the 14th ASEAN Summit, Cha-am Hua Hin, Thailand, 1 March 2009, Section A, para. 2.5. See also Vientiane Action Programme 2004–2010, adopted at the 10th ASEAN Summit, Vientiane, Lao PDR, 29 November 2004, Annex 1: ASEAN Security Community, Programme Areas and Measures Ref 1.2.7.

[20] Termsak Chalermpalanupap and Mayla Ibañez, 'ASEAN Measures in Combating Piracy and Other Maritime Crimes' in Robert C. Beckman and J. Ashley Roach (eds.), *Piracy and International Maritime Crimes in ASEAN: Prospects for Cooperation* (Cheltenham: Edward Elgar, 2012) 139, 143–4.

[21] ADMM Three-Year Work Programme, adopted at the 2nd ASEAN Defence Ministers' Meeting, Singapore, 14 November 2007, para. 2.1.6.

[22] Bandar Seri Begawan Joint Declaration on the Second ASEAN Defence Ministers' Meeting Plus, Bandar Seri Begawan, Brunei Darussalam, 29 August 2013, para. 3.

for the commencement of work on 'crafting protocols of interaction to maintain open communications, to avoid misunderstanding and prevent undesirable incidents'.[23]

ASEAN member states have also worked cooperatively to facilitate the internalisation of various rules of international law in addressing specific maritime security issues. For example, the ARF issued the Statement on Cooperation against Piracy and Other Threats to Security in 2003,[24] which sought to build upon the LOSC, the SUA Convention and relevant International Maritime Organization (IMO) initiatives dealing with piracy.[25] A similar initiative was taken in relation to maritime terrorism, with the adoption of the 2004 ARF Statement on Strengthening Transport Security against International Terrorism, which was intended to fully implement obligations under the IMO's International Ship and Port Facility Security Code.[26] Another example is the 2010 ASEAN Declaration on Cooperation in Search and Rescue of Persons and Vessels in Distress at Sea, which was adopted, at the initiative of Vietnam, to facilitate coordination of maritime search and rescue efforts in the region.[27]

---

[23] Joint Declaration of the ASEAN Defence Ministers on Promoting Defence Cooperation for a Dynamic ASEAN Community, adopted at the 10th ASEAN Defence Ministers' Meeting, Vientiane, Lao PDR, 25 May 2016, para. 13.

[24] Adopted at the 10th ARF, Phnom Penh, Cambodia, 17 June 2003.

[25] Chalermpalanupap and Ibañez, above n. 20, 152.

[26] Adopted at the 11th ARF Meeting, Jakarta, Indonesia, 2 July 2004. The Code sits within the framework of the International Convention for the Safety of Life at Sea, adopted 1 November 1974, 1184 UNTS 278 (entered into force 25 May 1980) as amended.

[27] Adopted at the 17th ASEAN Summit, Hanoi, Vietnam, 27 October 2010.

Outside the framework of ASEAN, Southeast Asian nations have been very active in associated regional forums designed to promote maritime confidence-building mechanisms. These forums include the Council for Security Cooperation in the Asia Pacific, the Combined Maritime Forces naval partnership that was developed post-9/11, the Western Pacific Naval Symposium, the Shangri-La Dialogue and the Shanghai Cooperation Organisation. Eight ASEAN member states are also party to the 2004 Regional Cooperation Agreement on Combating Piracy and Armed Robbery against Ships in Asia (ReCAAP Agreement), which entered into force in 2006 and established the ReCAAP Information Sharing Centre as an international organisation on 30 January 2007.[28]

ASEAN members and other East Asian states have also considered and developed mechanisms to respond to non-traditional maritime security issues relating to the marine environment and resource management. The 2005 Bali Plan of Action 'Towards Healthy Oceans and Coasts for Sustainable Growth and Prosperity of the Asia-Pacific Community' was adopted within an APEC framework, and

---

[28] Regional Cooperation Agreement on Combating Piracy and Armed Robbery against Ships in Asia, adopted 11 November 2004, 2398 UNTS 199 (entered into force 4 September 2006). Indonesia and Malaysia are not party to the ReCAAP. For discussion, see Miha Hribernik, 'Countering Maritime Piracy and Robbery in Southeast Asia: The Role of the ReCAAP Agreement' (European Institute for Asian Studies, Briefing Paper 2013/2); Robin Geiß and Anna Petrig, *Piracy and Armed Robbery at Sea: The Legal Framework for Counter-Piracy Operations in Somalia and the Gulf of Aden* (Oxford: Oxford University Press, 2011) 45–8.

was designed to promote sustainable management of the marine environment, sustainable economic benefits from the oceans and sustainable development of coastal communities.[29] The Bali Plan of Action built upon the 2005 State of the World Fisheries and Aquaculture Report, published by the Food and Agricultural Organization (FAO).[30] This initiative complemented parallel measures undertaken by some individual states to combat illegal fishing throughout the region. However, a limitation of these initiatives has been the 'soft' ASEAN framework within which they have been adopted, which has been a characteristic of ASEAN environmental initiatives.[31]

4.3 Maritime Security Law and Policy in ASEAN Member States

Despite their shared position on maritime security through regional cooperation, ASEAN member states have different levels of interest in and policy approaches to maritime security issues, as reflected in the case of counter-piracy.[32] These differences are illustrated by the ways in which several ASEAN member states have contributed to the development of the international law of the sea and have implemented the

---

[29] Adopted at the APEC Ocean-Related Ministerial Meeting, Bali, Indonesia, 16 September 2005.

[30] FAO, *State of the World Fisheries and Aquaculture Report 2005* (Rome: FAO, 2005).

[31] See Lorraine Elliott, 'ASEAN and Environmental Cooperation: Norms, Interests and Identity' (2003) 16(1) *The Pacific Review* 29.

[32] Chalermpalanupap and Ibañez, above n. 20, 139.

relevant rules. The variance in practice amongst ASEAN member states is to be expected, given the differential sizes in the maritime domains of some states: Indonesia and the Philippines are 'Archipelagic States' under Part IV of the LOSC; Brunei and Singapore have very short coastlines;[33] and Lao PDR is landlocked.

The regime of transit passage is especially prominent in the region, because the Straits of Malacca and Singapore are some of the most heavily transited international straits in the world.[34] Indonesia, Malaysia and Singapore, as the adjoining strait states, have in recent decades been able to assert a relatively common position on matters concerning the straits. During the LOSC negotiations they increasingly shared a common position on international straits, and took joint initiatives with the IMO to address navigational and maritime safety issues through the straits.[35] This level of cooperation was highlighted in April 1982, when Indonesia, Malaysia and Singapore indicated to the President of the Third UN Conference on the Law of the Sea that they had reached agreement with certain major maritime states on the application of the LOSC to the Straits of Malacca and Singapore, in particular with respect to the issue of laws and

---

[33] The coastal length of Brunei is 161 km and Singapore 193 km; compared to Indonesia (57,716 km) and the Philippines (36,289 km): Central Intelligence Agency, 'The World Factbook', available at www.cia.gov/library/publications/the-world-factbook/.

[34] See generally, Michael Leifer, *International Straits of the World: Malacca, Singapore and Indonesia* (Alphen aan den Rijn: Sijthoff & Noordhoff, 1978).

[35] Ibid., 141–8; Kheng Lian Koh, *Straits in International Navigation: Contemporary Issues* (London: Oceana, 1982) 55–95, 175–94.

regulations concerning traffic separation schemes in the Straits and also under keel clearance for certain ships.[36]

The level of legislative implementation of maritime security measures also varies (see Table 4.1), though this may be explained by differences in legal systems, including requirements for passing new laws and regulations to give effect to international legal commitments.[37] As archipelagic states whose status is recognised consistent with the LOSC, Indonesia and the Philippines have declared archipelagic baselines, thereby enclosing waters within their respective archipelagos. Consequently, within the 'archipelagic waters' that fall on the landward side of the archipelagic baselines, Indonesia and the Philippines enjoy virtually complete sovereignty, subject to certain navigational freedoms for foreign ships.[38] For example, in 2002 Indonesia adopted Government Regulation No. 37, which deals with the rights and obligations of foreign ships

[36] José Antonia de Yturriaga, *Straits Used for International Navigation: A Spanish Perspective* (Dordrecht: Martinus Nijhoff, 1991) 148–9. This 'understanding' was confirmed in letters of concurrence from representatives of Australia, France, the UK, the US, Japan and the Federal Republic of Germany. For the subsequent development, see Joshua H. Ho, 'Enhancing Safety, Security, and Environmental Protection of the Straits of Malacca and Singapore: The Cooperative Mechanism' (2009) 40 *Ocean Development and International Law* 233, 237–42.

[37] Robert C. Beckman and J. Ashley Roach, 'Ratification and Implementation of Global Conventions on Piracy and Maritime Crimes' in Robert C. Beckman and J. Ashley Roach (eds.), *Piracy and International Maritime Crimes in ASEAN: Prospects for Cooperation* (Cheltenham: Edward Elgar, 2012) 165, 170.

[38] LOSC, above n. 11, art. 53. For discussion, see Donald R. Rothwell and Tim Stephens, *The International Law of the Sea* (2nd edn, Oxford: Hart/Bloomsbury, 2016) 197–201.

Table 4.1 *Status of Maritime Security-Related Treaties and Legislation*

LOSC: Convention on the Law of the Sea

SUA Convention: Convention for the Suppression of Unlawful Acts against the Safety of Maritime Navigation

ReCAAP: Regional Cooperation Agreement on Combating Piracy and Armed Robbery against Ships in Asia

a: accession   s: signature   n: notification   r: ratification

	LOSC	SUA Convention	ReCAAP	Primary Legislative Instruments
Brunei	s (5 Dec. 1984) r (5 Nov. 1996)	r (4 Dec. 2003)	a (28 Oct. 2006)	Merchant Shipping (Safety Convention) Regulations 2003 (amended in 2004); Maritime Offences (Ships and Fixed Platforms) Order 2007
Cambodia	s (1 Jul. 1983)	a (18 Aug. 2006)	n (3 May 2006)	Law on Counter-Terrorism 2007 (ch 7)
Indonesia	s (10 Dec. 1982) r (3 Feb. 1986)	–	–	Law on Indonesian Waters 1996; Regulation No. 37/2002
Lao PDR	s (10 Dec. 1982) r (5 Jun. 1998)	a (20 Mar. 2012)	n (11 Jul. 2005)	–
Malaysia	s (10 Dec. 1982) r (14 Oct. 1996)	–	–	Malaysian Maritime Enforcement Agency Act 2004
Myanmar	s (10 Dec. 1982) r (21 May 1996)	a (19 Sep. 2003)	n (6 Feb. 2006)	–

Philippines	s (10 Dec. 1982) r (8 May 1984)	r (6 Jan. 2004)	n (31 Jan. 2006)	Republic Act No. 3046/1961 to Define the Baselines of the Territorial Sea of the Philippines, as amended by Republic Act No. 5446/1968 and No. 9522/2009; Executive Order No. 57/2011
Singapore	s (10 Dec. 1982) r (17 Nov. 1994)	a (3 Feb. 2004)	n (28 Apr. 2005)	Maritime Offences Act 2003
Thailand	s (10 Dec. 1982) r (15 May 2011)	–	n (3 Sep. 2005)	Prevention and Suppression of Piracy Act 1991
Vietnam	s (10 Dec. 1982) r (25 Jul. 1994)	a (12 Jul. 2002)	n (26 May 2006)	Law on Maritime Code 2005; Law of the Sea of Vietnam 2012

and aircraft in passage,[39] and makes direct reference to archipelagic sea lanes passage by foreign ships and aircraft as a right recognised under Indonesian law.[40]

The Philippines, on the other hand, has yet to adopt equivalent laws;[41] nor has it enacted legislation to implement its obligations under the SUA Convention and the associated Protocol on Fixed Platforms, which it ratified on 6 January 2004.[42] For the Philippines, maritime security issues such as piracy and armed robbery at sea are nearly indistinguishable from maritime terrorism due to the political context in which these activities have taken place. Groups such as Abu Sayyaf Group commit piracy and armed robbery for sources of funding and as political tools, and hence these activities have been addressed within the context of counter-terrorism laws.[43] In

---

[39] Regulation No. 37/2002 on the Rights and Obligations of Foreign Ships and Aircraft Exercising the Right of Archipelagic Sea Lanes Passage through Designated Sea Lanes (Indonesia), reproduced in (2003) 52 *Law of the Sea Bulletin* 20.

[40] Law on Indonesian Waters 1997 (Indonesia); see also Regulation No. 37/2002 on the Rights and Obligations of Foreign Ships and Aircraft Exercising the Right of Archipelagic Sea Lanes Passage through Designated Sea Lanes (Indonesia) art. 2.

[41] For discussion, see Tara Davenport, 'The Archipelagic Regime' in Donald R. Rothwell, Alex G. Oude Elferink, Karen N. Scott and Tim Stephens (eds.), *The Oxford Handbook of the Law of the Sea* (Oxford: Oxford University Press, 2015) 134, 150–4.

[42] For discussion of the consequences of not implementing legislation, see Robert Beckman, 'Piracy and Armed Robbery against Ships in Southeast Asia' in Douglas Guilfoyle (ed.), *Modern Piracy: Legal Challenges and Responses* (Cheltenham: Edward Elgar, 2013) 13, 31.

[43] Sandra L. Hodgkinson, 'The Incorporation of International Law to Define Piracy Crimes, National Laws, and the Definition of Piracy' in

2009, the Philippines reached an agreement with the US to undertake a programme of counter-piracy training and education, in direct response to the security threats posed by piracy to shipping.[44] Nevertheless, the Philippines has also adopted policy responses to ASEAN regional cooperative initiatives against maritime security threats and challenges. An example is the establishment of a National Coast Watch System in 2011, which was designed to provide for a 'coordinated and coherent approach on maritime issues and maritime security operations'.[45]

While neither Indonesia nor Malaysia are party to the SUA Convention or the ReCAAP Agreement, both have been actively participating in joint maritime operations, because of concerns about allowing a foreign military presence – such as US navy vessels and Japanese patrol ships – in the Straits of Malacca to combat piracy and maritime terrorism.[46] The 2004

Michael P. Scharf, Michael A. Newton and Milena Sterio (eds.), *Prosecuting Maritime Piracy: Domestic Solutions to International Crimes* (Cambridge: Cambridge University Press, 2015) 32, 51–2. See also Chapter 3.3 for analysis of the implementation of counter-terrorism law and policy in the Philippines.

[44] Memorandum of Cooperation between the Government of the United States of America and the Government of the Republic of the Philippines on Maritime Counter-Piracy Training and Education, signed in Washington DC, US, 31 July 2009.

[45] Executive Order No. 57/2011 'Establishing a National Coast Watch System, Providing for its Structure and Defining the Roles and Responsibilities of Member Agencies in Providing Coordinated Inter-Agency Maritime Security Operations and for Other Purposes' (Philippines) s. 1.

[46] For details, see Yann-huei Song, 'Regional Maritime Security Initiative (RMSI) and Enhancing Security in the Straits of Malacca: Littoral States' and Regional Responses' in Shicun Wu, Keyuan Zou and Tim Benbow (eds.), *Maritime Security in the South China Sea: Regional Implications and*

trilateral agreement between Indonesia, Malaysia and Singapore to undertake coordinated counter-piracy patrols in the Straits of Malacca, and the associated 'Eyes in the Sky' patrols under the Malacca Straits Patrol Network, is a prominent example of regional maritime cooperation.[47] Further, in May 2016, Indonesia, Malaysia and the Philippines agreed to conduct coordinated maritime patrols and to establish a hotline to respond to piracy and kidnapping in their adjoining waters.[48] Additional agreements were reached in August 2016 to support joint patrols that facilitate aspects of 'hot pursuit', with a view to combating piracy, terrorism and transnational crimes at sea.[49] These joint patrols were expanded in 2017 to include Brunei in response to the maritime security issues arising from the activities of Abu Sayyaf in the southern Philippines and adjacent Sulu Sea.[50]

International Cooperation (Abingdon: Routledge, 2009) 109, 111–20; J. N. Mak, 'Securitizing Piracy in Southeast Asia: Malaysia, the International Maritime Bureau and Singapore' in Mely Caballero-Anthony, Ralf Emmers and Amitav Acharya (eds.), *Non-Traditional Security in Asia: Dilemmas in Securitization* (Aldershot: Ashgate, 2006) 66, 82.

[47] Carolin Liss, *Oceans of Crime: Maritime Piracy and Transnational Security in Southeast Asia and Bangladesh* (Singapore: Institute of Southeast Asian Studies, 2011) 295; Song, above n. 46, 124–5.

[48] Joe Cochrane, 'Indonesia, Malaysia and Philippines to Bolster Security at Sea', *New York Times*, 5 May 2016, available at www.nytimes.com/2016/05/06/world/asia/indonesia-malaysia-philippines-naval-patrols.html?_f=0.

[49] Ben Otto, 'Indonesia, Malaysia, Philippines Agree on Maritime "Hot Pursuit"', *The Wall Street Journal*, 2 August 2016, available at www.wsj.com/articles/indonesia-malaysia-philippines-agree-on-maritime-hot-pursuit-1470139890.

[50] Ana Jacinta Olabre and Alexis Romero, 'Philippines, Indonesia, Malaysia Kick Off Joint Patrols in Sulu Sea', *The Philippine Star*, 19 June 2017,

In Brunei,[51] Cambodia[52] and Myanmar,[53] although the number of piracy and armed robbery incidents are relatively low, authorities have nonetheless been concerned about their capability to deal with non-traditional maritime security issues effectively. These states have benefitted from information-sharing and capacity-building through the ReCAAP Information Sharing Centre. In Thailand, the Maritime Enforcement Coordinating Centre has been the main mechanism to coordinate maritime operations, with its maritime enforcement functions being upgraded in 2005 to handle a variety of maritime security issues including piracy and armed robbery at sea, illegal fishing and trafficking in persons.[54] Vietnam is a party to the SUA Convention and the ReCAAP Agreement,[55] but its primary

available at www.philstar.com/headlines/2017/06/19/1711573/philippines-in donesia-malaysia-kick-joint-patrols-sulu-sea.

[51] Brunei Darussalam ratified the SUA Convention and its Protocol (above n. 9) on 4 December 2003 and implemented its obligations by promulgating the Merchant Shipping (Safety Convention) Regulations 2003 (amended in 2004) and the Maritime Offences (Ships and Fixed Platforms) Order 2007.

[52] Chheang Vannarith, 'Cambodia: Maritime Security Challenges and Priorities' (Cambodian Institute for Cooperation and Peace, Working Paper No. 32, 2010) 9–10, 13; Chap Sotharith, 'Maritime Security in Cambodia: A Critical Assessment (Cambodian Institute for Cooperation and Peace, Working Paper No. 21, 2007) 13–15.

[53] See Jürgen Haacke, 'Myanmar and Maritime Security', The Asian Forum, 22 February 2016, available at www.theasanforum.org/myan mar-and-maritime-security/.

[54] Somjade Kongrawd, 'Legal Frameworks for Combating IUU Fishing in Thailand' in Vijay Sakhuja and Kapil Narula (eds.), Maritime Safety and Security in Indian Ocean (Delhi: Vij Books India, 2016) ch 8.

[55] There is no specific legislation to implement its obligations under the SUA Convention or the ReCAAP Agreement, while the Law on

maritime security concern is the territorial and maritime dispute in the East Sea (South China Sea) with the PRC.[56] Vietnam has been the recipient of significant naval capability development assistance from extra-regional powers such as Japan and the US.[57]

4.4 ASEAN's Engagement with the South China Sea Dispute

The South China Sea has proven to be a particularly contentious maritime security challenge for ASEAN because of the differing positions and interests of ASEAN member states, and the role of the PRC and to a lesser extent the Republic of China (Taiwan).[58] The region has long been the subject of

Maritime Code 2005 provides detailed regulation of shipping: Beckman and Roach, above n. 37, 194.

[56] See discussion in Carlyle A. Thayer, 'Vietnam's Strategy of "Cooperating and Struggling" with China over Maritime Disputes in the South China Sea' (2016) 3 *Journal of Asian Security and International Affairs* 200.

[57] See e.g., Wendell Minnick, 'Vietnam Pushes Modernization as China Challenge Grows', *Defense News*, 30 August 2015, available at www.defensenews.com/story/defense/naval/2015/08/30/vietnam-pushes-modernization-china-challenge-grows/32042259/.

[58] There are hundreds of small islands, rocks and low tide elevations scattered throughout the South China Sea which are the subject of competing claims by Brunei, Malaysia, the Philippines, the PRC, Taiwan and Vietnam. Indonesia also claims islands that fall within the South China Sea, but those claims are uncontested and are at the southern extremity of the region. See generally, Keyuan Zou, 'The South China Sea' in Donald R. Rothwell, Alex G. Oude Elferink, Karen N. Scott and Tim Stephens (eds.), *The Oxford Handbook of the Law of the Sea* (Oxford: Oxford University Press, 2015) 626; Robert Beckman, 'The UN Convention on the Law of the Sea and the Maritime Disputes in the South China Sea' (2013) 107 *American Journal of International Law* 142.

both territorial and maritime disputes, and since the 1970s small-scale military clashes and stand-offs have occurred between the PRC and Vietnam (in 1974, 1988 and 2014),[59] and the PRC and the Philippines (over Scarborough Shoal in 2012). Terse diplomatic exchanges have also occurred following the arrest of fishing vessels alleged to have engaged in illegal fishing.[60] In 2013, the Philippines commenced proceedings against the PRC before an Arbitral Tribunal pursuant to Annex VII of the LOSC in relation to their South China Sea maritime disputes. The Award of the Tribunal, delivered on 12 July 2016, found unanimously for the Philippines in holding that the PRC had committed numerous breaches of the LOSC.[61]

[59] The most recent of these clashes arose in 2014 following the positioning by the Chinese National Offshore Oil Company of an oil rig in waters between the Vietnamese coast and the Chinese claimed and occupied Paracel Islands: 'China Sends Four Oil Rigs to South China Sea amid Regional Tensions over Territorial Claims', *ABC News*, 21 June 2014, available at www.abc.net .au/news/2014–06-20/china-sends-four-oil-rigs-to-south-china-sea-amid-tensions/5540432.

[60] See generally, Leszek Buszynski, 'The Origins and Development of the South China Sea Maritime Dispute' in Leszek Buszynski and Christopher B. Roberts (eds.), *The South China Sea Maritime Dispute: Political, Legal and Regional Perspectives* (Abingdon: Routledge, 2015) 1; Nong Hong, *UNCLOS and Ocean Dispute Settlement: Law and Politics in the South China Sea* (Abingdon: Routledge, 2012) 5–33; J. N. Mak, 'Sovereignty in ASEAN and the Problem of Maritime Cooperation in the South China Sea' in Sam Bateman and Ralf Emmers (eds.), *Security and International Politics in the South China Sea: Towards a Cooperative Management Regime* (Abingdon: Routledge, 2009) 110.

[61] *In the Matter of the South China Arbitration before an Arbitral Tribunal Constituted under Annex VII to the 1982 United Nations Convention on*

As discussed in the Introduction and Chapter 1, ASEAN is not well equipped to deal with an inter-state dispute involving an extra-regional power despite the fact that the contracting parties to the TAC, to which the PRC has acceded, may form a High Council with the power to recommend appropriate means of settlement and appropriate measures for the prevention of a deterioration of the dispute or the situation.[62] Nevertheless, ASEAN has played a limited role in facilitating the peaceful management of the dispute with a dual approach.

The first is to engage the PRC in preventing escalation of the disputes, with the adoption of the 2002 Declaration on the Conduct of Parties in the South China Sea (DOC) between the ten ASEAN member states and the PRC;[63] and a proposed 'Code of Conduct'. The DOC sought to promote a 'peaceful, friendly and harmonious environment' in the South China Sea, and reaffirmed a commitment towards the provisions of the LOSC and the TAC. In particular, the DOC reaffirmed a commitment to the LOSC freedoms of navigation and overflight; the resolution of disputes without recourse to the use of force; the 'exercise of self-restraint in the conduct of activities that would complicate or escalate disputes', including

the *Law of the Sea between the Republic of the Philippines and the People's Republic of China* (Award), PCA Case No. 2013–19 (12 July 2016), para. 1203. For analysis of different aspects of the decision, see contributions to the South China Sea Agora in (2016) 34 *Australian Year Book of International Law* 21–86.

[62] Treaty of Amity and Cooperation in Southeast Asia, adopted 24 February 1976, 1025 UNTS 319 (entered into force 15 July 1976) arts. 14 and 15.

[63] Adopted at the 8th ASEAN Summit, Phnom Penh, Cambodia, 4 November 2002, reproduced in (2003) 2 *Chinese Journal of International Law* 418.

inhabiting what were at the time uninhabited maritime features; and the undertaking of a range of cooperative activities with respect to marine environmental protection, marine scientific research, the safety of navigation and search and rescue.

The DOC thus provided a legal framework within which ASEAN member states re-affirmed the application of existing rules and principles, and clarified what those rules and principles would require in managing the South China Sea dispute.[64] However, ASEAN member states are not necessarily united beyond this minimum common denominator, as demonstrated most notably by the failure of the 45th ASEAN Ministerial Meeting in 2012 to adopt a joint communiqué, for the first time in ASEAN history, because of disagreement about a reference to the South China Sea dispute.[65] Despite its centrality to ASEAN's shared approach to South China Sea dispute management, the DOC remains a legally non-binding instrument. Indeed, it was treated as such by the South China Sea Arbitral Tribunal, which

[64] Rob McLaughlin and Hitoshi Nasu, 'The Law's Potential to Break – Rather Than Entrench – the South China Sea Deadlock?' (2016) 21 *Journal of Conflict & Security Law* 305, 315–16; Robert C. Beckman, 'Legal Regimes for Cooperation in the South China Sea' in Sam Bateman and Ralf Emmers (eds.), *Security and International Politics in the South China Sea: Towards a Cooperative Management Regime* (Abingdon: Routledge, 2009) 222, 227–8; Kriangsak Kittichaisaree, 'A Code of Conduct for Human and Regional Security around the South China Sea' (2001) 32 *Ocean Development & International Law* 131, 134–40.

[65] For details, see Carlyle A. Thayer, 'ASEAN's Code of Conduct in the South China Sea: A Litmus Test for Community-Building' (2012) 10(34) *The Asia-Pacific Journal* No. 4.

observed that 'the DOC was not intended to be a legally binding instrument with respect to dispute resolution', and that 'the Parties' subsequent conduct further confirms that the DOC is not a binding agreement'.[66]

The DOC envisaged the eventual adoption of a Code of Conduct,[67] for which ASEAN and the PRC have engaged in multiple intermittent negotiations in the intervening period.[68] Notwithstanding some simmering tensions following the 2016 Arbitral Award,[69] significant progress was made in

[66] *In the Matter of an Arbitration before an Arbitral Tribunal Constituted under Annex VII to the 1982 United Nations Convention on the Law of the Sea between the Republic of the Philippines and the People's Republic of China* (Award on Jurisdiction and Admissibility), PCA Case No. 2013–19 (29 October 2015), paras. 217–18.

[67] DOC, above n. 63, para. 11.

[68] See generally, Carlyle A. Thayer, 'ASEAN, China and the Code of Conduct in the South China Sea' (2013) 33(2) *SAIS Review of International Affairs* 75.

[69] See e.g., Chairman's Statement of the 28th and 29th ASEAN Summits, Vientiane, Lao PDR, 6–7 September 2016, para. 121; Ministry of Foreign Affairs (Singapore), 'MFA Spokesman's Comments on the Ruling of the Arbitral Tribunal in the Philippines v China Case under Annex VII to the 1982 United Nations Convention on the Law of the Sea (UNCLOS)' (Press Release, 12 July 2016), available at www.mfa.g ov.sg/content/mfa/media_centre/press_room/pr/2016/201607/pres s_20160712_2.html. For differing views on ASEAN's response to the 2016 Arbitral Award, see Elina Noor, 'ASEAN not so Divided on the South China Sea', *East Asia Forum*, 17 August 2016, available at www. eastasiaforum.org/2016/08/17/asean-not-so-divided-the-south-china-se a/; Adam Leong Kok Wey, 'Is the South China Sea Fracturing ASEAN?', *East Asia Forum*, 25 August 2016, available at www.east asiaforum.org/2016/08/25/is-the-south-china-sea-fracturing-ASEAN; Prashanth Parameswaran, 'Assessing ASEAN's South China Sea Position in its Post-Ruling Statement', *The Diplomat*, 25 July 2016,

2017 with the parties agreeing to a timetable to start negotiations on the final text of a legally binding Code of Conduct in 2018.[70] However, it remains to be seen whether these negotiations within the agreed framework will succeed in bringing ASEAN's efforts to manage the dispute into fruition,[71] and what this will mean for the exercise of ASEAN's legal authority in dealing with a regional security issue involving the interests of an extra-regional power.

The second approach pursued by ASEAN with respect to the South China Sea dispute has been the prevention of maritime incidents through ASEAN maritime security initiatives. One of these initiatives is the preparation of the 'Guidelines' for maritime interaction among ASEAN member states in response to maritime emergencies. In 2017, the ADMM adopted a Concept Paper on the Guidelines for Maritime Interaction,[72] designed to address the diverse maritime security challenges faced by ASEAN, and to be observed by naval ships

available at http://thediplomat.com/2016/07/assessing-aseans-south-china-sea-position-in-its-post-ruling-statement/.

[70] Framework of a Code of Conduct for the South China Sea, adopted at the 14th ASEAN-China Senior Officials Meeting on the Declaration on the Conduct of Parties in the South China Sea, Guiyang, PRC, 18 May 2017 and endorsed by the Joint Communiqué of the 50th ASEAN Foreign Ministers' Meeting, Manila, Philippines, 5 August 2017, para. 195.

[71] For critical assessment, see Thayer, above n. 68, 82; Lee YingHui, 'A South China Sea Code of Conduct: Is Real Progress Possible?', *The Diplomat*, 18 November 2017, available at https://thediplomat.com/2017/11/a-south-china-sea-code-of-conduct-is-real-progress-possible/.

[72] Concept Paper on the Guidelines for Maritime Interaction (19 September 2017), adopted at the 11th ASEAN Defence Ministers' Meeting, Clark, Philippines, 23 October 2017.

and naval aircraft.[73] The Concept Paper envisages the Guidelines to, inter alia, uphold existing maritime arrangements between ASEAN member states including the LOSC, complement various regional security forums that address maritime security issues and reaffirm ASEAN member states' commitment to the resolution of disputes through peaceful means without resorting to the use of force.[74] The Guidelines are expected to help prevent undesirable incidents that might occur in and over the South China Sea due to miscalculation.[75]

In addition, a Joint Statement was issued on the Application of the Code for Unplanned Encounters at Sea (CUES) in the South China Sea.[76] The CUES had previously been agreed upon in 2014 at a meeting of the Western Pacific Naval Symposium, and while not a legally binding instrument, it is designed to achieve a 'coordinated means of communication to maximise safety at sea', consistent with existing international law and maritime practice.[77] The 2017 Concept Paper

---

[73] Ibid., paras. 6–7. [74] Ibid., paras. 9–12.

[75] Joint Declaration of the ASEAN Defence Ministers on Partnering for Change, Engaging the World, adopted at the 11th ASEAN Defence Ministers' Meeting, Manila, Philippines, 23 October 2017, para. 14.

[76] Joint Statement of the 19th ASEAN-China Summit to Commemorate the 25th Anniversary of ASEAN-China Dialogue Relations, Vientiane, Lao PDR, 7 September 2016, para. 6; see also, Ministry of Foreign Affairs (PRC), 'The 19th China-ASEAN Summit Adopts Guidelines for Hotline Communications among Senior Officials of the Ministries of Foreign Affairs of China and ASEAN Member States in Response to Maritime Emergencies' (Press Release, 8 September 2016), available at www.fmprc.gov.cn/mfa_eng/zxxx_662805/t1396703.shtml.

[77] Code for Unplanned Encounters at Sea, adopted at the Western Pacific Naval Symposium, Qing Dao, PRC, 22 April 2014, s. 1.1.1, available at https://news.usni.org/2014/06/17/document-conductunplanned-encounters-sea.

on Guidelines for Maritime Interaction also reaffirmed the importance of CUES to prevent maritime incidents.[78]

These developments are arguably reflective of ASEAN's greater willingness to exercise its authority regarding norm development and localisation, to the extent that a dispute threatens regional security and stability. ASEAN has resolutely continued with its commitment to the DOC and the negotiation of a Code of Conduct, while developing a regional norm on maritime interaction to prevent maritime incidents in the South China Sea. However, ASEAN's institutional ability to engage in normative processes with regard to the South China Sea dispute has been significantly constrained, given the different national interests that are at stake and the strong political interest of extra-regional powers involved in the dispute.

4.5 Concluding Observations

Although there is some shared ground for regional cooperation, Southeast Asian nations have different maritime security interests, concerns and levels of capability to undertake naval and maritime law enforcement activities. Indonesia, Malaysia and Singapore have primarily been concerned about ensuring safety and security in major sea lanes, including international straits and archipelagic waters, as well as combating piracy and armed robbery at sea through coordinated or joint

Western Pacific Naval Symposium members include the PRC and the eight maritime ASEAN member states.
[78] Concept Paper on the Guidelines for Maritime Interaction, above n. 72, paras. 7 and 10.

patrols. Piracy and armed robbery issues are enmeshed with maritime terrorism in the Philippines due to their political struggle with various non-state armed groups, whereas the same issues intersect with human trafficking in Thailand. For Vietnam, Malaysia and, until very recently, the Philippines, the modernisation of naval and maritime law enforcement capabilities has been their priority, to deal with territorial and maritime disputes with the PRC in the South China Sea.

With these disparate maritime security interests, the potential for ASEAN to exercise its legal authority to engage in normative processes to address regional maritime security issues is somewhat compromised. Nevertheless, ASEAN has engaged in maritime security initiatives in areas such as counter-piracy, counter-robbery at sea, ship and port facility security, maritime search and rescue of persons, and communication hotlines in the case of maritime emergencies. Many of these initiatives have then been internalised in ASEAN member states through the enactment or amendment of relevant legislation, capacity-building or policy implementation, either individually or jointly, as international concern over maritime security in the region intensifies. By contrast, ASEAN's institutional ability to engage in normative processes with regard to the South China Sea dispute has been significantly constrained despite various efforts to build upon a shared interest in the maintenance of maritime security and stability in the region.

Chapter 5

Cyber Security

5.1 Introduction

According to analysis by the Organisation for Economic Co-operation and Development (OECD), most domestic cyber security policies focus on achieving two interconnected objectives: 'strengthening cyber security for the internet economy to further drive economic and social prosperity; and protecting cyber-space reliant societies against cyber-threats'.[1] ASEAN's cyber security policy has indeed developed along this line of dual functions, although with some modification towards further regional integration and more active engagement with external actors. On one hand, ASEAN has attempted to secure cyberspace through regional cooperation in building national cyber security resilience. On the other hand, ASEAN has realised the need for more comprehensive cyber security efforts in order to secure cyberspace from common threats such as transnational cyber intrusions by criminal and terrorist

---

[1] OECD, 'Cybersecurity Policy Making at a Turning Point: Analysing a New Generation of National Cybersecurity Strategies for the Internet Economy' (OECD Digital Economy Papers No. 211, 2012) 6, available at https://ccdcoe.org/sites/default/files/documents/OECD-121116-Cyber securityPolicyMaking.pdf.

organisations.[2] The present and future uncertainty about the cyber security landscape and its implications for geopolitical rivalry, both within ASEAN and with extra-regional powers, pose challenges to ASEAN's ability to galvanise members into cooperative action on cyber security.[3]

Further challenges arise from the lack of a uniform legal framework governing conduct in cyberspace.[4] There is limited guidance available in existing international legal instruments including the Council of Europe's Convention on Cybercrime[5] and UN General Assembly Resolution 55/63.[6] An authoritative study has also been compiled in the Tallinn Manual on the International Law Applicable to Cyber Operations,[7] which clarifies how existing rules of international

---

[2] For details, see Hitoshi Nasu and Helen Trezise, 'Cyber Security in the Asia-Pacific' in Nicholas Tsagourias and Russell Buchan (eds.), *Research Handbook on International Law and Cyberspace* (Cheltenham: Edward Elgar, 2015) 446, 451–5; Nicholas Thomas, 'Cyber Security in East Asia: Governing Anarchy' (2009) 5 *Asian Security* 3, 11.

[3] See Nicholas Rees, 'EU and ASEAN: Issues of Regional Security' (2010) 47 *International Politics* 402, 408.

[4] Cf. Martha Finnemore and Duncan B. Hollis, 'Constructing Norms for Global Cybersecurity' (2016) 110 *American Journal of International Law* 425.

[5] Adopted 23 November 2001, ETS No. 185, 2296 UNTS 167 (entered into force 1 July 2004).

[6] UN Doc A/RES/55/63 (4 December 2000) ('Combating the Criminal Misuse of Information Technologies').

[7] Michael N. Schmitt (ed.), *Tallinn Manual on the International Law Applicable to Cyber Warfare* (Cambridge: Cambridge University Press, 2013); Michael N. Schmitt (ed.), *Tallinn Manual 2.0 on the International Law Applicable to Cyber Operations* (Cambridge: Cambridge University Press, 2017).

law would apply to the use of cyberspace. However, critical differences exist at the fundamental level in the understanding of how principles of international law apply, or ought to be applied, to ensure a secure and stable cyberspace. At one end of the spectrum, for those who consider cyberspace as a 'free space', cyber security policies need to respect human rights such as freedom of expression and privacy. At the other end of spectrum, a top-down governmental regulatory approach demands the imposition of law and order, including the ban on the use of the Internet 'to incite ethnic hatred and separatism, to promote cult and to distribute salacious, pornographic, violent or terrorist information'.[8] These critical differences in the legal approach to regulating cyberspace also cast a shadow on the cyber security debate in ASEAN forums.[9]

ASEAN is one of the first regional institutions that started collectively engaging in cyber capacity-building as the age of information technology commenced. While the international legal framework was still evolving, ASEAN had to tackle various security dimensions of cyberspace within the context of existing socio-political situations, geopolitical rivalry and the 'digital divide' among its member states in terms of cyber capabilities and vulnerabilities. This chapter examines ASEAN's evolving practice in building relevant legal infrastructure to secure cyberspace in each member state

---

[8] ASEAN Regional Forum, *Annual Security Outlook 2013* (Jakarta: ASEAN Secretariat, 2013) 46.

[9] See e.g., Co-Chair's Summary Report on ARF Workshop on Measures to Enhance Cyber Security – Legal and Cultural Aspects, Beijing, the PRC, 11–12 September 2013, paras. 33–7.

and considers how it has facilitated the development, localisation and internalisation of relevant norms as cyber infrastructure matures and societies become increasingly interconnected online.

5.2 ASEAN's Engagement with Cyber Security

ASEAN started its engagement with cyberspace by adopting the 1999 e-ASEAN initiative, which focused on the establishment of cyber infrastructure through facilitation of e-commerce, trade, investment and capacity-building. At the Fourth ASEAN Informal Summit in Singapore in 2000, the e-ASEAN Framework Agreement was signed to provide a legal foundation for a structural implementation of the initiative.[10] The Agreement required member states to 'adopt electronic commerce regulatory and legislative frameworks that create trust and confidence for consumers and facilitate the transformation of businesses towards the development of e-ASEAN'.[11] However, as cyber infrastructure continues to develop at an alarmingly rapid pace, and the government and the whole of society becomes reliant on it, some states – most notably Singapore, Thailand and Lao PDR – have increasingly become concerned by the potential vulnerability of governments in cyberspace.

---

[10] Adopted 24 November 2000 (not in force). It requires the deposit of instruments of ratification or acceptance by all signatory governments for its entry into force: ibid., art. 15. As at 1 September 2018, Cambodia, Lao PDR, Malaysia and Vietnam have not ratified or accepted this agreement.
[11] Ibid., art. 5(1).

Such recognition of government vulnerability in cyberspace has a logical fit with the ethos of ASEAN, which was established to cooperatively ensure the political stability of each member state, as well as to protect regional security from external interference.[12] However, the increased recognition of cyberspace as the fifth domain of warfare poses challenges to the development of regional cyber security architecture within the ASEAN legal framework. Hostile or malicious use of cyberspace has the potential to amplify existing geopolitical tensions in the region and could even trigger a spiral of conflict. These mixed motives for cyber security regulation are reflected, with varying degrees of success, in the three different ways that cyber security has been addressed within ASEAN and through its external relations with major extra-regional powers.

First, a common regional framework for cyber security capacity-building has been developed with particular focus on the establishment of national Computer Emergency Response Teams (CERTs), as envisaged in the 2003 Singapore Declaration.[13] This common regional framework was needed to enable the sharing of cyber expertise and cyber security threat and vulnerability assessment information so as to 'help develop cybersecurity policies and exchange real-time information on cybersecurity issues'.[14] This is particularly vital to

---

[12] See Introduction and Chapter 1.2.
[13] See Singapore Declaration, adopted at the 3rd Meeting of ASEAN Telecommunications & IT Ministers, Singapore, 19 September 2003.
[14] Joint Media Statement of the Third ASEAN Telecommunications & IT Ministers, Singapore, 19 September 2003, para. 4. See also, ASEAN Economic Community Blueprint, adopted at the 13th ASEAN Summit, Singapore, 20 November 2007, para. 51.

cyber security in Southeast Asia as less developed countries are at greater risk of cyber intrusion, creating an imperative for regional cooperation in capacity-building exercises and other cyber security measures aimed at mitigating potential 'weak links'.[15] Recognising that a significant digital divide remains in the region, the ASEAN ICT Masterplan 2015 calls for the establishment of common minimum standards for network security, the promotion of CERT cooperation, as well as the sharing of expertise and best practices.[16]

Second, ASEAN has sought to address cyber insecurity, particularly threats posed by non-state actors, along with other common security challenges within the region through its Political-Security Community. Within this Community, cyber security has primarily been the domain of the ARF, as part of its focus on counter-terrorism and transnational crime. Since 2004, the ARF has conducted regular seminars and workshops on cyberspace, with particular focus on cyber terrorism, incident response, capacity-building and the threat of proxy actors.[17] In 2006, ARF member states issued the Statement on

[15] Caitríona H. Heinl, 'Regional Cyber Security: Moving towards a Resilient ASEAN Cyber Security Regime' (Working Paper No. 263, S Rajaratnam School of International Studies, 9 September 2013) 12, available at www .rsis.edu.sg/wp-content/uploads/rsis-pubs/WP263.pdf.

[16] ASEAN ICT Masterplan 2015, adopted at the 10th Meeting of ASEAN Telecommunications & IT Ministers, Kuala Lumpur, Malaysia, 13–14 January 2011, Initiative 4.2. See also, ASEAN ICT Masterplan 2020, adopted at the 15th Meeting of ASEAN Telecommunications & IT Ministers, Da Nang, Vietnam, 27 November 2015, Initiatives 8.1 and 8.2.

[17] Recent examples include: ARF Workshop on Operationalising Confidence Building Measures for Cooperation during Cyber-incident Response, Kuala Lumpur, Malaysia, 2–3 March 2016; ARF Seminar on

Cooperation in Fighting Cyber Attack and Terrorist Misuse of Cyberspace,[18] which encouraged enhanced national and regional cyber security regimes on the grounds that 'an effective fight against cyber-attacks and terrorist misuse of cyber space requires increased, rapid and well-functioning legal and other forms of cooperation'.[19] This policy was endorsed in the Hanoi Plan of Action to Implement the ARF Vision Statement by the ARF SOM in May 2010.[20] In 2012, the ARF adopted the Statement on Cooperation in Ensuring Cyber Security,[21] with a view to developing a cyber security specific work plan.[22]

A counter-terrorism approach to cyber security has been further promoted by APEC's Counter Terrorism Action Plans,[23] which devote a section to 'promoting cyber security' and reaffirm the commitment to 'counter . . . terrorism by implementing and

Operationalizing Cyber CBMs in the ARF, Singapore, 21–22 October 2015; ARF Workshop on Cyber Security Capacity Building, Beijing, PRC, 29–30 July 2015; ARF Workshop on Cyber Confidence Building Measures, Kuala Lumpur, Malaysia, 25–26 March 2014. See also, Co-Chairs' Summary Report of the Thirteenth ASEAN Regional Forum Inter-Sessional Meeting on Counter-Terrorism and Transnational Crime, Nanning, PRC, 14–15 May 2015, section 5.1.3.

[18] Adopted at the 13th ARF Meeting, Kuala Lumpur, Malaysia, 28 July 2006.
[19] Ibid.
[20] Hanoi Plan of Action to Implement the ASEAN Regional Forum Vision Statement, adopted at the 17th ARF Meeting, Hanoi, Vietnam, 20 May 2010, para. 2.
[21] Adopted at the 19th ARF Meeting, Phnom Penh, Cambodia, 12 July 2012.
[22] ASEAN Regional Forum Work Plan on Security of and in the Use of Information and Communications Technologies (ICTs), adopted at the 22nd ARF Meeting, Kuala Lumpur, Malaysia, 6 August 2015.
[23] See Chapter 3.2.

enhancing critical information infrastructure protection and cyber security to ensure a trusted, secure and sustainable online environment'.[24] This voluntary measure allows member economies to detail their cyber security measures and cyber capacity-building needs, with an emphasis on proactive engagement with the private sector. Significantly for the wider Asia-Pacific region, this initiative provides a pragmatic solution to the sovereignty issue that the PRC's 'One China' policy poses to ASEAN and its related forums, as the reach of APEC's cyber security activities extends to Taiwan and Hong Kong – two of the most networked economies in the region.[25]

Third, ASEAN has more recently provided a forum in which military cyber security capabilities and threats can be discussed, particularly through the ADMMs, and often involving dialogues with extra-regional powers. Despite the cooperative security foundation set out in the 2006 ARF Cyber Security Statement, the 2012 ARF Statement on Cooperation in Ensuring Cyber Security implicitly recognises the growing correlation between cyberspace and national security concerns.[26] In August 2013 at the Second

---

[24] See e.g., 2014 APEC Counter Terrorism Action Plan – Singapore (2015/SOM1/CTWG/018), submitted to the APEC 4th Counter-Terrorism Working Group Meeting, Subic, Philippines, 31 January to 1 February 2015, 21. The plans also include the 2010 commitment to 'enhance mutual cooperation on countering malicious online activities and engage in efforts to increase cybersecurity awareness'.

[25] See Nasu and Trezise, above n. 2, 459–62.

[26] ARF Statement on Cooperation in Ensuring Cyber Security, above n. 21, preamble para. 9 (highlighting 'the need for further dialogue on the development of confidence-building and other transparency measures to reduce the risk of misperception, escalation and conflict').

ADMM-Plus Meeting, ASEAN Defence Ministers and eight ASEAN Dialogue Partners discussed what role the defence sector had to play in addressing emerging non-traditional security threats, including cyber security.[27] In May 2016 ASEAN Defence Ministers adopted the Concept Paper on the Establishment of the ADMM-Plus Experts' Working Group on Cyber Security,[28] which focused solely on cyber security issues related to the defence and military sectors.[29]

A critical challenge to the e-ASEAN initiative and the three areas of regional cooperation for cyber security outlined above lies with the different socio-political systems prevailing in ASEAN.[30] Indeed, during the 12th Asia Security Summit (Shangri-La Dialogue), held in Singapore from 31 May to 2 June 2013, concerns were raised about 'ideological and political differences' inhibiting the development of a cohesive international legal framework for addressing cyber issues and

---

[27] ASEAN Secretariat, 'ASEAN Defence Ministers and their Plus Counterparts Reaffirm Commitment for Regional Peace and Security at the 2nd ADMM-Plus', *ASEAN Secretariat News*, 3 September 2013, available at http://asean .org/asean-defence-ministers-and-their-plus-counterparts-reaffirm-com mitment-for-regional-peace-and-security-at-the-2nd-admm-plus/.

[28] Joint Declaration of the ASEAN Defence Ministers on Promoting Defence Cooperation for a Dynamic ASEAN Community, adopted at the 10th ASEAN Defence Ministers' Meeting, Vientiane, Lao PDR, 25 May 2016, para. 5.

[29] Establishment of the ADMM-Plus Experts' Working Group on Cyber Security: Concept Paper, adopted at the 10th ASEAN Defence Ministers' Meeting, Vientiane, Lao PDR, 25 May 2016, para. 6.

[30] Xiudian Dai, 'e-ASEAN and Regional Integration in South East Asia' in Ari-Veikko Anttiroiko and Matti Mälkiä (eds.), *Encyclopedia of Digital Government* (Hershey, PA: Idea Group Reference, 2007) 416, 418.

the increasing militarisation of cyberspace.[31] A critical question for the purpose of this chapter is whether and to what extent the same problem has inhibited ASEAN's efforts to facilitate the development of national legal infrastructure to secure cyberspace in each member state.

5.3 Cyber Security Law and Policy in ASEAN Member States

Pursuant to the 2003 Singapore Declaration, the establishment of CERTs in each ASEAN member state was – belatedly as it was originally to be achieved by 2005 – completed in February 2012 following the inauguration of LaoCERT. In the same year, a multi-stakeholder ASEAN Network Security Action Council was established to promote CERT cooperation and the sharing of expertise through annual meetings.[32] The Mactan Cebu Declaration, adopted in 2012, also seeks to boost cyber security by strengthening regional CERTs through, for example, ASEAN CERT Incident Drills, which aim to enhance 'incident investigation and coordination amongst [ASEAN and other regional] CERTs'.[33]

---

[31] International Institute for Strategic Studies (IISS), 'The Shangri-La Dialogue Report 2013' (Conference Proceedings of the 12th Asia Security Summit, Singapore, 31 May to 2 June 2013) 46, available at www.iiss.org/-/media// silos/shangrila/the-shangri-la-dialogue-report-2013/shangri-la-dialogue-report-2013.pdf.

[32] Heinl, above n. 15, 29.

[33] Mactan Cebu Declaration: 'Connected ASEAN – Enabling Aspirations', adopted at the 12th Meeting of ASEAN Telecommunications & IT Ministers, Mactan Cebu, Philippines, 15–16 November 2012, para. 16.

However, writing in 2013, Caitríona H. Heinl observed that these efforts to establish a regional comprehensive framework based on national-level cyber security programmes remained piecemeal and fragmented, demonstrating a lack of region-wide cohesiveness.[34] As discussed below, the difficulty in establishing a region-wide comprehensive cyber security framework lies largely with differences in the level and aspect of cyber security concerns among ASEAN member states, derived from their pre-existing socio-political situations.

ASEAN member states share an understanding that there is a need for strengthening capacities in certain legal areas, such as the harmonisation of e-commerce laws and the cross-border investigation of cyber-crime for law enforcement purposes.[35] Even though the 2000 e-ASEAN Framework Agreement is not in force, most ASEAN member states have enacted legislation on electronic transactions and cyber-crime (see Table 5.1), especially in relation to the prevention and criminalisation of unauthorised access, interception, alteration and use of computer materials and services.[36]

The first country to introduce cyber-specific legislation in the region was Singapore, with the enactment of the Computer Misuse and Cybersecurity Act 1993 (Singapore). This legislation was used as a model to develop the Computer Crimes Act 1997 (Malaysia) and the Computer Misuse Act

[34] Heinl, above n. 15, 2.
[35] UN Conference on Trade and Development (UNCTAD), *Review of E-Commerce Legislation Harmonization in the Association of Southeast Asian Nations* (New York and Geneva: UN, 2013) 12–14.
[36] Ibid., xi. As at 1 September 2018, Cambodia is the only country without cyber-specific legislation.

Table 5.1 *Status of Cyber Security-Related Treaty and Legislation*
e-ASEAN: e-ASEAN Framework Agreement   r: ratification

	e-ASEAN	Primary Legislative Instruments
Brunei	r (30 May 2002)	Computer Misuse Act 2000 (amended in 2007); Electronic Transactions Act 2001 (amended in 2008)
Cambodia		
Indonesia	r (4 Jul. 2001)	Law on Electronic Information and Transactions 2008
Lao PDR		Law on Electronic Transactions 2012; Decree No. 327 on Internet-Based Information Control and Management 2014; Law on Prevention and Combating Cyber Crime 2015
Malaysia		Computer Crimes Act 1997
Myanmar	r (10 Sep. 2002)	Electronic Transactions Law 2004
Philippines	r (10 Dec. 2001)	Act Providing and Use of Electronic Commercial and Non-Commercial Transactions, Penalties for Unlawful Use Thereof, and Other Purposes 2000
Singapore	r (24 May 2002)	Computer Misuse and Cybersecurity Act 1993 (amended in 2007)
Thailand	r (13 Jun. 2008)	Electronic Transaction Act 2001 (amended in 2008); Computer Crime Act 2007 (amended in 2017)
Vietnam		Law on Information Technology 2006; Joint Circular on Assurance of Infrastructure Safety and Information Security in Post, Telecommunications and Information Technology Activities 2008; Law on Network Information Security Law 2015 Law on Cybersecurity 2018

2000 (Brunei Darussalam). In 2000, the Philippines enacted a more comprehensive regulation of the use of information technology for commercial and non-commercial transactions.[37] Subsequently, Brunei Darussalam, Myanmar, Indonesia, Thailand and Lao PDR followed by enacting electronic transactions law.[38]

The general purposes of these computer-related laws are tame and unobjectionable due to the clear need for legal infrastructure to regulate various activities in cyberspace in an age of information technology. However, these regulatory rules are not merely designed to ensure the security of cyberspace as a new domain of human interactions, but are also used to create a regulatory space where existing national security concerns are projected. Illustrative is the Electronic Transactions Law 2004 (Myanmar), which makes it an offence to use information technology for an 'act detrimental to the security of the State or prevalence of law and order or community peace and tranquillity or national solidarity or national economy or national culture'.[39] This provision is an extension of the suite of repressive legislation that exists in Myanmar in relation to cyberspace, and was allegedly used to suppress critics of Myanmar's military regime

---

[37] Act Providing and Use of Electronic Commercial and Non-Commercial Transactions, Penalties for Unlawful Use Thereof, and Other Purposes 2000 (Philippines).

[38] Electronic Transactions Act 2001 (amended in 2008) (Brunei); Electronic Transaction Act 2001 (amended in 2008) (Thailand); Electronic Transactions Law 2004 (Myanmar); Law on Electronic Information and Transactions 2008 (Indonesia); Law on Electronic Transactions 2012 (Lao PDR).

[39] Electronic Transactions Law 2004 (Myanmar) s. 33(a).

through prison sentences of up to fifteen years.[40] Likewise, Vietnam has criminalised the use of digital information for the purpose of '[o]pposing the State of the Socialist Republic of Vietnam or undermining the all-people unity block'.[41]

A similar observation can be made in relation to cyber-crime legislation, particularly when the creation of new offences is combined with strengthened investigatory powers of competent authorities, including the access to and interception of computer communications. The Computer Crime Act 2007 (Thailand), for example, has been instrumental to the Government's ability to maintain strict control of the Internet, as highlighted by the heavy censorship of online content following the 2006 coup.[42] In 2015, the National Cybersecurity Bill was introduced to Thailand's National Legislative Assembly with the aim of enacting into permanent law the emergency surveillance powers authorised under the Martial Law Order No. 29 of 2014.[43] The Bill was designed to

[40] Amnesty International, 'Myanmar: Amnesty International Submission to the UN Universal Periodic Review' (presented at the 10th session of the Universal Periodic Review Working Group, January 2011) 2, available at http://lib.ohchr.org/HRBodies/UPR/Documents/Session10/MM/AI_AmnestyInternational_eng.pdf.

[41] Law on Information Technology 2006 (Vietnam) art. 12(2). See also, Joint Circular on Assurance of Infrastructure Safety and Information Security in Post, Telecommunications and Information Technology Activities 2008 (Vietnam) art. 4(a); Law on Cybersecurity 2018 (Vietnam) art. 16.

[42] See Chalisa Magpanthong, 'Thailand's Evolving Internet Policies: The Search for a Balance between National Security and the Right to Information' (2013) 23 *Asian Journal of Communication* 1.

[43] National Cybersecurity Bill 2015 (Thailand). An unofficial English translation of the Bill is available at https://thainetizen.org/wp-content/uploads/2015/03/cybersecurity-bill-20150106-en.pdf.

provide the Government with authority to access information without a court order and has been criticised as another means to suppress freedom of expression.[44]

Similarly, Lao PDR issued Decree No. 327 in 2014, which extended the exercise of governmental control over the Internet by introducing new cyber offences, including disseminating false and misleading information against the government, and providing competent authorities with the mandate to conduct online surveillance.[45] In 2015, another controversial piece of legislation, intended to comprehensively prevent and combat cyber-crimes, passed the National Assembly of Lao PDR.[46] The same attempt was made in Cambodia, where a cyber-crime law was drafted with a view to strengthening Cambodia's legal and institutional framework to combat all kinds of offences committed through

[44] Suchit Leesa-nguansuk, 'Cybersecurity Bill Needs Revising', *Bangkok Post*, 13 January 2015, available at www.bangkokpost.com/archive/ana lyst-cybersecurity-bill-needs-revising/456524. The Bill has since then been revised for public consultation in March 2018: Kowit Somwaiya and Paramee Kerativitayanan, 'Thailand's Draft Cyber Security Bill Open for Public Hearing Again', *LawPlus*, 25 March 2018, available at www .lawplusltd.com/2018/03/thailands-draft-cyber-security-bill-open-pub lic-hearing-2/.

[45] Decree No. 327 on Internet-Based Information Control and Management 2014 (Lao PDR) arts. 9 and 19. For criticisms, see Report of the Working Group on the Universal Periodic Review: Lao People's Democratic Republic, UN Doc A/HRC/29/7 (23 March 2015) paras. 53, 70, 101; Mong Palatino, 'Laos' Internet Law Undermines Free Speech', *The Diplomat*, 5 November 2014, available at http://thediplomat.com/ 2014/11/laos-internet-law-undermines-free-speech/.

[46] Law on Prevention and Combating Cyber Crime 2015 (Lao PDR) arts. 13(2) and 29.

computer systems.[47] This legislative process has been put on hold after the public revelation of the draft text in April 2014 caused public outcry.[48]

The use of a regional framework as an opportunity to advance national security agendas is not unique to the field of cyber security. As observed with regard to counter-terrorism law and policy in Chapter 2, domestic political considerations, unique historical backgrounds and international pressure have often taken precedence over regional initiatives. With its cyber security initiatives, ASEAN has facilitated the development by member states of legal tools to address a new national security issue, as part of the regional security agenda to harmonise e-commerce and cyber-crime legislation.[49] This role has been particularly significant for those ASEAN

[47] See Mong Palatino, 'Cambodia's "Cyber War" Legislation Targets Online Critics', *The Diplomat*, 27 May 2015, available at http://thediplo mat.com/2015/05/cambodias-cyber-war-legislation-targets-online-crit ics/; Joshua Wilwohl and Hul Reaksmey, 'Cybercrime Law May Silence Critics, NGOs Say', *The Cambodia Daily*, 10 April 2014, available at www .cambodiadaily.com/archives/cybercrime-law-may-silence-critics-ngos-say-56288/.

[48] Chris Mueller and Khuon Narim, 'Controversial Cybercrime Law "Scrapped"', *The Cambodia Daily*, 12 December 2014, available at www .cambodiadaily.com/news/controversial-cybercrime-law-scrapped-7405 7/. The drafting of a new bill gained momentum in 2017, with the rise of malware attack on computer systems: Chea Vannak, 'Cybercrime Law on the Way', *Khmer Times*, 3 July 2017, available at www .khmertimeskh.com/news/39866/cybercrime-law-on-the-way/.

[49] ASEAN Declaration to Prevent and Combat Cybercrime, adopted at the 31st ASEAN Summit, Manila, Philippines, 13 November 2017, para. 1 (acknowledging the importance of harmonisation of laws concerning cyber-crime and electronic evidence).

member states that are increasingly concerned about the rise of a new social platform to voice and coordinate dissent against the governing regime. In other words, the ASEAN-led initiative for cyber security has provided a regional support for member states to address their own emerging national security problems under the auspices of the e-ASEAN Framework.

Despite this additional benefit of the regional cyber security agenda, not all ASEAN member states have an officially recognised national cyber security policy or strategy. For those that do, the perception and readiness of cyber security against external threats varies in different countries. Brunei understands that '[t]hreats to information systems can undermine competitive advantage and reveal sensitive national information' but is mainly focused on the survivability of its defence force's own communication systems to ensure operational effectiveness in situations of emergency.[50] Malaysia and the Philippines, on the other hand, consider cyber security to be part of the protection of national critical infrastructures from various threats including accidents and malfunction, terrorism, cyber terrorism and cyber warfare.[51] In Thailand, the focus of cyber security efforts has shifted since the 2014 coup, from the protection of information systems against various malicious means such as crimes and acts of terrorism,[52] to a more national security-centric view under

---

[50] Defence White Paper 2011: Defending the Nation's Sovereignty, Expanding Roles in Wider Horizons (Brunei Darussalam, 2011) 7, 16, 36.

[51] National Cyber-Security Policy (Malaysia, 2006); National Cyber Security Plan (Philippines, 2004) 1–2.

[52] Second Thailand Information and Communication Technology (ICT) Master Plan 2009–2013 (Thailand, 2009) 25.

the military regime that encompasses military security, domestic peace and order, and economic stability.[53] Singapore's Cybersecurity Strategy, launched at the inaugural Singapore International Cyber Week in October 2016, represents a more comprehensive approach to cyber security through the protection of essential services, securing government networks and the establishment of a professional cyber security workforce, while working with ASEAN member states to coordinate a regional approach to cyber-crime.[54]

5.4 ASEAN's Role in Cyber Warfare

It has been suggested that an expanded regional arrangement with extra-regional powers in relation to cyber security issues would be beneficial for the entire region, given that ASEAN's perception as a 'neutral broker' positions it well to mitigate tensions between great power rivalries. Indeed, the political interest ASEAN member states have in the regulation of cyberspace is much more limited compared, for example, to their vested interests in the South China Sea dispute, in which some member states are directly involved as claimants. As discussed above, however, ASEAN member states have only recently started demonstrating concerns about the military use of cyberspace, and their national security concerns regarding cyberspace have primarily remained inward-looking. This means that ASEAN member states are yet to

---

[53] Cyber Crime Act 2007 (as amended in 2017) (Thailand) ss. 12 and 14(2); National Cybersecurity Bill 2015 (Thailand) ss. 3 and 5.

[54] Singapore's Cybersecurity Strategy (Singapore, 2016).

be ready for the full implications of the security threats posed to the interconnected network societies within Southeast Asia.

In the absence of a specific regional arrangement, any military use of cyberspace against and within ASEAN member states is subject to the relevant rules of general international law, particularly those concerning state responsibility, the use of force and international humanitarian law.[55] When the cyber capabilities for military purposes have matured, the real question that will be posed to ASEAN is: what measures will be taken to ensure respect for the relevant principles of the association? Of particular relevance is the respect for the right of every member state to lead its national existence free from external interference, subversion and coercion,[56] given the highly intrusive and subversive nature of cyber capabilities.

As cyber infrastructure develops and societies become increasingly interconnected online, ASEAN and its member states will find themselves vulnerable to covert cyber intrusions.[57] When those incidents are investigated and interpreted in light of the prevailing geopolitical circumstances, there is a risk that the targeted state will misperceive the situation and

---

[55] See especially, Schmitt (ed.), *Tallinn Manual 2.0*, above n. 7, chs. 4, 14 and 16–20.

[56] Charter of the Association of Southeast Asian Nations, adopted 20 November 2007, 2624 UNTS 223 (entered into force 15 December 2008) art. 2(f).

[57] On the legality of cyber espionage, see Schmitt (ed.), *Tallinn Manual 2.0*, above n. 7, 168–74.

react in such a way that escalates the existing tension between itself and another member state, or an extra-regional power.

This concern was already identified by the ARF in its 2012 Statement on Cooperation in Ensuring Cyber Security, which urged member states to consider 'confidence-building and other transparency measures' necessary to 'reduce the risk of misperception, escalation and conflict'.[58] Given all the different political interests, strategic considerations and the uncertainty in the strategic and tactical use of cyberspace, it remains to be seen how effective those confidence-building and other transparency measures can be to defend cyber infrastructure within ASEAN member states.

As a cooperative security institution, ASEAN is not well equipped to resolve inter-state disputes between member states, let alone regional conflicts involving extra-regional powers.[59] Instead, as it has done in dealing with terrorism and human trafficking,[60] ASEAN may choose to exercise its legal authority to build a uniform law enforcement approach, particularly in the areas of cyber-crime investigation and extradition. This will be consistent with the principles of comprehensive security and collective responsibility for regional security by ensuring that the benefits of normative processes in the region outweigh incentives for resorting to unilateral cyber security operations.

---

[58] ARF Statement on Cooperation in Ensuring Cyber Security, above n. 21, preamble para. 9.

[59] See Introduction (fns 7–11) and Chapter 1.2.

[60] See Chapter 3.2 and Chapter 6.2 respectively.

5.5 Concluding Observations

At a special session entitled 'the cyber dimension to Asian security' during the 12th Asia Security Summit (Shangri-La Dialogue), it was widely acknowledged that in moving forward, states would have to 'identify shared goals and the lowest denominator of interest and priorities' in relation to cyber security.[61] ASEAN's cyber security initiatives have focused upon regional cooperation in building national cyber security resilience and more comprehensive efforts to address common threats such as malicious cyber activities by criminal and terrorist organisations. It has been observed above that most ASEAN member states have enacted electronic transaction and cyber-crime legislation pursuant to the 2000 e-ASEAN Framework Agreement. Some states have also taken advantage of this regional effort to fill a perceived gap in their own national security laws.

It may be argued that such cyber security laws were enacted for ulterior motives, including the suppression of dissidents who use information technology. As is often the case with any legislative motion, however, the impact of ASEAN's initiative on national efforts to build legal infrastructure for cyberspace cannot be dismissed just for one ulterior motive that might well have been mixed with other policy rationales. Indeed, one of the primary purposes of ASEAN is to respect and reinforce the national security of each member state through regional cooperation, with which the exercise of its authority examined above is consistent.

---

[61] IISS, above n. 31, 47.

More concerning is the prospect of cyberspace being used for covert cyber intrusions and offensive activities, which exposes vulnerability of Southeast Asian nations to external interferences by cyber means. It remains to be seen how ASEAN might react to these emerging challenges to securing cyberspace beyond the realm of regional cooperation, with a view to achieving its shared commitment and collective responsibility in cyberspace. However, ASEAN's practice in dealing with terrorism and human trafficking indicates the possibility that ASEAN can do more to exercise its legal authority in building a uniform law enforcement approach to common cyber threats.

Chapter 6

Human Trafficking and People Smuggling

6.1 Introduction

Due to the close geographical proximity of neighbouring states and the high traffic on major sea lanes Southeast Asia has been the home of transnational crimes such as piracy, drug trafficking, smuggling of small arms, money laundering, cyber-crime, terrorism and other issues affecting 'human security'.[1] The concept of human security espouses a human or people-centred approach to security,[2] encompassing issues such as the protection of civilians in armed conflict, the protection of refugees and the protection of other migrants from human trafficking,[3] as well as people

---

[1] East Asia Study Group, 'Final Report of the East Asia Study Group' (adopted at ASEAN+3 Summit, Phnom Penh, 4 November 2002) para. 104, available at www.mofa.go.jp/region/asia-paci/asean/pmv0211/report .pdf.

[2] Commission on Human Security, 'Human Security Now' (2003) 5, available at www.humansecurity-chs.org/finalreport/index.html. For details, see especially, Barbara von Tigerstrom, *Human Security and International Law: Prospects and Problems* (Oxford and Portland, OR: Hart Publishing, 2007).

[3] Human trafficking is generally defined as 'the recruitment, transportation, transfer, harbouring or receipt of persons, by means of the threat or use of force or other forms of coercion, of abduction, of fraud, of deception, of the abuse of power or of a position of vulnerability or of the

smuggling.[4] In particular, the issues of human trafficking and people smuggling have attracted significant attention over the last two decades, with an exponential increase in the number of migrants in the region due to the growth of social networks and a 'migration industry', improved transport systems, as well as the internationalisation of business and labour markets.[5]

In Southeast Asia, however, these transnational crimes have been addressed as 'non-traditional security' issues rather

giving or receiving of payments or benefits to achieve the consent of a person having control over another person, for the purpose of exploitation': Protocol to Prevent, Suppress and Punish Trafficking in Persons Especially Women and Children, supplementing the United Nations Convention against Transnational Organized Crime, adopted 15 November 2000, 2237 UNTS 319 (entered into force 25 December 2003) art. 3(a) (hereinafter UN Trafficking Protocol).

[4] People smuggling is generally defined as 'the procurement, in order to obtain, directly or indirectly, a financial or other material benefit, of the illegal entry of a person into a State Party of which the person is not a national or a permanent residence': Protocol against the Smuggling of Migrants by Land, Sea and Air, Supplementing the United Nations Convention against Transnational Organized Crime, adopted 15 November 2000, 2241 UNTS 507 (entered into force 28 January 2004) art. 3(a) (hereinafter UN Smuggling Protocol).

[5] For historical analysis of the movement of migrants and refugees in the Asia-Pacific, see Stephen Castles, Hein de Haas and Mark J. Miller, *The Age of Migration: International Population Movements in the Modern World* (5th edn, Basingstoke: Palgrave Macmillan, 2013) 147–71; Graeme Hugo, 'Migration in the Asia-Pacific Region' (A paper prepared for the Policy Analysis and Research Programme of the Global Commission on International Migration, September 2005), available at www.iom.int/jahia/webdav/site/myjahiasite/shared/shared/mainsite/policy_and_research/gcim/rs/RS2.pdf.

than as 'human security' issues – 'widening' the traditionally narrow scope of security, while refusing to 'deepen' it by shifting the focus to people as the referent object of security.[6] This characterisation is not mere semantic choice, but rather reflects the view traditionally shared within the region towards irregular migrants – particularly labour migrants – as a threat to the territorial integrity of the state,[7] rather than as a human security issue.[8] The consistent application of this approach culminated in the adoption of the 2015 ASEAN Convention against Trafficking in Persons, Especially Women and Children.[9] The Convention presents a shared norm for the region's approach to the issue of human trafficking, 15 years after the US-led negotiations produced the UN Trafficking Protocol.[10]

With a focus on ASEAN's responses to human trafficking and people smuggling issues in Southeast Asia, this chapter examines how ASEAN has facilitated the development, localisation and internalisation of relevant norms and rules within the rubric of comprehensive security and non-interference, while interacting with political interests of extra-regional powers such as Australia, the PRC and the US.

---

[6] For usage of these terms, see Peter Hough, *Understanding Global Security* (Abingdon: Routledge, 2004) 2–21.

[7] See Mely Caballero-Anthony, 'Reflections on Managing Migration in Southeast Asia: Mitigating the Unintended Consequences of Securitisation' in Melissa G. Curley and Wong Siu-Lun (eds.) *Security and Migration in Asia: The Dynamics of Securitisation* (Abingdon: Routledge, 2008) 165, 166–7.

[8] See Chapter 1.4.2.

[9] Adopted 21 November 2015 (entered into force 8 March 2017).

[10] See above n. 3.

6.2 ASEAN's Response to Human Trafficking

A significant part of the regional response to human trafficking has arisen from different multilateral consultative processes outside of ASEAN. The initial regional responses to human trafficking emerged in 1996 when the Manila Process and the Asia-Pacific Consultations on Refugees, Displaced Persons and Migrants were established. The Manila Process was an initiative of the International Organization for Migration, set up as one of the regional consultative processes to address irregular migration and trafficking, its root causes, repatriation and reintegration of migrants, and border control.[11] On the other hand, the Asia-Pacific Consultations were established by the Australian Government and the UN High Commissioner for Refugees as an informal forum for discussion of a much wider range of issues relating to population movements in the Asia-Pacific. In addition, the US and the Philippines convened the Asian Regional Initiative against Trafficking in Women and Children, in Manila on 1 March 2000.

The Manila Process and the Asia-Pacific Consultations played a significant role in setting the normative foundation

[11] The participants included Australia, Brunei Darussalam, Cambodia, Indonesia, Japan, Lao PDR, Malaysia, Myanmar, New Zealand, Papua New Guinea, the Philippines, the PRC, the Republic of Korea, Singapore, Thailand, Vietnam and Hong Kong. For detailed analysis of these regional consultative processes, see Amanda Klekowski von Koppenfels, 'Informal but Effective: Regional Consultative Processes as a Tool for Managing Migration' (2001) 39(6) *International Migration* 61; Andreas Schloenhardt, 'Trafficking in Migrants in the Asia-Pacific: National, Regional and International Responses' (2001) 5 *Singapore Journal of Comparative and International Law* 696, 726–7.

upon which regional responses to human trafficking and people smuggling were to be developed, leading to the adoption of the Bangkok Declaration on Irregular Migration on 23 April 1999.[12] This Declaration, although legally non-binding, has important normative value in noting that, when dealing with irregular migration, there is a need for states to balance 'their sovereign rights and legitimate interests', including safeguarding their national borders, against the 'obligations of the country of origin to accept its nationals back, and the obligation of the countries of transit and destination to provide protection and assistance where appropriate, in accordance with their national laws'.[13] The Declaration also promotes an inclusive approach to irregular migration, encouraging comprehensive analysis of and responses to the issue by linking it to development efforts as well as educational and information activities.[14]

However, as Samuel Cheung observes, these processes based on an inclusive approach 'struggle[d] to gain traction when outnumbered by other predominantly migration-oriented bodies [such as the UN High Commissioner for Refugees and the International Organization for Migration], where progress is measured by the slow and gradual insertion of human rights language rather than a direct discussion of the root causes of displacement or proposals for comprehensive

[12] Adopted at the International Symposium on Migration: 'Towards Regional Cooperation on Irregular/Undocumented Migration', Bangkok, Thailand, 23 April 1999. The text is available at www.iom.int/jahia/webdav/site/myjahiasite/shared/shared/mainsite/policy_and_research/rcp/APC/BANGKOK_DECLARATION.pdf.
[13] Ibid., preamble para. 12.   [14] Ibid., paras. 4 and 5.

solutions'.[15] By contrast, the legal responses, adopted by ASEAN and the ARF in particular, are best characterised as an exclusive approach focusing primarily on criminalising human trafficking and improving law enforcement capacity, almost to the exclusion of promoting the protection of and respect for the interests of irregular migrants themselves.

ASEAN's response to human trafficking emerged as part of a larger transnational security cooperation initiative, as reflected in the ASEAN Vision 2020, announced on 15 December 1997. In this statement, regional leaders committed themselves to the development of 'agreed rules of behaviour and cooperative measures to deal with problems that can be met only on a regional scale, including environmental pollution and degradation, drug trafficking, trafficking in women and children, and other transnational crimes'.[16]

Five days later, at the inaugural meeting of ASEAN Ministers of Interior/Home Affairs on Transnational Crime held in Manila, ASEAN member states adopted the ASEAN Declaration on Transnational Crime. In the Declaration, they expressed concerns about 'the pernicious effects of transnational crime, such as terrorism, illicit drug trafficking, arms smuggling, money laundering, traffic[king] in persons and piracy on regional stability and development, the maintenance of the rule of law and the welfare of the region's

---

[15] Samuel Cheung, 'Migration Control and the Solutions Impasse in South and Southeast Asia: Implications from the Rohingya Experience' (2011) 25 *Journal of Refugee Studies* 50, 65.

[16] ASEAN Vision 2020, adopted by ASEAN Heads of State/Government at the 2nd Informal Summit, Kuala Lumpur, Malaysia, 15 December 1997.

peoples'.[17] While providing very few tangible outcomes, this Declaration had a significant impact in 'securitising' the issue of human trafficking in the ASEAN rhetoric by positioning it next to terrorism, piracy and illicit drug trafficking – transnational crimes that had traditionally been more prevalent in the region.[18]

Following the commitments made in the 1997 Declaration, the ASEAN Plan of Action to Combat Transnational Crime was adopted in June 1999 to develop 'a more cohesive, regional strategy' and, through the ASEAN Senior Officials Meeting on Transnational Crime (SOMTC), to promote regional cooperation and coordination in dealing with transnational crime.[19] On 18 October 2000, the ASEAN Plan of Action for Cooperation on Immigration Matters was adopted as a complement to the 1999 Plan of Action in order to 'forge and strengthen immigration cooperation'.[20] The prompt

[17] ASEAN Declaration on Transnational Crime, adopted at the 1st ASEAN Conference on Transnational Crime, Manila, Philippines, 20 December 1997, preamble.
[18] See Ralf Emmers, 'ASEAN and the Securitisation of Transnational Crime in Southeast Asia' (2003) 16 *Pacific Review* 419, 424–5.
[19] Adopted at the 2nd ASEAN Ministerial Meeting on Transnational Crime, Yangon, Myanmar, 23 June 1999, Section B-(b) para. 1 and Section D-(b). For implementation of the Plan of Action, see Ralf Emmers, Beth Greener-Barcham and Nicholas Thomas, 'Institutional Arrangements to Counter Human Trafficking in the Asia Pacific' (2006) 28 *Contemporary Southeast Asia* 490, 496–7.
[20] ASEAN Plan of Action for Cooperation on Immigration Matters, adopted at the 4th Meeting of ASEAN Directors-General of Immigration Departments and Heads of Consular Affairs of ASEAN Ministries of Foreign Affairs, Davao City, Philippines, 16–18 October 2000, Section II-A.

adoption of these action plans stood in marked contrast to the absence of an action plan in the procrastinated Manila Process which soon became dormant as a result.[21]

The gradual shift in focus from transnational crime to human trafficking was highlighted when ASEAN leaders signed the ASEAN Declaration against Trafficking in Persons Particularly Women and Children at the Tenth ASEAN Summit in Vientiane on 29 November 2004.[22] This instrument recognised 'the urgent need for a comprehensive regional approach to prevent and to combat trafficking in persons, particularly women and children'.[23] While the Declaration can be seen as a regional response to the entry into force of the UN Trafficking Protocol, its terms are aspirational and require member states to take measures only 'to the extent permitted by their respective domestic laws and policies'.[24] As Nicholas Rees observes, in relation to this Declaration as well as regional engagement in other areas of transnational crime, '[t]he problem remains, however, that much depends on the ability of individual states to address transnational crime and this is linked to the capacity of the state to implement appropriate measures via national laws'.[25]

---

[21] Klekowski von Koppenfels, above n. 11, 78.
[22] ASEAN Declaration against Trafficking in Persons, Particularly Women and Children, adopted at the 10th ASEAN Summit, Vientiane, Lao PDR, 29 November 2004.
[23] Ibid., preamble para. 3.
[24] Ibid., preamble para. 9; Susan Kneebone and Julie Debeljak, *Transnational Crime and Human Rights: Responses to Human Trafficking in the Greater Mekong Subregion* (Abingdon: Routledge, 2012) 191.
[25] Nicholas Rees, 'EU and ASEAN: Issues of Regional Security' (2010) 47 *International Politics* 402, 412.

Perhaps the more significant impact of the adoption
of the 2004 Declaration was the impetus – as well as the policy
rationale – for national authorities to strengthen their law
enforcement capacity and criminal justice approach to
human trafficking. Indeed, in conjunction with the ASEAN
Mutual Legal Assistance Treaty (MLAT),[26] a set of guidelines
on law enforcement against trafficking in persons was developed to assist criminal justice practitioners, which was
endorsed by the SOMTC in 2007. The SOMTC also developed
a work plan to implement the 2004 Declaration, which was to
strengthen 'the legal and policy framework around trafficking
in order to promote more effective national responses as well
as greater regional and international cooperation especially in
relation to the investigation and prosecution of trafficking
cases and the protection of victims'.[27]

One of the commitments made by ASEAN leaders in
the Declaration was implemented in the form of supporting,
jointly with the UN Office on Drugs and Crime and the
Australian-funded Asia Regional Trafficking in Persons
Project, the development of the *ASEAN Handbook on
International Legal Cooperation in Trafficking in Persons*

---

[26] Treaty on Mutual Legal Assistance in Criminal Matters, adopted
29 November 2004 (entered into force 28 April 2005 for Singapore,
25 October 2005 for Vietnam, 1 June 2005 for Malaysia, 15 February 2006
for Brunei Darussalam, 25 June 2007 for Lao PDR, 9 September 2008 for
Indonesia, 12 December 2008 for the Philippines, 22 January 2009 for
Myanmar, 8 April 2010 for Cambodia, and 31 January 2013 for Thailand).
[27] 2007–2009 Work Plan to Implement the ASEAN Declaration against
Trafficking in Persons, Particularly Women and Children, endorsed by
the 7th ASEAN Senior Officials Meeting on Transnational Crime,
Vientiane, Lao PDR, 27 June 2007, s. 1.2.

Cases. The Handbook aims to provide guidance to regional criminal justice officials on how the key tools of international cooperation such as mutual legal assistance and extradition might be relevant to the investigation and prosecution of trafficking-in-persons cases.[28]

As stated at the outset of this chapter, ASEAN has characterised human trafficking as a non-traditional security issue. This is reflected in the 2009 ASEAN Political-Security Community Blueprint, in which ASEAN member states agreed to strengthen cooperation in addressing non-traditional security issues including 'criminal justice responses to trafficking in persons'.[29] The 'securitisation' of human trafficking issues as new challenges to regional stability is acknowledged in ASEAN's external relations as well.[30] In particular, the Memorandum of Understanding on Cooperation in the Field of Non-Traditional Security Issues, concluded on 10 January 2004 between ASEAN and

---

[28] Pauline David, Fiona David and Anne Gallagher, *ASEAN Handbook on International Legal Cooperation in Trafficking in Persons Cases* (Jakarta: ASEAN Secretariat, 2010) 2.

[29] ASEAN Political-Security Community Blueprint, adopted at the 14th ASEAN Summit, Cha-am Hua Hin, Thailand, 1 March 2009, Section B.4.1, para. iv.

[30] Joint Declaration of ASEAN and China on Cooperation in the Field of Non-traditional Security Issues, adopted at the 6th ASEAN-China Summit, Phnom Penh, Cambodia, 4 November 2002; Joint Statement of the First ASEAN-India Summit, Phnom Penh, Cambodia, 5 November 2002; Joint Declaration of the Foreign Ministers of the Russian Federation and the Association of Southeast Asian Nations on Partnership for Peace and Security, and Prosperity and Development in the Asia-Pacific Region, adopted in Phnom Penh, Cambodia, 19 June 2003.

the PRC, reinforced extra-ASEAN regional cooperation in law enforcement and criminal justice responses to human trafficking.[31] As David Arase observes, 'the China-ASEAN concept of NTS [non-traditional security] should not be confused with human security because NTS excludes, or at least fails to mention, human security as a guiding principle' and instead cites 'only the protection of state sovereignty'.[32] These institutional responses have thus effectively transformed what is essentially a human security agenda into a policy platform for advancing security cooperation to enhance national security and regional stability.

An alternative approach emerged when ASEAN leaders signed the ASEAN Declaration on the Protection and Promotion of the Rights of Migrant Workers on 13 January 2007.[33] This Declaration sets out and emphasises the commitments by ASEAN to protect and promote the rights of migrant workers, rather than the need for states to strengthen their law enforcement capabilities. Although considered a significant milestone in advancing a rights-based approach to regional migration, the Declaration excludes irregular

---

[31] Memorandum of Understanding Between the Governments of the Member Countries of the Association of Southeast Asian Nations (ASEAN) and the People's Republic of China on Cooperation in the Field of Non-Traditional Security Issues, adopted in Bangkok, Thailand, 10 January 2004.

[32] David Arase, 'Non-Traditional Security in China-ASEAN Cooperation: The Institutionalization of Regional Security Cooperation and the Evolution of East Asian Regionalism' (2010) 50 *Asian Survey* 808, 812.

[33] ASEAN Declaration on the Protection and Promotion of the Rights of Migrant Workers, adopted at the 12th ASEAN Summit, Cebu, Philippines, 13 January 2007.

migrants from the scope of protection.[34] Also, its proposed measures did not depart significantly from the traditional criminal justice approach adopted by ASEAN member states. The 2007 Declaration reiterates that in accordance with their national laws, member states will 'take concrete measures to prevent or curb the smuggling and trafficking in persons by, among others, introducing stiffer penalties for those who are involved in these activities'.[35]

On 21 November 2015, ASEAN finally adopted the ASEAN Convention against Trafficking in Persons, Especially Women and Children. All ASEAN member states, with the exception of Brunei, are parties to the 2000 UN Trafficking Protocol and the 2015 ASEAN Convention. Although in substance there is a striking similarity with the 2000 UN Trafficking Protocol, the 2015 Convention recognises the need for greater protection of trafficking victims. It requires each party, for example, to 'consider not holding victims of trafficking in persons criminally or administratively liable, for unlawful acts committed by them, if such acts are directly related to the acts of trafficking' and to 'not unreasonably hold ... victims of trafficking in persons in detention or in prison'.[36] These additional requirements not only reflect the policy debates that followed during the

---

[34] Caballero-Anthony, above n. 7, 172–3.

[35] ASEAN Declaration on the Protection and Promotion of the Rights of Migrant Workers, above n. 33, para. 17.

[36] ASEAN Convention against Trafficking in Persons, Especially Women and Children, above n. 9, arts. 14(7) and 14(8). For detailed comparison with the UN Trafficking Protocol, see Ranyta Yusran, 'The ASEAN Convention Against Trafficking in Persons: A Preliminary Assessment' (2018) 8 *Asian Journal of International Law* 258–92.

intervening period, but also illustrate ASEAN's role in localising international norms and rules to address particular concerns shared within the region. The fact that the Convention is designed to come into force upon ratification of the sixth member state, and indeed entered into force within a very short period of time, also demonstrates ASEAN's resolve to combat human trafficking and to protect the victims of trafficking.[37]

Although it is too early to make any assessment on the 2015 Convention, notable lessons can be drawn from the criticisms that have been directed towards the South Asian Association for Regional Cooperation (SAARC) Convention on Preventing and Combating Trafficking in Women and Children for Prostitution.[38] Despite its similarly victim-centred approach to human trafficking and all the institutional mechanisms that have been put in place, Anne Gallagher observes that '[t]o date, there is little evidence that the Convention has exerted any influence over anti trafficking law, policy, or practice at either the regional or national levels'.[39] Mely Caballero-Anthony considers that this is due to the opaque language used in the Convention, which allows member states to implement their own migration policies

---

[37] ASEAN Convention against Trafficking in Persons, Especially Women and Children, above n. 9, art. 29. It entered into force on 8 March 2017, the thirtieth day following the deposit of the sixth instrument of ratification by the Philippines.

[38] Adopted 5 January 2002 (entered into force 15 November 2005).

[39] Anne T. Gallagher, *The International Law of Human Trafficking* (Cambridge: Cambridge University Press, 2010) 130–1. See also Roza Pati, 'Trading in Humans: A New Haven Perspective' (2012) 20 *Asia Pacific Law Review* 135, 156.

where they see fit with regard to their own national or border security.[40] Indeed, since the Fourteenth SAARC Summit held in New Delhi on 3–4 April 2007, the victim-centred approach has faded due to increased attention to the alleged connection between terrorism and other organised criminal activities including human trafficking.[41]

The 2015 Convention may well follow a similar path, given the use of qualifying language such as 'subject to its domestic laws' and 'in appropriate cases' diluting the legal significance of the obligations for the protection of trafficking victims.[42] The ASEAN Intergovernmental Commission on Human Rights (AICHR), established in 2009, and the ASEAN Commission on the Promotion and Protection of the Rights of Women and Children (ACWC), established in 2010, are both competent to address human trafficking issues.[43] Yet, it remains to be seen how these regional human rights bodies might influence the way in which ASEAN member states implement their obligations under the 2015 Convention to address human trafficking issues.[44]

---

[40] Caballero-Anthony, above n. 7, 173–4.

[41] Declaration of the Fourteenth SAARC Summit, New Delhi, India, 3–4 April 2007, para. 26; Declaration of the Fifteenth SAARC Summit, Colombo, Sri Lanka, 2–3 August 2008, para. 35; Declaration of the Sixteenth SAARC Summit, Thimphu, Bhutan, 28–29 April 2010, para. 34; Declaration of the Seventeenth SAARC Summit, Addu City, Maldives, 10–11 November 2011, preamble para. 6, all available via http://saarc-sec.org/saarc-summit/7/.

[42] ASEAN Convention against Trafficking in Persons, Especially Women and Children, above n. 9, arts. 14(4), 14(6) and 14(7).

[43] AICHR Terms of Reference, s. 4.6; ACWC Terms of Reference, s. 5.1.

[44] For a critical view, see Naparat Kranrattanasuit, *ASEAN and Human Trafficking: Case Studies of Cambodia, Thailand and Vietnam* (Leiden: Brill, 2014) 84–94.

6.3 ASEAN's Response to People Smuggling

The consideration of people smuggling by ASEAN, in contrast, has been limited to discussion of broader transnational security issues – often in conjunction with human trafficking – in the ARF. The reference to 'the problem of illegal migration' first appeared as one of the 'transboundary problems that could have a significant impact on regional security' at the ARF's Sixth Meeting in Singapore on 26 July 1999.[45] In the wake of the 9/11 terrorist attacks in New York and the Bali Bombings on 12 October 2002, the ARF started characterising people smuggling as a security issue through its linkage with terrorism and other organised crimes, such as money laundering and arms trafficking, which formed 'part of a complex set of new security challenges'.[46]

As the Indian Co-Chair observed at the Sixth ARF Inter-Sessional Meeting on Counter-Terrorism and Transnational Crime in 2008, this joint commitment reflects the shared understanding that 'in [an] inter-connected world, the fight against terrorism and transnational crimes would have to be addressed in [a] comprehensive manner'.[47] The 2010 Hanoi Plan of Action to Implement the ASEAN Regional Forum Vision Statement identifies one of its aims as

---

[45] Chairman's Statement of the 6th ASEAN Regional Forum, Singapore, 26 July 1999.

[46] ARF Statement on Cooperative Counter-Terrorist Action on Border Security, adopted at the 10th ARF Meeting, Phnom Penh, Cambodia, 17 June 2003.

[47] Co-Chairs' Summary Report of the Sixth ASEAN Regional Forum Inter-Sessional Meeting on Counter-Terrorism and Transnational Crime, Semarang, Indonesia, 21–22 February 2008, para. 4.

'forg[ing] closer cooperation in combating maritime terrorism and transnational maritime crimes such as ... smuggling,
and trafficking in person[s], in accordance with national and
international laws through concrete and practical activities'.[48]

As far as the ARF is concerned, people smuggling has
thus been absorbed into a broader transnational security
agenda as an example of the cross-border movements that
are to be regulated through an effective network of law enforcement authorities and armed forces in the region. Yet, while
people smuggling – or irregular migration more broadly – has
been noted, recognised and discussed as a transnational
security threat and challenge at almost every meeting over
the last decade, no concrete action has resulted other than
Chairman's Statements expressing support for initiatives elsewhere, such as the Bali Process.[49]

Formally known as the Regional Ministerial Conference
on People Smuggling, Trafficking in Persons and Related
Transnational Crime, the Bali Process has provided an alternative Asia-Pacific region-wide framework in which member states
and institutions coordinate their policy on counter-smuggling
and assist each other in establishing counter-smuggling programmes, law-making and capacity-building on a voluntary

---

[48] Hanoi Plan of Action to Implement the ASEAN Regional Forum Vision
Statement, adopted at the 17th ARF Meeting, Hanoi, Vietnam,
20 July 2010, para. 3.8.

[49] See e.g., Chairman's Statement of the 17th ASEAN Regional Forum,
Hanoi, Vietnam, 23 July 2010, para. 26; Chairman's Statement of the 12th
ASEAN Regional Forum, Vientiane, Lao PDR, 29 July 2005, para. 30;
Chairman's Statement of the 10th ASEAN Regional Forum, Phnom
Penh, Cambodia, 18 June 2003, para. 17.

basis.[50] The emergence of the Bali Process was precipitated by a sizable increase in boat arrivals and a number of highly politicised incidents since 1999; the most infamous being the *MV Tampa* affair in 2001, which sparked controversy over the Australian Government's handling of the event.[51]

However, the Bali Process does not necessarily share the same normative foundation as the ARF's conception of people smuggling issues in that the former regards people smuggling as creating significant political, economic, social and 'national security' challenges. According to Reinhard Drifte, this characterisation of people smuggling was appealing directly to links with traditional security discourse when it was understood in the context of predominant concern about sovereignty among Asian nations.[52]

Built upon this conceptual foundation, the 'inclusive but non-binding' Regional Cooperation Framework was adopted at the Fourth Bali Regional Ministerial Conference on People Smuggling, Trafficking in Persons and Related

---

[50] For details, see Anne T. Gallagher and Fiona David, *The International Law of People Smuggling* (Cambridge: Cambridge University Press, 2014) 121–2; Susan Kneebone, 'The Bali Process and Global Refugee Policy in the Asia-Pacific Region' (2014) 27 *Journal of Refugee Studies* 596.

[51] There is voluminous literature on this incident, but see especially, Mary Crock, Ben Saul and Azadeh Dastyari, *Future Seekers II: Refugees and Irregular Migration in Australia* (Sydney: Federation Press, 2006) 113–30.

[52] Reinhard Drifte, 'Migrants, Human Security and Military Security' in Harald Kleinschmidt (ed.), *Migration, Regional Integration and Human Security: The Formation and Maintenance of Transnational Spaces* (Aldershot: Ashgate, 2006) 103, 118.

Transnational Crime on 29–30 March 2011. It sets out the following five principles:

i. Irregular movement facilitated by people smuggling syndicates should be eliminated and States should promote and support opportunities for orderly migration.

ii. Where appropriate and possible, asylum seekers should have access to consistent assessment processes, whether through a set of harmonised arrangements or through the possible establishment of regional assessment arrangements, which might include a centre or centres, taking into account any existing sub-regional arrangements.

iii. Persons found to be refugees under those assessment processes should be provided with a durable solution, including voluntary repatriation, resettlement within and outside the region and, where appropriate, possible 'in country' solutions.

iv. Persons found not to be in need of protection should be returned, preferably on a voluntary basis, to their countries of origin, in safety and dignity. Returns should be sustainable and States should look to maximise opportunities for greater cooperation.

v. People smuggling enterprises should be targeted through border security arrangements, law enforcement activities and disincentives for human trafficking and smuggling.[53]

Since 2011, this Framework has been used as the basis upon which participating states develop practical arrangements,

---

[53] The text is available at www.baliprocess.net/regional-cooperation-framework.

including those towards consistent assessment processes for asylum seekers. The Regional Support Office was established in 2012 to facilitate the implementation of the Framework and its objectives.[54] Neither ASEAN nor the ARF has been brought into this Framework with a view to facilitating its implementation within ASEAN member states.

6.4 Legal and Policy Responses to Human Trafficking and People Smuggling in ASEAN Member States

While the formal institutional responses by ASEAN and the ARF remain focused upon policy coordination, more tangible outcomes in the form of norm internalisation have resulted from both assistance and pressure from extra-regional actors. One of the key achievements of the Bali Process, for example, is the drafting of the Model Legislation to Criminalise People Smuggling and Trafficking, at the joint initiative of Australia and the PRC. This initiative has proven successful, with more than eighteen regional countries making use of the model legislation.[55]

---

[54] See Co-Chairs' Statement, Fifth Bali Regional Ministerial Conference on People Smuggling, Trafficking in Persons and Related Transnational Crime, Bali, Indonesia, 2 April 2013, para. 2, available via www .baliprocess.net.

[55] Joseph H. Douglas and Andreas Schloenhardt, 'Combating Migrant Smuggling with Regional Diplomacy: An Examination of the Bali Process' (Research Paper, Migrant Smuggling Working Group, The University of Queensland, February 2012) 13–14, available at https:// law.uq.edu.au/files/6723/Douglas-Schloenhardt-Bali-Process.pdf.

As an extra-regional power, Australia also led the Asia Regional Cooperation to Prevent People Trafficking Project from 2003 to 2006, the Asia Regional Trafficking in Persons Project from 2007 to 2012 and the Australia-Asia Program to Combat Trafficking in Persons from 2013 to 2018.[56] These programmes were developed at the initiative of the Australian Government to support the criminal justice systems of participating governments and to enhance investigative and judicial cooperation in the prosecution of human traffickers, in close coordination with the ASEAN SOMTC.[57]

Another multilateral process that has facilitated norm internalisation regarding human trafficking in Southeast Asia is the Coordinated Mekong Ministerial Initiative against Trafficking (COMMIT), which was established in October 2004 by Cambodia, Lao PDR, Myanmar, the PRC, Thailand and Vietnam. With its secretariat located at the UN Inter-Agency Project on Human Trafficking in the Greater Mekong Subregion in Bangkok, COMMIT has institutionalised a multi-sectoral approach to implement the commitments

---

[56] For details, see Kneebone and Debeljak, above n. 24, 192–200; Peter Bazeley and Mike Dottridge, 'Asia Regional Trafficking in Persons (ARTIP) Project: Independent Completion Report' (Department of Foreign Affairs and Trade, Australia, 2011), available at http://aid.dfat.gov.au/countries/eastasia/regional/Documents/asia-regional-trafficking-in-persons-report.pdf; Department of Foreign Affairs and Trade (Australia), 'Australia-Asia Program to Combat Trafficking in Persons' (Fact Sheet, January 2016), available at https://dfat.gov.au/about-us/publications/Documents/aaptip-fastfacts.pdf.

[57] Interview with Willem Pretorius, Deputy Team Leader at the Australia-Asia Program to Combat Trafficking in Persons, Bangkok, Thailand, 17 June 2016.

made in the Memorandum of Understanding on Cooperation against Trafficking in Persons in the Greater Mekong Sub-region.[58] While adopting the UN Trafficking Protocol's definition of human trafficking, COMMIT has facilitated the internalisation of these commitments among the Greater Mekong Subregion countries through the adoption of the COMMIT Sub-Regional Plans of Action and reviews of their implementation, with a comprehensive, victim-centred approach to trafficking, particularly in the area of repatriation and victim support.[59]

However, the internalisation of legal responses to human trafficking appears to have been more heavily influenced by the US Department of State's annual Trafficking in Persons (TIP) Reports. Notwithstanding their dubious legitimacy due to the US-biased approach, the TIP Reports have been influential in prompting individual governments to take concrete action to address human trafficking. This is because the US withholds non-humanitarian, non-trade related assistance to any government that fails to comply with, or to make significant efforts to comply with, the standards set by the US.[60]

---

[58] Memorandum of Understanding on Cooperation against Trafficking in Persons in the Greater Mekong Sub-Region, adopted in Yangon, Myanmar, 29 October 2004.

[59] For detailed analysis, see Kneebone and Debeljak, above n. 24, 201–11; Ratchada Jayagupta, 'The Thai Government's Repatriation and Reintegration Programmes: Responding to Trafficked Female Commercial Sex Workers from the Greater Mekong Subregion' (2009) 47 *International Migration* 227, 237–47.

[60] For details, see Gallagher, above n. 39, 480–6; Janie Chuang, 'The United States as Global Sheriff: Using Unilateral Sanctions to Combat Human Trafficking' (2006) 27 *Michigan Journal of International Law* 437.

Indeed, the Law on the Suppression of Human Trafficking and Sexual Exploitation 2008 was passed in Cambodia in response to severe pressure from the US,[61] with a view to implementing the UN Trafficking Protocol and purportedly reinforcing its criminal justice approach by adopting a narrower and more precise definition of human trafficking offences.[62]

In Indonesia, the Parliament enacted the Law on the Protection of Children 2002, and the President issued Decree No. 88/2002 on the National Plan of Action for the Elimination of Trafficking in Women and Children, in response to the Tier 3 ranking it received in the 2001 and 2002 TIP Reports. Although the Indonesian government signed the UN Trafficking Protocol in 2000 and the ASEAN Declaration against Trafficking in Persons in 2004, it did not enact the Law on the Eradication of the Criminal Act of Trafficking in Persons 2007 until it was demoted to the Tier 2 Watch List in the 2006 TIP Report.[63]

---

[61] It replaced the Law on the Suppression of the Kidnapping, Trafficking, and Exploitation of Human Beings 1996 (Cambodia), which was described as 'poorly written, ambiguous, [having] confounded trafficking, smuggling, illegal migration, and prostitution, and cast a wide net over many ill-defined behaviors': Chenda Keo, *Human Trafficking in Cambodia* (Abingdon: Routledge, 2014) 5.

[62] For details, see ibid., 60–1, 90–2. For critical analysis of the new human trafficking law in Cambodia, see Kneebone and Debeljak, above n. 24, 138–42; Cambodian Center for Human Rights, 'Human Trafficking Trials in Cambodia' (Report, July 2010), available at http://asiafounda tion.org/publications/pdf/756.

[63] See Wayne Palmer, 'Discretion in the Trafficking-like Practices of the Indonesian State' in Michele Ford, Lenore Lyons and Willem van Schendel (eds.), *Labour Migration and Human Trafficking in Southeast Asia: Critical Perspectives* (Abingdon: Routledge, 2012) 149, 151.

Other countries – namely Brunei,[64] Lao PDR,[65] Malaysia,[66] Myanmar,[67] the Philippines,[68] Singapore[69] and

[64] See Quratul-Ain Bandial, '46 Cases of Human Trafficking Probed', *The Brunei Times*, 24 November 2014, available at http://bt.com.bn/news/national?page=740&%24domain=aysnfipmttrmfxp (the Deputy Public Prosecutor, Chris Ng, reportedly stating that the Attorney General's Chamber is considering amendment to the Trafficking and Smuggling of Persons Order, in light of the recommendation in the Trafficking in Persons Report).

[65] See Kneebone and Debeljak, above n. 24, 129. Cf. Anne Gallagher, 'A Shadow Report on Human Trafficking in Lao PDR: The US Approach vs. International Law' (2006) 15 *Asia and Pacific Migration Journal* 525, 533. Having more recently been placed in the Tier 2 Watch List for three years, Lao PDR enacted the Law on Anti-Trafficking in Persons in 2015, which was promulgated in 2016.

[66] See Lenore Lyons and Michele Ford, 'Trafficking versus Smuggling: Malaysia's Anti-Trafficking in Persons Act' in Sallie Yea (ed.), *Human Trafficking in Asia: Forcing Issues* (Abingdon: Routledge, 2014) 35, 37–8; Pooja Theresa Stanslas, 'Transborder Human Trafficking in Malaysian Waters: Addressing the Root Causes' (2010) 41 *Journal of Maritime Law & Commerce* 595, 597–9.

[67] See e.g., Ministry of Home Affairs (Myanmar), 'Statement on Allegations of the US State Department in its Trafficking in Persons Report 2011' (Press Release, 2011), available at www.mehanoi.org/news/88-human-trafficking-english.html.

[68] See e.g., Dioniso P. Tubianosa, 'Congress to Patch Loopholes in Anti-Trafficking Law' (Press Release, House of Representatives, Republic of the Philippines, 11 November 2011), available at http://congress.gov.ph/press/details.php?pressid=5618. Ranking the Philippines in the Tier 2 Watch List of the 2011 TIP Report led to the 2012 amendments to the Anti-Trafficking in Persons Act 2003 (Philippines).

[69] See e.g., Ministry of Manpower (Singapore), 'Singapore Inter-Agency Taskforce's Official Statement in response to the 2013 US State Department's Trafficking in Persons Report' (Press Release, 24 June 2013), available at www.mom.gov.sg/newsroom/Pages/PressReleaseDetail.aspx?listid=511 (noting

Thailand[70] – have also been taking notice of the TIP Reports, while adopting legislative and policy measures to improve their capacity to address human trafficking, in some cases even before becoming a party to the UN Trafficking Protocol (see Table 6.1).

These external factors led many Southeast Asian nations to adopt the definition of human trafficking in the UN Trafficking Protocol,[71] with little variation, for domestic legislative instruments.[72] The virtually uniform criminalisation of human trafficking is striking, particularly when it is compared with the fragmented criminalisation of people smuggling and its varied definitions among Southeast Asian nations (see Table 6.2).[73] Whether such internalisation of

> that the Singaporean government introduced its National Plan of Action in 2012, partly to bolster its ranking in the TIP Reports).
>
> [70] See e.g., Anne Gallagher, 'Human Rights and Human Trafficking in Thailand: A Shadow TIP Report' in Karen Beeks and Delila Amir (eds.), *Trafficking and the Global Sex Industry* (Lanham, MD: Lexington Books, 2006) 139.
>
> [71] See the definition of human trafficking under the UN Trafficking Protocol cited above n. 3.
>
> [72] See e.g., Trafficking and Smuggling in Persons Order 2004 (Brunei) ss. 2 and 4; Law on the Eradication of the Criminal Act of Trafficking in Persons 2007 (Indonesia) art. 1(1); Law on Development and Protection of Women 2004 (Lao PDR) art. 24 and Penal Code 1990 (as amended in 2005) (Lao PDR) art. 134; Anti-Trafficking in Persons Law 2005 (Myanmar) s. 3(a); Anti-Trafficking in Persons Act 2003 (Philippines) s. 3 (a); Prevention of Human Trafficking Act 2015 (Singapore) s. 3; Anti-Trafficking in Persons Act 2008 (Thailand) s. 6; Law on Prevention and Suppression against Human Trafficking 2012 (Vietnam) art. 3.
>
> [73] Compare, e.g., Trafficking and Smuggling in Persons Order 2004 (Brunei) ss. 2 and 7–9; with Law on Immigration 2011 (Indonesia) arts. 1(32) and 120; Anti-Trafficking in Persons and Anti-Smuggling of Migrants Act 2007 (as amended in 2010 and 2015) (Malaysia) s. 2.

Table 6.1 *Status of UN Trafficking Protocol, Legislation and TIP Ranking*

a: accession s: signature r: ratification
T1: Tier 1 T2: Tier 2 T2WL: Tier 2 Watch List (introduced in 2004) T3: Tier 3

	UN Trafficking Protocol	Primary Legislative Instruments	TIP Ranking
Brunei		Trafficking and Smuggling of Persons Order 2004	T2 (2003, 2009, 2012–2017); T2WL (2010–2011)
Cambodia	s (11 Nov. 2001); r (2 Jul. 2007)	Law on Suppression of Human Trafficking and Sexual Exploitation 2008	T2 (2001, 2003–2004, 2008, 2010–2012, 2016–2017); T3 (2002, 2005); T2WL (2006–2007, 2009, 2013–2015)
Indonesia	s (12 Dec. 2000); r (28 Sep. 2009)	Decrees No. 88 (2002); Law on the Eradication of the Criminal Act of Trafficking in Persons 2007	T3 (2001–2002); T2 (2003–2005, 2007–2017); T2WL (2006)
Lao PDR	a (26 Sep. 2003)	Law on Development and Protection of Women 2004; Penal Code 1990 (as amended in 2005) art. 134; Law on the Protection of the Rights and Interests of Children 2007; Law on Anti-Trafficking in Persons 2015	T2 (2001–2003, 2005, 2007–2009, 2011–2013); T2WL (2004, 2010, 2014–2017); T3 (2006)
Malaysia	a (26 Feb. 2009)	Anti-Trafficking in Persons and Anti-Smuggling of Migrants Act 2007 (amended in 2010 and 2015)	T3 (2001, 2007, 2009, 2014); T2 (2002–2005, 2017); T2WL (2006, 2008, 2010–2013, 2015–2016)

Table 6.1 (*cont.*)

	UN Trafficking Protocol	Primary Legislative Instruments	TIP Ranking
Myanmar	a (30 Mar. 2004)	Anti-Trafficking in Persons Law 2005	T3 (2001–2011, 2016); T2WL (2012–2015, 2017)
Philippines	s (14 Dec. 2000); r (28 May 2002)	Anti-Trafficking in Persons Act 2003 (amended in 2012)	T2 (2001–2003, 2006–2008, 2011–2015); T2WL (2004–2005, 2009–2010); T1 (2016–2017)
Singapore	a (28 Sep. 2015)	Prevention of Human Trafficking Act 2015	T2 (2001–2002, 2004–2005, 2007–2009, 2011–2017); T1 (2006); T2WL (2010)
Thailand	s (18 Dec 2001); r (17 Oct. 2013)	Measures in the Prevention and Suppression of Trafficking in Women and Children Act 1997; Anti-Trafficking in Persons Act 2008 (amended in 2015)	T2 (2001–2003, 2005–2009); T2WL (2004, 2010–2013, 2016–2017); T3 (2014–2015)
Vietnam	a (8 Jun. 2012)	Penal Code 1999 (amended in 2009 and 2015) arts. 150–1; Law on Prevention and Suppression against Human Trafficking 2012	T2 (2001–2003, 2005–2009, 2012–2017); T2WL (2004, 2010–2011)

Table 6.2 *Status of UN Smuggling Protocol and Legislation*
a: accession   s: signature   r: ratification

	UN Smuggling Protocol	Primary Legislative Instruments
Brunei		Trafficking and Smuggling of Persons Order 2004
Cambodia	s (11 Nov. 2001); r (12 Dec. 2005)	
Indonesia	s (12 Dec. 2000); r (28 Sep. 2009)	Law on Immigration 2011
Lao PDR	a (26 Sep. 2003)	Penal Code 1990 (as amended in 2005) art. 75
Malaysia		Anti-Trafficking in Persons and Anti-Smuggling of Migrants Act 2007 as amended in 2010 and 2015
Myanmar	a (30 Mar. 2004)	
Philippines	s (14 Dec. 2000); r (28 May 2002)	
Singapore		
Thailand	s (18 Dec. 2001)	
Vietnam		Penal Code 1999 (amended in 2009 and 2015) art. 275

human trafficking norms is resulting in successful prosecutions and stemming the flow of human trafficking networks is beyond the scope of this chapter. Relevant to this chapter is the fact that regional multilateral processes, at the initiative or with the involvement of extra-regional powers, have had a significant impact on the development and internalisation of regional legal responses to human trafficking, even prior to ASEAN's adoption of a legally binding regional instrument.

These external influences could well be seen as violating the principle of non-interference, particularly given that legal responses involve changes to criminal justice and migration policy, which are typically considered matters within the domestic jurisdiction of a state. However, by characterising human trafficking and people smuggling as non-traditional security or transnational security issues commonly shared within the region, ASEAN has arguably provided the normative foundation upon which its member states can consider these agendas as vehicles to reinforce their own law enforcement capabilities, rather than as a form of interference that challenges their authority.

Nevertheless, in cases where a different position is adopted, national authorities find it useful to rely upon the principle of non-interference to protect themselves from criticism. For example, the 2010 amendments to the Anti-Trafficking in Persons and Anti-Smuggling of Migrants Act 2007 in Malaysia have been criticised for narrowing the legal definition of human trafficking to exploitation through 'coercion' only, and for conflating other aspects of human trafficking with the immigration offences of people smuggling.[74] The Malaysian Government responded to this criticism by stating that the definition of human trafficking 'may vary from one country to another based on its historical dimension, different resources and national security concerns'.[75]

---

[74] See 'Letter from Human Rights Watch to the Prime Minister of Malaysia' (8 September 2010), available at www.hrw.org/news/2010/09/08/malaysia-letter-prime-minister-regarding-amendments-anti-trafficking-persons-act.

[75] Permanent Mission of Malaysia to the United Nations, Geneva, '26th HRC: Statement Delivered during Interactive Dialogue with SR on Trafficking in Persons & IE on International Solidarity' (Ministry of

This response is illustrative of the more traditional reaction by Southeast Asian nations to external intrusion into a state's internal affairs. Wary of potentially obstructing the effect of this regional principle, Australia needed to carefully manage the Bali Process so as not to appear to interfere with domestic migration and refugee policies, while at the same time promoting the criminalisation of people smuggling and law enforcement cooperation, in order to achieve Australia's political interest by appealing to the mutual interests of neighbouring states to control irregular migration.[76]

6.5 Concluding Observations

Human trafficking has been widely recognised as a prominent non-traditional security issue within ASEAN, and as part of a broader transnational security agenda shared within the ARF. The adoption of the ASEAN Convention against Trafficking in Persons, Especially Women and Children, in 2015, and its prompt entry into force in 2017 has signalled ASEAN's willingness to exercise its authority in localising the relevant norms and rules of international law to facilitate the region's collective response to shared security concerns. By contrast, the institutional practices relating to people smuggling are limited to policy coordination with very little

Foreign Affairs, Malaysia, 12 June 2014) para. 4, available at www
.kln.gov.my/web/che_un-geneva/home/-/asset_publisher/8pPT/blog/
26th-hrc:-statement-delivered-during-interactive-dialogue-with-sr-on-
trafficking-in-persons-&-ie-on-internaitonal-solidarity-12-june-2014?re
direct=%2Fweb%2Fche_un-geneva%2Fhome.
[76] For details, see Kneebone, above n. 50, 600–1.

bearing upon the actual development, localisation and internalisation of legal responses. Instead, different multilateral processes and other extra-regional factors have hijacked the ASEAN-based institutional efforts to facilitate legislative responses and law enforcement capacity-building.

These extra-regional factors involving major powers such as Australia and the US have allowed human trafficking and people smuggling issues to be framed more flexibly with a particular political agenda, through the promotion of various implementation programmes and action plans. This flexibility also means that the internalisation of legal and policy responses to human trafficking and people smuggling has, more or less, taken place outside ASEAN's institutional and legal constraints. This has allowed Southeast Asian governments to capitalise on the political interests of extra-regional powers to reinforce their law enforcement capacity, particularly in dealing with irregular migrants.

Chapter 7

Food Security

7.1 Introduction

The issue of food security was first recognised in policy discourse in the 1970s with a focus on food supply problems. At that time, the dominant perspective was that food security would be achieved when adequate availability of food was secured at all times.[1] Since then, the definition of food security has evolved to one that emphasises, on the demand side, physical, social and economic access to sufficient, safe and nutritious food.[2] This is reflected in the widely accepted definition of food security adopted at the World Food Summit in 1996, which reads:

> Food security, at the individual, household, national, regional and global levels is achieved when all people, at all times, have physical and economic access to sufficient, safe

---

[1] See Universal Declaration on the Eradication of Hunger and Malnutrition, preamble para. (g), reprinted in *Report of the World Food Conference, Rome, 5–16 November 1974* (New York: UN, 1975) 1.

[2] For discussion of the shifts in focus of food security policy and debate, see especially FAO, *Trade Reforms and Food Security: Conceptualizing the Linkages* (Rome: FAO, 2003) ch 2; Jessica Duncan, *Global Food Security Governance: Civil Society Engagement in the Reformed Committee on World Food Security* (Abingdon: Routledge, 2015) 43–8; Simon Maxwell, 'Food Security: A Post-Modern Perspective' (1996) 21(2) *Food Policy* 155.

and nutritious food to meet their dietary needs and food preferences for an active and healthy life.[3]

Food insecurity can manifest as an acute, short-term food shortage crisis or as chronic, long-term food inaccessibility, and can be characterised differently according to the focus of inquiry as a national security,[4] non-traditional security,[5] human security[6] or international security issue.[7] Food security is often closely linked with other traditional security issues such as armed conflict, as well as non-traditional security issues such as famine and public health, which are exacerbated by threat multiplier events such as climate change and natural disasters.[8]

---

[3] World Food Summit Plan of Action, adopted at the World Food Summit, Rome, Italy, 13–17 November 1996, para. 1.

[4] See e.g., National Food Security Act 2013 (India).

[5] See e.g., Irene A. Kuntjoro, Sofiah Jamil and Arpita Mathur, 'Food' in Mely Caballero-Anthony and Alistair D. B. Cook (eds.), *Non-Traditional Security in Asia: Issues, Challenges and Framework for Action* (Singapore: Institute of Southeast Asian Studies, 2013) 41–65.

[6] See e.g., Commission on Human Security, 'Human Security Now' (Report, 2003) 14, available at www.humansecurity-chs.org/finalreport/index.html.

[7] See the UN Security Council's debates on food security with respect to its 'incontrovertible link' to international peace and security: UN Security Council Official Records, UN Doc S/PV.5220 (30 June 2005); UN Doc S/PV.4736 (7 April 2003); UN Doc S/PV.4652 (3 December 2002).

[8] See e.g., Ferne Edwards et al., 'Climate Change Adaptation at the Intersection of Food and Health' 23(2) *Asia-Pacific Journal of Public Health* 91S; Yi-Yuan Su, Yi-Hao Weng and Ya-Wen Chiu, 'Climate Change and Food Security in East Asia' (2009) 18 *Asia-Pacific Journal of Clinical Nutrition* 674.

The causes of food insecurity are multifaceted and range from natural hazards like famine, to over-production of foodstuffs, agricultural subsidies and the existing global food supply structure. Law and policy are part of this structural problem. Many states have domestic legislation and regulations to govern food production, stockpiling, supply, sale, distribution and quality control. The implementation of such domestic laws has cross-border effects on the stability of the world food market due to the expansion of international trade – for example, the strict food safety standards in developed countries may adversely affect food security in developing countries.[9]

There are also various rules of international law that contribute to the structural causes of food insecurity, such as international trade, investment and intellectual property rules.[10] The concept of the right to food, by contrast, attempts

---

[9] For discussion, see especially, Julie A. Caswell and Christian Friis Bach, 'Food Safety Standards in Rich and Poor Countries' in Per Pinstrup-Andersen and Peter Sandøe (eds.), *Ethics, Hunger and Globalization: In Search of Appropriate Policies* (Berlin: Springer, 2007) 281.

[10] See e.g., Dilan Thampapillai, 'The Food and Agriculture Organization and Food Security in the Context of International Intellectual Property Rights Protection' in Hitoshi Nasu and Kim Rubenstein (eds.), *Legal Perspectives on Security Institutions* (Cambridge: Cambridge University Press, 2015) 269; Christian Häberli, 'The WTO and Food Security: What's Wrong with the Rules?' in Rosemary Rayfuse and Nicole Weisfelt (eds.), *The Challenge of Food Security: International Policy and Regulatory Frameworks* (Cheltenham: Edward Elgar, 2012) 149; Christian Häberli and Fiona Smith, 'Food Security and Agri-Foreign Direct Investment in Weak States: Finding the Governance Gap to Avoid "Land Grab"' (2014) 77 *Modern Law Review* 189; Melaku Geboye Desta, 'Food Security and International Trade Law: An Appraisal of the World Trade Organization Approach' (2001) 35 *Journal of World Trade* 449.

to address food insecurity within the framework of international law.[11] Both strands necessarily shape the legal parameters of national and regional food security policy-making. It is this legal quagmire that ASEAN has had to navigate through in developing its legal and policy responses to food insecurity.

7.2 ASEAN's Engagement with Food Security

As the economic impact of the oil crisis reached Southeast Asia in the 1970s, ASEAN member states perceived the challenge of food security as a real issue and, on 4 October 1979, signed the Agreement on the ASEAN Food Security Reserve with a view to establishing the ASEAN Emergency Rice Reserve (AERR).[12] Under the agreement, ASEAN member states committed themselves to earmarking an agreed amount of rice, which was to be released in an emergency when a member state, 'having suffered extreme and unexpected natural or man-induced calamity, is unable to cope with such state or condition through its national reserve and is unable to procure the needed supply through normal trade'.[13] The prices, terms and conditions of payment were to be

[11] See e.g., Report of the Special Rapporteur on the Right to Food, UN Doc A/64/170 (23 July 2009); Wenche Barth Eide, 'From Food Security to the Right to Food' in Wenche Barth Eide and Uwe Kracht (eds.), *Food and Human Rights in Development: Volume I, Legal and Institutional Dimensions and Selected Topics* (Antwerp: Intersentia, 2005) 67; Kerstin Mechlem, 'Food Security and the Right to Food in the Discourse of the United Nations' (2004) 10 *European Law Journal* 631.

[12] Agreement on the ASEAN Food Security Reserve, adopted 4 October 1979 (entered into force 17 July 1980), amended in 1982 and 1997.

[13] Ibid., art. IV(5).

subject to direct negotiations between the states concerned.[14] However, the AERR was never activated to release the earmarked rice reserve primarily due to the small size of the reserve and the requirement of bilateral negotiations for the release.[15] Even when the region experienced sharp increase in food prices in 2007–2008 (particularly the price of rice),[16] it failed to provide support.[17]

Following the 2007–2008 food crisis, ASEAN member states pledged 'to embrace food security as a matter of permanent and high priority policy' in the ASEAN Statement on Food Security in the ASEAN Region, adopted on 1 March 2009, and established the ASEAN Integrated Food Security (AIFS) Framework and the Strategic Plan of Action on Food Security (SPA-FS). The AIFS sets out the scope for joint pragmatic approaches for cooperation among ASEAN member states, which are grouped into four components and six strategic thrusts with a view to

---

[14] Ibid., art. V.

[15] For detailed analysis, see Japan International Cooperation Agency, *The Development Study on East Asia: ASEAN Rice Reserve System, Final Report* (Tokyo: Pacific Consultants International, 2002).

[16] For detailed analysis of the crisis, see e.g., David Dawe (ed.), *The Rice Crisis: Markets, Policies and Food Security* (London and Washington DC: Earthscan, 2010); Milan Brahmbhatt and Luc Christiaensen, 'The Run on Rice' (2008) 25(2) *World Policy Journal* 29.

[17] For a review of ASEAN member states' response to the 2007–2008 food crisis, see e.g., Mulat Demeke, Guendalina Pangrazio and Materne Maetz, 'Country Responses to the Food Security Crisis: Nature and Preliminary Implications of the Policies Pursued' (FAO, 2009), available at www.fao.org/fileadmin/user_upload/ISFP/pdf_for_site_Country_Response_to_the_Food_Security.pdf.

promoting long-term food security in Southeast Asia.[18] The Strategic Plan of Action, on the other hand, tailors an operational plan outlining detailed action programmes and activities to be undertaken under each strategic thrust.[19] During the ASEAN Consultative Meeting on Integrating Nutrition into the AIFS Framework and the SPA-FS, ASEAN member states agreed to add a new nutrition component and three related strategic thrusts on nutrition sensitive policies and programmes.[20]

The 2007–2008 food crisis also prompted ASEAN to institutionalise regional cooperation on food security, with involvement of the ASEAN Plus Three process. For example, the first component of the AIFS – on food security emergency and shortage relief – expressly refers to the ASEAN Plus Three as the forum through which a long-term, effective and timely mechanism for food supply in emergency relief is to be established in the region. Correspondingly, on 24 October 2009, the ASEAN Plus Three issued the Cha-am Hua Hin Statement on ASEAN Plus Three Cooperation on Food Security and Bio-Energy Development,[21] which

---

[18] ASEAN Integrated Food Security (AIFS) Framework and Strategic Plan of Action on Food Security in the ASEAN Region (SPA-FS) 2009–2013, adopted at the 14th ASEAN Summit, Cha-am Hua Hin, Thailand, 1 March 2009.

[19] Ibid.

[20] Report of the ASEAN Consultative Meeting on Integrating Nutrition into ASEAN Integrated Food Security Framework and Strategic Plan of Action on Food Security (2015–2019), Pattaya, Thailand, 6–7 February 2014, available at www.fao.org/fileadmin/templates/rap/files/meetings/2014/140206-report.pdf.

[21] Adopted at the 12th ASEAN+3 Summit, Cha-am Hua Hin, Thailand, 24 October 2009.

subsequently led to the adoption of the ASEAN Plus Three Emergency Rice Reserve (APTERR) Agreement on 7 October 2011.[22]

The APTERR is an extension of the East Asia Emergency Rice Reserve (EAERR), a three-year pilot programme which was established at Japan's initiative as part of the 2004 Strategic Plan of Action on Cooperation in Food, Agriculture and Forestry. Built upon the scheme established by the 1979 AERR, the EAERR extended its coverage with the maintenance of physical stocks, rather than mere earmarked stocks, and the establishment of more elaborate mechanisms to facilitate rice trade in situations of food emergency.[23] Hidetaka Yoshimatsu observes that although ASEAN policy-makers were generally cautious about developing the EAERR project into a permanent institution, the 2007–2008 food crisis made them realise the risk of social unrest and political instability that could be triggered by food emergencies.[24] This realisation led them to consider the APTERR as an effective institution to stabilise the prices of staple foods.

With respect to the trigger mechanism of food supply, the AIFS and the APTERR apply the same

[22] ASEAN Plus Three Emergency Rice Reserve Agreement, adopted 7 October 2011 (entered into force 12 July 2012).

[23] For details, see Elenita Daño, 'ASEAN's Emergency Rice Reserve Schemes: Current Developments and Prospects for Engagement' (2006) 3 *Women in Action* 35, 36–8.

[24] Hidetaka Yoshimatsu, *Comparing Institution-Building in East Asia: Power Politics, Governance, and Critical Junctures* (Basingstoke: Palgrave Macmillan, 2014) 110–11.

definition of 'emergency' as the one originally adopted for the 1979 AERR in the Agreement on the ASEAN Food Security Reserve, namely: (1) the extreme and unexpected calamity; and (2) the affected state's inability to address the situation through its own national reserve or normal trade. There is no clarification of 'the extreme and unexpected calamity'. This phrase remains vague compared to the same notion adopted under the ASEAN Petroleum Security Agreement, which provides specific examples of unexpected natural calamities such as an 'earthquake, an explosion of production facilities, storage or refinery plants or an abrupt stoppage of import due to war or other similar crises'.[25] Therefore, concerns remain that the mechanism to trigger release may be too rigid to be effective, or too sensitive so that large-scale withdrawals from earmarked reserves in excess of actual needs may cause distortions to normal international trade.

The APTERR addresses these concerns by introducing a three-tiered triggering mechanism, modelled upon the EAERR.[26]

---

[25] ASEAN Petroleum Security Agreement, adopted 24 June 1986 (entered into force 2 April 1987) art. 2(vi); ASEAN Petroleum Security Agreement, adopted 1 March 2009 (entered into force 22 March 2013) art. 2(5).

[26] See Roehlano M. Briones, 'Regional Cooperation for Food Security: The Case of Emergency Rice Reserves in the ASEAN Plus Three' (Sustainable Development Working Paper Series No. 18, Asian Development Bank, 2011) 14–15, available at www.adb.org/sites/default/files/publication/29275/adb-wp18-regional-cooperation-food-security.pdf.

Tier 1: a release from earmarked rice reserves under commercial terms;

Tier 2: a release from earmarked rice reserves under long-term loan or grant; and

Tier 3: a release from stockpiled rice reserves in the case of an acute and urgent emergency (or if stockpiled rice is not utilised within twelve months, as food aid for poverty alleviation).[27]

As Michael Ewing-Chow and others observe, these rules governing the operation of the APTERR have been shaped largely by legal considerations for compliance with various international trade law rules.[28] This demonstrates ASEAN's normative contribution, through ASEAN Plus Three process, to the development of regional rules, while respecting the applicable rules of general international law.

---

[27] For details, see e.g., Roehlano M. Briones, 'Climate Change and Price Volatility: Can We Count on the ASEAN Plus Three Emergency Rice Reserve?' (Sustainable Development Working Paper Series No. 24, Asian Development Bank, 2012) 3–4, available at www.adb.org/sites/default/files/publication/29971/adb-wp-24-climate-change-price-volatility.pdf.

[28] Michael Ewing-Chow, Melanie V. Slade and Lui Gehuan, 'Rice is Life: Regional Food Security, Trade Rules and the ASEAN+3 Emergency Rice Reserve' in Hitoshi Nasu and Kim Rubenstein (eds.), *Legal Perspectives on Security Institutions* (Cambridge: Cambridge University Press, 2015) 292; Michael Ewing-Chow and Melanie Vilarasau Slade, 'A Case Study of Regional Food Security: APTERR' in Michael Ewing-Chow and Melanie Vilarasau Slade (eds.), *International Trade and Food Security: Exploring Collective Food Security in Asia* (Cheltenham: Edward Elgar, 2016) 62.

7.3 Comparison with APEC's Food Security Policy

ASEAN's food security policy can be characterised as being based on the food 'self-reliance' approach, as opposed to the food 'self-sufficiency' approach.[29] The former aims to promote availability of various food items for domestic consumption through various means, including international trade as an essential component of food security strategy. The latter, on the other hand, emphasises the production of various food items by domestic producers without relying on imports as a major source of domestic food supplies. The ASEAN food security measures agreed upon in the AIFS Framework, such as sustainable food trade development and integrated food security information systems, as well as the APTERR mechanism to address regional food security emergencies, are all oriented towards a cooperative security arrangement to stabilise food prices by achieving regional food 'self-reliance'.

APEC, by contrast, has adopted a food security policy that focuses on food productivity and 'self-sufficiency', despite the fact that it emerged specifically with a regional trade liberalisation agenda.[30] Initially, APEC developed the

[29] For discussion of these different approaches, see Alexander C. Chandra and Lucky A. Lontoh, 'Regional Food Security and Trade Policy in Southeast Asia: The Role of ASEAN' (Policy Report No. 3, International Institute for Sustainable Development Series on Trade and Food Security, 2010) 2–3, available at www.iisd.org/tkn/pdf/regional_food_trade_asean.pdf.

[30] Shanghai Accord, adopted at the 9th APEC Leaders' Meeting, Shanghai, PRC, 21 October 2001, Section I; APEC Economic Leaders' Declaration

APEC Food System with a focus on three areas of food security concern: rural infrastructure development; the promotion of trade in food products; and the dissemination of technological advances in food production and processing.[31] However, the 2007–2008 food crisis alerted APEC nations to the vulnerability of food security in the Asia-Pacific, which led to a series of declarations adopted at the Ministerial Meetings on Food Security.[32]

While promoting investment and trade in food and agricultural products, these declarations emphasise the significance of sustainable development in the agricultural sector.[33] This is most clearly demonstrated in the 2014 Beijing Declaration adopted at the Third Ministerial Meeting on Food Security. Expanding the ambit of the first goal articulated in the 2010 Niigata Declaration – sustainable development of the agricultural sector – the 2014 Beijing Declaration promotes sustainable agricultural and food production, based on: progress in agricultural science and technology; improved post-harvest management to

of Common Resolve, adopted at the 2nd APEC Leaders' Meeting, Bogor, Indonesia, 15 November 1994, para. 1.

[31] Auckland Declaration, adopted at the 7th APEC Leaders' Meeting, Auckland, New Zealand, 13 September 1999.

[32] Niigata Declaration on APEC Food Security, adopted at the 1st APEC Ministerial Meeting on Food Security, Niigata, Japan, 17 October 2010; Kazan Declaration on APEC Food Security, adopted at the 2nd APEC Ministerial Meeting on Food Security, Kazan, Russia, 31 May 2012; Beijing Declaration on APEC Food Security, adopted at the 3rd APEC Ministerial Meeting on Food Security, Beijing, PRC, 19 September 2014.

[33] Niigata Declaration, above. n 32, paras. 8–12; Kazan Declaration, above. n 32, paras. 6–12; Beijing Declaration, above n. 32, paras. 5–11.

reduce food loss; and strengthened research and development cooperation.[34]

This shift in emphasis of APEC food security policy is driven by the lure of food 'self-sufficiency', which has commonly been identified as a shortcoming of the APEC food security policy. Indeed, the APEC Policy Support Unit observes:

> The concept of self-sufficiency has grown in popularity among APEC economies because of growing mistrust in many developing and net food importing economies about the reliability of international markets as suppliers of affordable food ... Thus, several economies, notably Brunei Darussalam; China; Indonesia; Japan; Korea; Malaysia; Mexico; Papua New Guinea; Philippines; Russia; Chinese Taipei; and Viet Nam have called for increased self-sufficiency and food independence versus continued reliance on the international market for the availability of food in the domestic market.[35]

The drive for food self-sufficiency is further derived from concerns of agrarian stability, foreign currency conversion, potential political influences from exporting countries,[36] as well as the preferential adoption of short-term, domestic advantages over the regional cooperative approach espoused by ASEAN.[37]

---

[34] Beijing Declaration, above n. 32.

[35] APEC Policy Support Unit, *Food Security Policies in APEC* (Singapore: APEC Secretariat, 2012) 22.

[36] Ching-Cheng Chang, Huey-Lin Lee and Shih-Hsun Hsu, 'Food Security: Global Trends and Regional Perspective with reference to East Asia' (2013) 26 *The Pacific Review* 589, 596.

[37] Paul Teng and Maria C. S. Morales, 'Food Security Robustness: A Driver of Enhanced Regional Cooperation?' (Policy Brief, S. Rajaratnam School

7.4 Food Security Law and Policy in ASEAN Member States

Despite ASEAN member states' commitment to joint pragmatic approaches for cooperation under the AIFS Framework, and its operationalisation through the SPA-FS, the focus of national food security policy and related legislation among the region's food importers largely remains food 'self-sufficiency'. This is presumably because they are particularly vulnerable to dramatic increases in food prices.[38] Brunei Darussalam, for example, launched Vision 2035 in the middle of the 2007–2008 food crisis, which set out one of its primary goals as improving the rice self-sufficiency rate to at least 60 per cent by 2015.[39] Likewise, Malaysia introduced its National Food Security Policy in April 2008, with the production-centric objective to meet a higher self-sufficiency level by increasing rice production.[40] The Philippines released the

of International Studies, 2014) 3, available at www.rsis.edu.sg/wp-content/uploads/2014/07/PB140331_Food_Security_Robustness.pdf.

[38] According to the ASEAN Agricultural Commodity Outlook, the major rice importers in the region are Indonesia, Malaysia, the Philippines and Singapore: see ASEAN Food Security Information System, *ASEAN Agricultural Commodity Outlook No. 11* (Bangkok: ASEAN Food Security Information System Secretariat, 2013) 8 and 15.

[39] Jonatan A. Lassa, 'Brunei's Vision 2035: Can It Achieve Food Self-Sufficiency?' (Commentary No. 34, S. Rajaratnam School of International Studies, 2015) 1, available at www.rsis.edu.sg/wp-content/uploads/2015/02/CO15034.pdf.

[40] Ministry of Agriculture and Agro-based Industry (Malaysia), 'Malaysia National Report: Follow-up of the Implementation of the World Food Summit Plan of Action' (FAO, 2008) 16, available at ftp://ftp.fao.org/docrep/fao/meeting/013/ai699e.pdf. For details, see Y. S. Tey, 'Malaysia's

Food Staples Self-Sufficiency Roadmap 2011–2016, which aimed to attain self-sufficiency in staples with a focus on irrigation and institutional reforms.[41] Singapore is an exception as the second-most food secure country in the world despite its heavy reliance on food imports, pursuing its national food security through diversifying sources of food imports, optimising local food production and stockpiling.[42]

The idea of national food security with an emphasis on food self-sufficiency is most prominently expressed in Indonesia, where the 2012 Law on Food enshrines food sovereignty, food self-sufficiency and food security as the basic principles and objectives for planning, implementing and controlling food supply activities.[43] This 2012 Law replaced the 1996 Food Law, which focused on ensuring food safety, nutrition content and the quality of foods, on the grounds that it was 'no longer in line with the external and internal dynamic development conditions'.[44] Indonesia's national food security policy emerged in 2001 when Presidential Decree No. 132 was issued to establish the Food Security Board (*Dewan Ketahanan Pangan*), and with the subsequent adoption of the 2002 Regulation on Food Security.[45] The 2012 Law expands upon the previous food

Strategic Food Security Approach' (2010) 17 *International Food Research Journal* 501, 504.

[41] Philippine Development Plan 2011–2016 (Philippines, 2011) 113.
[42] See e.g., Cecilia Tortajada and Thinesh Kumar, 'Singapore's Impressive Food Security: How Has Singapore Become the Second-Most Food Secure Country in the World?', *The Diplomat* (6 September 2015), available at http://thediplomat.com/2015/09/singapores-impressive-food-security/.
[43] Law No. 18/2012 (Indonesia) arts. 2 and 3.   [44] Ibid., preamble para. d.
[45] Regulation No. 68/2002 (Indonesia).

security policy by committing the Government to prioritising domestic food production to meet food consumption needs, allowing food export only when the national food reserve and staple food consumption needs are satisfied and allowing food importation only when domestic food production is not sufficient or viable.[46]

The notion of food sovereignty is defined under this legislation, with a strong emphasis on national security, as 'the right of the state and nation that independently establishes a food policy that guarantees the right to food for the people and grants the right for the society to establish a food system that is appropriate with the local potential resources'.[47] Therefore, it must be distinguished from the notion of food sovereignty used elsewhere, particularly by non-governmental activists in promoting the interests of local and smallholder farmers.[48] As Zamroni Salim observes, Indonesia's food security policy based on the notion of food sovereignty 'emphasizes the supply of foods in the domestic market by domestic supplies only'.[49] This nationalistic approach to food security, rather than a regional cooperative approach, often entails significant trade restrictions, which compromises economic

---

[46] Law No. 18/2012 (Indonesia) arts. 15, 34 and 36.   [47] Ibid., art. 1(2).

[48] For discussion of various notions of food sovereignty, see especially, Priscilla Claeys, *Human Rights and the Food Sovereignty Movement: Reclaiming Control* (Abingdon: Routledge, 2015) 88–90.

[49] Zamroni Salim, 'Food Security Policies in Maritime Southeast Asia: The Case of Indonesia' (Trade Network Knowledge Series on Trade and Food Security: Policy Report 1, International Institute for Sustainable Development, 2010) 15, available at www.iisd.org/sites/default/files/pub lications/food_security_policies_indonesia.pdf.

efficiency.[50] It has also been seen as a major weakness as it is 'more susceptible to domestic economic and natural disaster risks than international events'.[51]

On the other hand, the region's rice exporters – namely, Thailand, Cambodia, Myanmar, Lao PDR and Vietnam[52] – tend to incorporate food security policy into their overall national development and poverty reduction plan, without building any food security specific policy framework. Food security forms an integral part of Thailand's National Economic and Social Development Plans, which emphasise the need to increase agricultural productivity through support for scientific and technological development.[53]

Cambodia adopts its food security policy as part of a broad range of national economic growth and poverty reduction policies promulgated in the National Strategic Development Plans,[54] the Rectangular Strategy (Phases I–III)[55] and the Agricultural Sector Strategic Development

[50] FAO, *Regional Overview of Food Insecurity Asia and the Pacific: Towards a Food Secure Asia and the Pacific* (Bangkok: FAO, 2015) 31.

[51] OECD, 'Indonesian Policy Brief: Agriculture' (OECD Better Policy Series, 2015) 2, available at www.oecd.org/policy-briefs/indonesia-agriculture-improving-food-security.pdf.

[52] See ASEAN Food Security Information System, above n. 38, 8 and 14.

[53] See e.g., Twelfth National Economic and Social Development Plan 2017–2021 (Thailand, 2017) 77–8; Eleventh National Economic and Social Development Plan 2012–2016 (Thailand, 2012) ch 5.

[54] National Strategic Development Plan 2014–2018 (Cambodia, 2014) para. 2.200–2.202; National Strategic Development Plan 2006–2010 (Cambodia, 2006) para. 4.46.

[55] Rectangular Strategy for Growth, Employment, Equity and Efficiency Phase III (Cambodia, 2013) paras. 51–6; Rectangular Strategy for Growth, Employment, Equity and Efficiency Phase II (Cambodia, 2008) para. 46;

Plans.[56] These policies emphasise an integrated approach to enhance productivity, diversification and commercialisation of agricultural products for domestic consumption and for export. The most recent strategic policy document on Cambodia's food security concludes that food security at the national level has largely been achieved and is of no particular concern for Cambodia today, although problems remain at the household and individual level.[57]

Myanmar's Framework for Economic and Social Reforms identifies food security as one of the priority areas for the national development plan.[58] Lao PDR gives food security the first priority for the improvement of livelihoods in its Agriculture Development Strategy, which sets out a long-term framework for national socio-economic development and poverty reduction through modernised agriculture production, promotion of investment and sustainable environmental management.[59] Vietnam adopted the Comprehensive Poverty Reduction and Growth Strategy in 2002, in which food security was sought through agriculture and rural

Rectangular Strategy for Growth, Employment, Equity and Efficiency in Cambodia (Cambodia, 2004) 13–14.

[56] Agricultural Sector Strategic Development Plan 2014–2018 (Cambodia, 2015) 32–4; Agricultural Sector Strategic Development Plan 2006–2010 (Cambodia, 2006) 18–20.

[57] National Strategy for Food Security and Nutrition 2014–2018 (Cambodia, 2014) 22–3.

[58] Asian Development Bank Economics and Research Department, *Myanmar: Unlocking the Potential* (Mandaluyong City: Asian Development Bank, 2014) 4–5.

[59] Strategy for Agricultural Development 2011 to 2020 (Lao PDR, 2010) 32–5.

development.[60] In 2009, the Government of Vietnam passed a resolution on national food security, which sets out comprehensive and efficient agricultural production development plans as a basis for ensuring national food security.[61]

Notwithstanding the conspicuous absence of reference to the AIFS Framework in each member state's national food security legislation and policy, as examined earlier, there are somewhat clearer indications of the domestic implementation of their obligations under the APTERR. To the extent that the APTERR forms a subset of national reserves, ASEAN member states can arguably be considered to be implementing their obligations under the APTERR by establishing or maintaining their national food reserve in one form or another. Upon ratification of the APTERR in 2012, the Cambodian Government set up the Cambodia Food Reserve System as a permanent mechanism to assist people affected by disaster or crisis.[62] Indonesia also introduced a system of public food reserves through the 2012 Law on Food, upon ratification of the APTERR by a presidential decree in 2012.[63] Different forms and levels of rice stockpiling are also observed in other parts of the region.[64]

---

[60] Document No. 2685/VPCP-QHQT (21 May 2002) and Document No. 1649/CP-QHQT (26 November 2003) 9.

[61] Resolution No. 63/NQ-CP (23 December 2009).

[62] Food and Agriculture Policy Decision Analysis (FAPDA), 'Country Fact Sheet on Food and Agriculture Policy Trends: Cambodia' (FAO, April 2014) 4, available at www.fao.org/docrep/field/009/i3761e/i3761e.pdf.

[63] Decree No. 62/2012 (Indonesia).

[64] See Mely Caballero-Anthony, Paul P. S. Teng, Maxim Shrestha, Tamara Nair and Jonatan A Lassa, 'Public Stockpiling and Food Security' (Policy

However, it remains to be seen how their national food security policy, based on the notion of food sovereignty or centred upon the notion of food 'self-sufficiency', will be reconciled with their commitments under the APTERR. This is particularly so in situations where the level of domestic food production is not sufficient to fulfil the national food reserve, or to meet domestic food consumption needs.

7.5 Concluding Observations

The adoption of the 2009 AIFS Framework and the SPA-FS presented a model of ASEAN's cooperative security. The food 'self-reliance' approach adopted within this framework encompasses the promotion of sustainable food production and trade, the strengthening of integrated food information systems, the encouragement of greater investment in food and agri-based industries, as well as cooperation for food security emergency relief. While this may have added a normative value to the development of a regional response to food security in accordance with the principle of comprehensive security and collective responsibility, it can hardly be considered as being internalised. There has been no clear impact on domestic

Brief, S. Rajaratnam School of International Studies, 2015) 6, available at www.rsis.edu.sg/wp-content/uploads/2015/06/PB150603_Public-Stockpi ling.pdf; Roehlano M. Briones, 'Public Stockholding in Southeast Asia: Review and Prospects' (paper presented at FAO Expert Meeting on Stocks, Markets and Stability, Rome, 30–31 January 2014) 3–9, available at www.fao.org/fileadmin/templates/est/meetings/stocks/Briones_public_ stockholding_in_southeast_asia.pdf.

food security laws and policies, which are largely centred upon food 'self-sufficiency' in many ASEAN member states.

There are clearer indications of ASEAN member states implementing their obligations under the APTERR, to the extent that their national food reserve system forms part of this regional agreement. It is expected that the new three-tiered triggering mechanism will add clarity as to when and under what circumstances emergency food supplies must be made available to affected states. It remains to be seen, however, how such cooperative arrangement will be implemented in conjunction with the strong assertion of food sovereignty and national food security policy centred upon the idea of food 'self-sufficiency', as pursued by some member states. This is particularly the case when the level of their domestic food production is not sufficient to fulfil the national food reserve or to meet their own domestic food consumption needs.

Conclusion

Born out of the region's shared concern for stability and identity at the height of Cold War politics, ASEAN's institutional evolution has always been oriented towards the political legitimisation of domestic governmental regimes through security cooperation and economic development. The close examination of ASEAN's handling of various regional security issues in the previous chapters has revealed a symbiotic relationship between ASEAN and its member states: ASEAN needs member states to maintain its legal authority relevant to regional cooperation that addresses shared security concerns, while member states need ASEAN to develop or localise various norms and rules as they apply to the region, with a view to facilitating legislative responses and domestic policy-making to deal with those concerns. Thus, characterising ASEAN as a security institution is apt, in that it is this mutually constitutive interaction that creates 'persistent and connected sets of rules' that determine how regional security issues are to be addressed.[1]

However, this relationship is not always easy to maintain. For example, the AIFS Framework and SPA-FS developed by ASEAN for regional cooperation on food security has not been widely internalised into domestic food security law and policy because many ASEAN member states have pursued food

---

[1] See Chapter 1.1.

security as part of their national development agenda with a focus on the objective of food 'self-sufficiency'.[2] Likewise, ASEAN has faced difficulties in developing a region-wide nuclear security regime due to the tension between nuclear aspirational states, whose national development agenda drives their own nuclear power programme, and those that are concerned about possible nuclear fallout and its potential cross-border impact.[3] The principle of non-interference restricts ASEAN's ability to develop a regulatory mechanism that overrides the political and legal constraints that exist within each member state.

The political and legal constraints within each member state necessarily limit ASEAN's capacity to facilitate regional cooperation in Southeast Asia. However, those constraints should not be understood as obstacles to the exercise of ASEAN's legal authority, but rather as socio-political structures in which ASEAN engages in mutual social persuasion and forges deeper intra-regional cooperation. This is done in a manner that complements respective national efforts to develop domestic legal and policy responses to shared security issues, often in tandem with evolving international cooperation on the same issues. This was indeed the case with the regional norms that ASEAN developed to combat terrorism, piracy and cyber threats. In a mutually constitutive relationship, the parameters of ASEAN's legal authority are necessarily informed by the security imperatives of each member state, as these imperatives emerge from each member state's own socio-political condition and as they become shared or acknowledged by other member states.

---

[2] See Chapter 7.3 and 7.4.   [3] See Chapter 2.4.

This brings us to the fundamental question at the core of the inquiry of this book: what is ASEAN's legal authority? The legal authority of ASEAN is facilitative and complementary in nature in that it provides Southeast Asian nations with the collective means to enable them to exercise their sovereign powers in dealing with shared security threats in a way that does not jeopardise the peace and stability of the region. ASEAN does not possess the authority to act independently of its member states to make decisions,[4] let alone to impose decisions upon member states.[5] It does, however, have the institutional ability to develop regional norms and rules, and to turn international norms and obligations into more concrete sets of guidelines for internalisation by member states.

The extent to which ASEAN has actually exercised the legal authority to develop new norms and rules has not been extensive so far. More often than not, this has been due to the availability of international norms that member states are prepared to accept or technical expertise and resources at the international level (and the comparative lack thereof at the regional level), as is the case with nuclear regulation and maritime security activities. A notable exception is the regional norm of a nuclear weapon-free zone, with the adoption of the Bangkok Treaty at a time when there was no global treaty

---

[4] The ASEAN Summit has general competence to 'take action' in emergency situations affecting ASEAN: Charter of the Association of Southeast Asian Nations, adopted 20 November 2007, 2624 UNTS 223 (entered into force 15 December 2008) art. 7(2)(d). However, it remains to be seen what 'action' ASEAN is competent to take: see Chapter 1.5.

[5] See Chapter 1.4.3.

on the prohibition of nuclear weapons.[6] ASEAN also developed the e-ASEAN Framework, given the absence of an international norm and the development of cyber infrastructure at an alarmingly rapid pace;[7] and the AIFS Framework and the SPA-FS, together with the APTERR, in response to the 2007–2008 food crisis.[8]

In cases where relevant international norms and rules exist, ASEAN tends to localise them – as it did by adopting the ACCT and the ASEAN Convention against Trafficking in Persons – by making necessary alterations to incorporate regionally shared interests. ASEAN's legal authority in localising international norms and rules has been exercised with a view to facilitating the region's collective response to shared security concerns, through adaptation of the relevant norms and rules of international law in a way that complements respective national efforts without interfering with the internal or external affairs of each state.[9] The adaptation of international norms has also been made through the adoption of regional plans of action, which are aimed to facilitate the process of 'norm internalisation' – the process of incorporating

---

[6] See Chapter 2.2. ASEAN supported the Convention on the Prohibition of Nuclear Weapons, adopted 7 July 2017 (not in force): see ASEAN Statement at the UN Conference to Negotiate a Legally Binding Instrument to Prohibit Nuclear Weapons, Leading Towards Their Total Elimination, delivered by Hon Bayani S. Mercado, Assistant Secretary, Office of the United Nations and Other International Organizations, Department of Foreign Affairs of the Philippines, New York, US, 27 March 2017, available at http://statements.unmeetings.org/media2/14683410/asean-statement-delivered-on-27-march-2017.pdf.

[7] See Chapter 5.2.   [8] See Chapter 7.2.   [9] See Chapters 2.2 and 6.2.

international or regional norms as collectively interpreted and translated into a set of concrete actions.

There are various restrictions on the analysis of the extent to which, and the manner in which, regional norms and rules have been internalised through ASEAN. The absence of explicit reference or case law in implementing ASEAN instruments hinders an in-depth evaluation of this process. Evidence of internalisation tends to be sparse in the actual practice of ASEAN member states. The process of internalisation in each ASEAN member state is not regularised and tends to be informal in nature. These are the reasons why this study relies heavily on a descriptive approach with detailed narrative of facts as the basis for a holistic analysis. Nevertheless, this approach has provided a sufficient ground for clarifying the normative aspect of ASEAN's legal authority, if not for empirical evidence.

ASEAN's legal authority to internalise regional norms and rules is most clearly evident in regional plans of action. For example, ASEAN has promoted nuclear security agendas through the adoption of successive Plans of Action to Strengthen the Implementation of the Treaty on the Southeast Asia Nuclear Weapon-Free Zone, in order to facilitate incorporation of international regulatory standards for nuclear security and safety.[10] ASEAN's gradual development of a regional counter-terrorism framework, and in particular the implementation of the 2009 ASEAN Comprehensive Plan of Action on Counter Terrorism, has assisted its member states to internalise international norms and rules on counter-terrorism into their

---

[10] See Chapter 2.3.

own counter-terrorism laws and policies.[11] Similar initiatives have also been taken by the ARF, with the adoption of official statements, work plans and a series of follow-up seminars and workshops on counter-terrorism, ship and port security against piracy, and capacity-building and incident response against various cyber-attacks.[12]

These regional initiatives through the exercise of ASEAN's legal authority can be understood as attempts to overcome the limits of national efforts against transnational security challenges, such as the proliferation of nuclear materials, terrorism, piracy and cyber-attacks.[13] These exercises of ASEAN's legal authority complement the traditional national security strategies and structures that have been developed by member states to address pre-existing domestic security issues, such as internal conflicts with communist insurgents and dissidents. In this respect, ASEAN's legal authority shares the same conceptual ground as the principle of subsidiarity – simply put, a principle governing inter-institutional relations that allocates the locus of decision-making authority between a centre and various member units – which emerged in European legal contexts, with the potential for wider application in various areas of international law.[14]

---

[11] See Chapter 3.3.   [12] See Chapters 3.2, 4.2, 5.2.

[13] See Chapters 2.5, 3.4, 4.3, 5.3.

[14] See generally, Andreas Follesdal, 'The Principle of Subsidiarity as a Constitutional Principle in International Law' (2013) 2 *Global Constitutionalism* 37; Nicholas Tsagourias, 'Security Council Legislation, Article 2(7) of the UN Charter, and the Principle of Subsidiarity' (2011) 24 *Leiden Journal of International Law* 539; Paolo G Carozza, 'Subsidiarity

However, unlike the principle of subsidiarity as applied in European legal contexts, ASEAN's legal authority is not rooted in any libertarian vision of social organisation centred upon moral superiority and the dignity of each human individual.[15] Nor does it create any tension between the centre and the locals with countervailing interests of integration or centralisation on the one hand, and diversity or devolution on the other.[16] This is because ASEAN does not adopt one of the three strategies by which sovereign states can respond to transnational security threats, as articulated by Anne-Marie Slaughter and William Burke-White, namely: strengthening domestic institutions; backstopping domestic government; and compelling action by national governments.[17]

While ASEAN exercises its legal authority to strengthen domestic institutions and to require national authorities to enact legislation to achieve a shared policy objective, backstopping – an interference by, or transfer of authority to, an international institution – is absent in its institutional design. Even though there is no specific provision prohibiting ASEAN from intervening into matters within the domestic jurisdiction of a member state (much like Article 2(7) of the UN Charter), the regional norm of non-interference precludes ASEAN from performing

as a Structural Principle of International Human Rights Law' (2003) 97 *American Journal of International Law* 38.
[15] Cf. Carozza, above n. 14, 40–56.
[16] Cf. Machiko Kanetake, 'Subsidiarity in the Maintenance of International Peace and Security' (2016) 79 *Law and Contemporary Problems* 165.
[17] Anne-Marie Slaughter and William Burke-White, 'The Future of International Law Is Domestic (or, the European Way of Law)' (2006) 47 *Harvard International Law Journal* 327, 333–46.

a backstopping function – and therefore from evolving towards any form of supranational entity – even in cases where regional security concerns override the interest of national governments.

Thus, ASEAN has relied upon the other two strategies in exercising its legal authority to address regional security issues in the form of norm development, localisation and internalisation as identified above. As a result, their effects have so far been inward-looking, contributing to the collective efforts to strengthen legal institutions and capacity-building at the national level. On the other hand, its institutional ability to externally engage in normative processes with extra-regional powers appears to be substantially constrained, par-ticularly when those extra-regional powers have a strong political interest in the normative outcome.[18] As the domestic institutional capacity matures in each member state and the regional interest in this respect starts to wane, ASEAN may need to re-conceptualise this inward-looking form of legal authority in order to stay relevant as a regional security institution, based on 'ASEAN centrality'.

There are at least three challenges to the exercise and further development of ASEAN's legal authority that the association will face in the coming decades.

First, the fundamental rationale for ASEAN's role as a security institution may be brought into question when the collective maintenance of the political stability of each mem-ber state ceases to be the security imperative for some, as they

---

[18] As discussed in relation to ASEAN's engagement with the South China Sea dispute (Chapter 4.4) and its institutional practices in relation to human trafficking and people smuggling (Chapter 6.3–6.4).

manage to maintain a stable domestic political condition on their own. Indeed, there are indications that Indonesia is drifting away from ASEAN with a greater foreign policy focus on national interest-driven power politics and balancing behaviour.[19] Indonesia's independent pursuit of national security interests is also reflected in the notion of food sovereignty, as discussed in Chapter 7. The stable political condition and the greater ability of each member state to independently pursue their own national interests may intensify individual responses to security threats, especially when ASEAN is perceived to be too weak and disunited to adequately address them.

Second, the PRC's expanding military presence and influence within the region – as the power and influence of the US in the region predictably declines and enters into a period of uncertainty under the Trump Administration – particularly through the development of South China Sea military bases and the associated projection of Chinese naval power throughout the South China Sea and beyond, will test the agility of ASEAN and its legal authority to protect the national interests of member states. It is important to remind ourselves that ASEAN is not well equipped to deal with inter-state conflicts, especially when significant interests of extra-regional powers are

---

[19] See e.g., Vibhanshu Shekhar, 'Realist Indonesia's Drift Away from ASEAN', *Asia Pacific Bulletin*, 30 September 2015, available at www .eastwestcenter.org/system/tdf/private/apb323.pdf?file=1&type=no de&id=35328. Cf. See Seng Tan, 'Indonesia among the Powers: Should ASEAN Still Matter to Indonesia?' (National Security College Issue Brief No. 14, Australian National University, 2014), available at http://nsc .anu.edu.au/documents/Indonesia-Article14.pdf.

involved. Nevertheless, when the conflicts create a condition that destabilises the entire region – much like the precarious situation that has resulted from the South China Sea dispute – it is not in the collective interests for the region to become a proxy for strategic rivalry between major powers such as the PRC and the US.[20] ASEAN will have to continue exploring creative ways to further institutionalise mechanisms to uphold the principle of comprehensive security without interfering in these disputes.

Third, ASEAN regional security issues will become increasingly entwined with the broader security issues that exist in the wider Asia-Pacific region, especially when the issues are not geographically contained as is the case with the threat of so-called Islamic State or cyber security. When the security threat spreads beyond the geographical scope of the region, ASEAN will be required not only to find their common position to deal with the threat internally, but also represent its position to the wider international community. However, the parameters of ASEAN's legal authority to address security threats externally – for example, authorising the deployment of ASEAN combined forces or the establishment of a common

---

[20] The direct references to the DOC in numerous ASEAN instruments arguably indicate ASEAN's agreement to adopt a neutral position on the South China Sea dispute: see Carlyle A. Thayer, 'Managing Security Tensions in the South China Sea: The Role of ASEAN' in David Brewster (ed.), *Indo-Pacific Maritime Security: Challenges & Cooperation* (Canberra: National Security College, Australian National University, 2016) 24, 27–8. Cf. Ralf Emmers, 'ASEAN's Search for Neutrality in the South China Sea' (2014) 2 *Asian Journal of Peacebuilding* 61, 70–3.

cyber security regulatory framework to address external cyber threats – is yet to be clearly defined.

Concerned about these challenges, Razil Sukma, author of the original ASEAN Security Community concept paper,[21] has observed that ASEAN needs to embark upon new initiatives to maintain its relevance in a rapidly changing strategic environment in East Asia, through deeper intra-ASEAN cooperation rather than adopting a new vision or ideals.[22] ASEAN's Vision 2025 indeed reiterates a commitment to the effective implementation of existing instruments as a key element of the 'rules-based, people-oriented and people-centred community'.[23] ASEAN's aspiration for a rules-based community is critical to the maintenance of the peaceful, secure and stable region it aims to achieve. To that end, ASEAN member states should be aware that ASEAN can play a critical role by exercising its legal authority to set clearer expectations

[21] Rizal Sukma, 'The Future of ASEAN: Towards a Security Community' (paper presented at the seminar on 'ASEAN Cooperation: Challenges and Prospects in the Current International Situation', Permanent Mission of the Republic of Indonesia to the United Nations, New York, US, 3 June 2003), which was incorporated into the Concept Paper on ASEAN Security Community, tabled by Indonesia's Ministry of Foreign Affairs at the ASEAN Ministerial Meeting in Cambodia, 16–18 June 2003.

[22] Rizal Sukma, 'ASEAN and Regional Security in East Asia' in Wilhelm Hofmeister (ed.), *Security Politics in Asia and Europe* (Singapore: Konrad-Adenauer-Stiftung, 2010) 109, 120.

[23] ASEAN Political-Security Community Blueprint 2025, in Kuala Lumpur Declaration on ASEAN 2025: Forging Ahead Together, adopted at the 27th ASEAN Summit, Kuala Lumpur, Malaysia, 2 November 2015, Section A.

about how regional norms and rules are to be interpreted and applied to the respective responses by member states to security threats. The challenge is whether ASEAN can extend those expectations to extra-regional powers in their dealings with ASEAN member states, and to regional security relations in the wider Asia-Pacific to protect all Southeast Asian nations from threats of instability.

1. Official Documents

2007–2009 Work Plan to Implement the ASEAN Declaration against Trafficking in Persons, Particularly Women and Children, endorsed by the 7th ASEAN Senior Officials Meeting on Transnational Crime, Vientiane, Lao PDR, 27 June 2007.

2014 APEC Counter Terrorism Action Plan – Singapore (2015/SOM1/CTWG/018), submitted to the APEC 4th Counter-Terrorism Working Group Meeting, Subic, Philippines, 31 January to 1 February 2015.

ADMM Three-Year Work Programme, adopted at the 2nd ASEAN Defence Ministers' Meeting, Singapore, 14 November 2007.

ADMM-Plus Maritime Security Expert Working Group (EWG) Concept Paper, Yogyakarta, Indonesia, 28 April 2011.

ASEAN Chairman's Statement on the Humanitarian Situation in Rakhine State, New York, US, 23 September 2017.

ASEAN Comprehensive Plan of Action on Counter Terrorism, Nay Pyi Taw, Myanmar, 30 June 2009.

ASEAN Comprehensive Plan of Action on Counter Terrorism, adopted at the 11th ASEAN Ministerial Meeting on Transnational Crime, Manila, Philippines, 20 September 2017.

ASEAN Defence Ministers' Meeting-Plus (ADMM-Plus): Concept Paper, adopted at the 2nd ASEAN Defence Ministers' Meeting, Singapore, 13–15 November 2007.

ASEAN ICT Masterplan 2015, adopted at the 10th Meeting of ASEAN Telecommunications & IT Ministers, Kuala Lumpur, Malaysia, 13–14 January 2011.

ASEAN ICT Masterplan 2020, adopted at the 15th Meeting of ASEAN Telecommunications & IT Ministers, Da Nang, Vietnam, 27 November 2015.

ASEAN Plan of Action for Cooperation on Immigration Matters, adopted at the 4th Meeting of ASEAN Directors-General of Immigration Departments and Heads of Consular Affairs of ASEAN Ministries of Foreign Affairs, Davao City, Philippines, 16–18 October 2000.

ASEAN Plan of Action to Combat Transnational Crime, adopted at the 2nd ASEAN Ministerial Meeting on Transnational Crime, Yangon, Myanmar, 23 June 1999.

The ASEAN Regional Forum: A Concept Paper, adopted at the 2nd ARF Meeting, Bandar Seri Begawan, Brunei Darussalam, 1 August 1995.

ASEAN Regional Forum Work Plan on Security of and in the Use of Information and Communications Technologies (ICTs), adopted at the 22nd ARF Meeting, Kuala Lumpur, Malaysia, 6 August 2015.

ASEAN Security Community Plan of Action, adopted at the 10th ASEAN Summit, Vientiane, Lao PDR, 29 November 2004.

Bali Plan of Action: Towards Healthy Oceans and Coasts for Sustainable Growth and Prosperity of the Asia-Pacific, adopted at the APEC Ocean-Related Ministerial Meeting, Bali, Indonesia, 16 September 2005.

Chair's Statement of the 18th ASEAN Summit: 'ASEAN Community in a Global Community of Nations', Jakarta, Indonesia, 7–8 May 2011.

Chairman's Statement of the 3rd ASEAN Maritime Forum, Manila, Philippines, 9 October 2012.

Chairman's Statement of the 6th ASEAN Regional Forum, Singapore, 26 July 1999.

Chairman's Statement of the 7th ASEAN Regional Forum, Bangkok, Thailand, 27 July 2000.

Chairman's Statement of the 10th ASEAN Regional Forum, Phnom Penh, Cambodia, 18 June 2003.

Chairman's Statement of the 11th ASEAN Summit, Kuala Lumpur, Malaysia, 12 December 2005.

Chairman's Statement of the 12th ASEAN Regional Forum, Vientiane, Lao PDR, 29 July 2005.

Chairman's Statement of the 17th ASEAN Regional Forum, Hanoi, Vietnam, 23 July 2010.

Chairman's Statement of the 19th ASEAN Regional Forum, Phnom Penh, Cambodia, 12 July 2012.

Chairman's Statement of the 25th ASEAN Summit: 'Moving Forward in Unity to a Peaceful and Prosperous Community', Nay Pyi Taw, Myanmar, 12 November 2014.

Chairman's Statement of the 28th and 29th ASEAN Summits, Vientiane, Lao PDR, 6–7 September 2016.

Chairman's Statement of the 1st East Asia Summit, Kuala Lumpur, Malaysia, 14 December 2005.

Chairman's Statement of the 10th East Asia Summit, Kuala Lumpur, Malaysia, 2 November 2015.

Co-Chairs' Statement, Fifth Bali Regional Ministerial Conference on People Smuggling, Trafficking in Persons and Related Transnational Crime, Bali, Indonesia, 2 April 2013.

Co-Chair's Summary Report of the First ASEAN Regional Forum Inter-Sessional Meeting on Non-Proliferation and Disarmament, Beijing, PRC, 1–3 July 2009.

Co-Chairs' Summary Report of the Sixth ASEAN Regional Forum Inter-Sessional Meeting on Counter-Terrorism and Transnational Crime, Semarang, Indonesia, 21–22 February 2008.

Co-Chairs' Summary Report of the Thirteenth ASEAN Regional Forum Inter-Sessional Meeting on Counter-Terrorism and Transnational Crime, Nanning, PRC, 14–15 May 2015.

Co-Chair's Summary Report on ARF Workshop on Measures to Enhance Cyber Security – Legal and Cultural Aspects, Beijing, the PRC, 11–12 September 2013.

Concept Paper for the Establishment of the ASEAN Defence Ministers' Meeting, adopted at the 1st ASEAN Defence Ministers' Meeting, Kuala Lumpur, Malaysia, 9 May 2006.

Concept Paper on the Guidelines for Maritime Interaction (19 September 2017), adopted at the 11th ASEAN Defence Ministers' Meeting, Clark, Philippines, 23 October 2017.

Establishment of the ADMM-Plus Experts' Working Group on Cyber Security: Concept Paper, adopted at the 10th ASEAN Defence Ministers' Meeting, Vientiane, Lao PDR, 25 May 2016.

First Report on Subsequent Agreements and Subsequent Practice in relation to Treaty Interpretation: Georg Nolte, UN Doc A/CN.4/660 (19 March 2013).

Framework of a Code of Conduct for the South China Sea, adopted at the 14th ASEAN-China Senior Officials Meeting on the Declaration on the Conduct of Parties in the South China Sea, Guiyang, PRC, 18 May 2017.

Hanoi Plan of Action to Implement the ASEAN Regional Forum Vision Statement, adopted at the 17th ARF Meeting, Hanoi, Vietnam, 23 July 2010.

Joint Media Statement of the Third ASEAN Telecommunications & IT Ministers, Singapore, 19 September 2003.

Joint Ministerial Statement of the 25th ASEAN Ministers on Energy Meeting: 'Energising ASEAN to Power a Dynamic Asia', Singapore, 23 August 2007.

Joint Ministerial Statement of the 30th ASEAN Ministers of Energy Meeting (AMEM), Phnom Penh, Cambodia, 12 September 2012.

Joint Statement of Special ASEAN Defence Ministers' Meeting on Countering Violent Extremism (CVE), Radicalisation and Terrorism, Manila, Philippines, 23 October 2017.

Joint Statement of the First ASEAN-India Summit, Phnom Penh, Cambodia, 5 November 2002.

Joint Statement of the 19th ASEAN-China Summit to Commemorate the 25th Anniversary of ASEAN-China Dialogue Relations, Vientiane, Lao PDR, 7 September 2016.

Joint Statement on the Commission for the Treaty on the Southeast Asia Nuclear Weapon-Free Zone, Manila, Philippines, 30 July 2007.

Letter dated 14 November 2006 from the Permanent Representative of Myanmar to the United Nations addressed to the Chairman of the Counter-Terrorism Committee, UN Doc S/2006/902/Annex (14 November 2006).

Plan of Action to Strengthen the Implementation of the Treaty on the South East Asia Nuclear Weapon-Free Zone (2013–2017), adopted 30 June 2013.

Press Statement by the Chairman of the ASEAN Foreign Ministers Retreat, Vientiane, Lao PDR, 27 February 2016.

Report of the ASEAN Consultative Meeting on Integrating Nutrition into ASEAN Integrated Food Security Framework and Strategic Plan of Action on Food Security (2015–2019), Pattaya, Thailand, 6–7 February 2014.

Report of the Government of the Lao People's Democratic Republic to the Security Council on the Implementation of Resolution 1624 (2005), UN Doc S/2007/141 (13 March 2007).

Report of the Special Rapporteur on the Right to Food, UN Doc A/64/170 (23 July 2009).

Report of the Working Group on the Universal Periodic Review: Lao People's Democratic Republic, UN Doc A/HRC/29/7 (23 March 2015).

Report submitted to the Counter-Terrorism Committee on Implementation by Viet Nam of Security Council Resolution 1624 (2005) on Additional Measures to Combat Terrorism, UN Doc S/2007/425 (12 July 2007).

Second Report on Subsequent Agreements and Subsequent Practice in relation to the Interpretation of Treaties: Georg Nolte, UN Doc A/CN.4/671 (26 March 2014).

UN Security Council Official Records, UN Doc S/PV.4652 (3 December 2002).

UN Security Council Official Records, UN Doc S/PV.4736 (7 April 2003).

UN Security Council Official Records, UN Doc S/PV.5220 (30 June 2005).

Vientiane Action Programme 2004–2010, adopted at the 10th ASEAN Summit, Vientiane, Lao PDR, 29 November 2004.

Work Programme to Implement the ASEAN Plan of Action to Combat Transnational Crime, adopted at the Special Meeting of the ASEAN Ministerial Meeting on Transnational Crime, Kuala Lumpur, Malaysia, 17 May 2002.

2. Books, Book Chapters, Articles and Reports

Abad Jr., M. C., 'A Nuclear Weapon-Free Southeast Asia and Its Continuing Strategic Significance' (2005) 27 *Contemporary Southeast Asia* 165–87.

Abass, A., *Regional Organisations and the Development of Collective Security: Beyond Chapter VIII of the UN Charter* (Oxford and Portland, OR: Hart Publishing, 2004).

Abuza, Z., *Conspiracy of Silence: The Insurgency in Southern Thailand* (Washington, DC: United States Institute of Peace, 2009).

Acharya, A. (Amitav), 'Arguing about ASEAN: What Do We Disagree About?' (2009) 22 *Cambridge Review of International Affairs* 493–99.

Acharya, A. (Amitav), *Constructing a Security Community in Southeast Asia: ASEAN and the Problem of Regional Order* (3rd edn, Abingdon: Routledge, 2014).

Acharya, A. (Amitav), 'Regional Institutions and Security in the Asia-Pacific: Evolution, Adaptation, and Prospects for Transformation' in Amitav Acharya and Evelyn Goh (eds.), *Reassessing Security Cooperation in the Asia-Pacific: Competition, Congruence, and Transformation* (Cambridge, MA: The MIT Press, 2007) 1–40.

Acharya, A. (Amitav), 'Securitization in Asia: Functional and Normative Implication' in Mely Caballero-Anthony, Ralf Emmers, and Amitav Acharya (eds.), *Non-Traditional Security in Asia: Dilemmas in Securitization* (Aldershot: Ashgate, 2006) 247–50.

Acharya, A. (Amitav), *Regionalism and Multilateralism: Essays on the Cooperative Security in the Asia-Pacific* (Singapore: Eastern Universities Press, 2003).

Acharya, A. (Amitav), 'Regional Institutions and Asian Security Order: Norms, Power, and Prospects for Peaceful Change' in Muthiah Alagappa (ed.), *Asian Security Order: Instrumental and Normative Features* (Stanford, CA: Stanford University Press, 2003) 210–40.

Acharya, A. (Amitav), 'How Ideas Spread: Whose Norms Matter? Norm Localization and Institutional Change in Asian Regionalism' (2004) 58 *International Organization* 239–75.

Acharya, A. (Amitav), 'Culture, Security, Multilateralism: The "ASEAN Way" and Regional Order' (1998) 19(1) *Contemporary Security Policy* 55–84.

Acharya, A. (Amitav) and Tan, S. S., *Bandung Revisited: The Legacy of the 1955 Asian-African Conference for International Order* (Singapore: NUS Press, 2008).

Acharya, A. (Arabinda), *Whither Southeast Asia Terrorism?* (London: Imperial College Press, 2015).

Acharya, A. (Arabinda), *Targeting Terrorist Financing: International Cooperation and New Regimes* (Abingdon: Routledge, 2009).

Alagappa, M., 'Comprehensive Security: Interpretations in ASEAN Countries' in Robert A. Scalapino et al. (eds.), *Asian Security Issues: Regional and Global* (Berkeley, CA: Institute of East Asian Studies, 1988) 50–78.

Alagappa, M., *Towards a Nuclear-Weapons-Free Zone in Southeast Asia* (Kuala Lumpur: Institute of Strategic and International Studies, 1987).

Ali, M. and Ramakrishna, K., 'ASEAN-US Cooperation to Combat International Terrorism: A More Nuanced Approach Needed' (Commentary No. 10/2002, S. Rajaratnam School of International Studies, 29 August 2002), available at https://dr.ntu.edu.sg/handle/10220/3955.

APEC Policy Support Unit, *Food Security Policies in APEC* (Singapore: APEC Secretariat, 2012).

Arase, D., 'Non-Traditional Security in China-ASEAN Cooperation: The Institutionalization of Regional Security Cooperation and the Evolution of East Asian Regionalism' (2010) 50 *Asian Survey* 808–33.

ASEAN Food Security Information System, *ASEAN Agricultural Commodity Outlook No. 11* (Bangkok: ASEAN Food Security Information System Secretariat, 2013).

ASEAN Political-Security Department Security Cooperation Division, *ASEAN Documents on Combating Transnational Crime and Terrorism* (Jakarta: ASEAN Secretariat, 2012).

ASEAN Regional Forum, *Annual Security Outlook 2013* (Jakarta: ASEAN Secretariat, 2013).

Asian Development Bank Economics and Research Department, *Myanmar: Unlocking the Potential* (Mandaluyong City: Asian Development Bank, 2014).

Ba, A. D., 'The Institutionalization of Southeast Asia: ASEAN and ASEAN Centrality' in Alice D. Ba, Cheng-Chwee Kuik and Sueo Sudo (eds.), *Institiutionalizing East Asia: Mapping and Reconfiguring Regional Cooperation* (Abingdon: Routledge, 2016) 11–34.

Ba, A. D., 'ASEAN Centrality Imperiled?' ASEAN Institutionalism and Challenges of Major Power Institutionalisation' in Ralf Emmers (ed.), *ASEAN and Institutionalization of East Asia* (Abingdon: Routledge, 2011) 114–29.

Ba, A. D., *(Re)Negotiating East and Southeast Asia: Region, Regionalism, and the Association of Southeast Asian Nations* (Stanford, CA: Stanford University Press, 2009).

Ba, A., 'The ASEAN Regional Forum: Maintaining the Regional Idea in Southeast Asia' (1997) 52 *International Journal* 635–56.

Basrur, R., Collin, K. S. L., and Kemburi, K. M., 'Nuclear Energy and Energy Security in Asia: Through the Human Security Lens' in Rajesh M. Basrur and Koh Swee Lean Collin (eds.), *Nuclear Power and Energy Security in Asia* (Abingdon: Routledge, 2012) 1–23.

Bazeley, P. and Dottridge, M., 'Asia Regional Trafficking in Persons (ARTIP) Project: Independent Completion Report' (Department of Foreign Affairs and Trade, Australia, 2011) available at http:// aid.dfat.gov.au/countries/eastasia/regional/Documents/asia-regi onal-trafficking-in-persons-report.pdf.

Beckman, R., 'The UN Convention on the Law of the Sea and the Maritime Disputes in the South China Sea' (2013) 107 *American Journal of International Law* 142–63.

Beckman, R., 'Piracy and Armed Robbery against Ships in Southeast Asia' in Douglas Guilfoyle (ed.), *Modern Piracy: Legal Challenges and Responses* (Cheltenham: Edward Elgar, 2013) 13–34.

Beckman, R. C., 'Legal Regimes for Cooperation in the South China Sea' in Sam Bateman and Ralf Emmers (eds.), *Security and International Politics in the South China Sea: Towards a Cooperative Management Regime* (Abingdon: Routledge, 2009) 222–35.

Beckman, R., Bernard, L., Phan, H. D., Tan, H.-L. and Yusran, R., *Promoting Compliance: The Role of Dispute Settlement and Monitoring Mechanisms in ASEAN Instruments* (Cambridge: Cambridge University Press, 2016).

Beckman, R. C. and Roach, J. A., 'Ratification and Implementation of Global Conventions on Piracy and Maritime Crimes' in Robert C. Beckman and J. Ashley Roach (eds.), *Piracy and International Maritime Crimes in ASEAN: Prospects for Cooperation* (Cheltenham: Edward Elgar, 2012) 165–206.

Beeson, M., 'ASEAN's Ways: Still Fit for Purpose?' (2009) 22 *Cambridge Review of International Affairs* 333–43.

Beeson, M., *Institutions of the Asia Pacific: ASEAN, APEC and Beyond* (Abingdon: Routledge, 2009).

Bellamy, A. J. and Drummond, C., 'The Responsibility to Protect in Southeast Asia: Between Non-Interference and Sovereignty as Responsibility' (2011) 24 *The Pacific Review* 179–200.

Bliss, M., 'Amity, Cooperation and Understanding(s): Negotiating Australia's Entry into the East Asia Summit' (2007) 26 *Australian Year Book of International Law* 63–86.

Brahmbhatt, M. and Christiaensen, L., 'The Run on Rice' (2008) 25(2) *World Policy Journal* 29–37.

Briones, R. M., 'Public Stockholding in Southeast Asia: Review and Prospects' (Paper presented at FAO Expert Meeting on Stocks, Markets and Stability, Rome, 30–31 January 2014), available at. www.fao.org/fileadmin/templates/est/meetings/stocks/Briones_public_stockholding_in_southeast_asia.pdf.

Briones, R. M., 'Climate Change and Price Volatility: Can We Count on the ASEAN Plus Three Emergency Rice Reserve?' (Sustainable Development Working Paper Series No. 24, Asian Development Bank, 2012), available at www.adb.org/sites/default/files/publica tion/29971/adb-wp-24-climate-change-price-volatility.pdf.

Briones, R. M., 'Regional Cooperation for Food Security: The Case of Emergency Rice Reserves in the ASEAN Plus Three' (Sustainable Development Working Paper Series No. 18, Asian Development Bank, 2011), available at www.adb.org/sites/default/files/publica tion/29275/adb-wp18-regional-cooperation-food-security.pdf.

Busse, N., 'Constructivism and Southeast Asian Security' (1999) 12 *The Pacific Review* 39–60.

Buszynski, L., 'The Origins and Development of the South China Sea Maritime Dispute' in Leszek Buszynski and Christopher B. Roberts (eds.), *The South China Sea Maritime Dispute: Political, Legal and Regional Perspectives* (Abingdon: Routledge, 2015) 1–23.

Buszynski, L., 'Southeast Asia in the Post-Cold War Era: Regionalism and Security' (1992) 32(9) *Asian Survey* 830–47.

Caballero-Anthony, M., 'Non-Traditional Security in Asia: The Many Faces of Securitisation' in Andrew F. Cooper, Christopher W. Hughes and Philippe de Lombaerde (eds.), *Regionalism and Global Governance: The Taming of Globalisation* (Abingdon: Routledge, 2008) 187–209.

Caballero-Anthony, M., 'Reflections on Managing Migration in Southeast Asia: Mitigating the Unintended Consequences of Securitisation' in Melissa G. Curley and Wong Siu-Lun (eds.)

Security and Migration in Asia: The Dynamics of Securitisation (Abingdon: Routledge, 2008) 165–76.

Caballero-Anthony, M., *Regional Security in Southeast Asia: Beyond the ASEAN Way* (Singapore: Institute of Southeast Asian Studies, 2005).

Caballero-Anthony, M., 'Revisioning Human Security in Southeast Asia' (2004) 28(3) *Asian Perspective* 155–89.

Caballero-Anthony, M. and Cook, A. D. B. (eds.), *Non-Traditional Security in Asia: Issues, Challenges and Framework for Action* (Singapore: Institute of Southeast Asian Studies, 2013).

Caballero-Anthony, M., Emmers, R. and Acharya, A. (eds.), *Non-Traditional Security in Asia: Dilemmas in Securitization* (Aldershot: Ashgate, 2006).

Caballero-Anthony, M., Teng, P. P. S., Shrestha, M., Nair, T. and Lassa, J. A., 'Public Stockpiling and Food Security' (Policy Brief, S Rajaratnam School of International Studies, 2015), available at www.rsis.edu.sg/wp-content/uploads/2015/06/PB150603_Public-Stockpiling.pdf.

Cambodian Center for Human Rights, 'Human Trafficking Trials in Cambodia' (Report, July 2010), available at http://asiafoundation .org/publications/pdf/756.

Capie, D. and Taylor, B., 'The Shangri-La Dialogue and the Institutionalization of Defence Diplomacy in Asia' (2010) 23 *The Pacific Review* 359–76.

Carozza, P. G., 'Subsidiarity as a Structural Principle of International Human Rights Law' (2003) 97 *American Journal of International Law* 38–79.

Castles, S., de Haas, H. and Miller, M. J, *The Age of Migration: International Population Movements in the Modern World* (5th edn, Basingstoke: Palgrave Macmillan, 2013).

Caswell, J. A. and Bach, C. F., 'Food Safety Standards in Rich and Poor Countries' in Per Pinstrup-Andersen and Peter Sandøe (eds.), *Ethics, Hunger and Globalization: In Search of Appropriate Policies* (Berlin: Springer, 2007) 281–304.

Central Intelligence Agency, 'The World Factbook', available at www.cia.gov/library/publications/the-world-factbook/.

Chalermpalanupap, T. and Ibañez, M., 'ASEAN Measures in Combating Piracy and Other Maritime Crimes' in Robert C. Beckman and J. Ashley Roach (eds.), *Piracy and International Maritime Crimes in ASEAN: Prospects for Cooperation* (Cheltenham: Edward Elgar, 2012) 139–64.

Chalk, P., Rabasa, A., Rosenau, W. and Piggott, L., *The Evolving Terrorist Threat to Southeast Asia: A Net Assessment* (Santa Monica, CA, Arlington, VA and Pittsburgh, PA: RAND Corporation, 2009).

Chandra, A. C. and Lontoh, L. A., 'Regional Food Security and Trade Policy in Southeast Asia: The Role of ASEAN' (Policy Report No. 3, International Institute for Sustainable Development Series on Trade and Food Security, 2010), available at www.iisd.org/tkn/pdf/regional_food_trade_asean.pdf.

Chang, C.-C., Lee, H.-L. and Hsu, S.-H., 'Food Security: Global Trends and Regional Perspective with reference to East Asia' (2013) 26 *The Pacific Review* 589–613.

Chapman, J. W. M., Drifte, R. and Gow, I. T. M., *Japan's Quest for Comprehensive Security: Defense - Diplomacy - Dependence* (London: Frances Pinter, 1983).

Chau, A., 'Security Community and Southeast Asia: Australia, the U.S., and ASEAN's Counter-Terror Strategy' (2008) 48(4) *Asian Survey* 626–49.

Cheung, S., 'Migration Control and the Solutions Impasse in South and Southeast Asia: Implications from the Rohingya Experience' (2011) 25 *Journal of Refugee Studies* 50–70.

Chheang, V., 'Cambodian Security and Defence Policy' in *Security Outlook of the Asia Pacific Countries and Its Implications for the*

Defense Sector (Tokyo: National Institute of Defense Studies, 2013) 3–16.

Chow, J. T., 'ASEAN Counterterrorism Cooperation since 9/11' (2005) 45 *Asian Survey* 302–21.

Chuang, J., 'The United States as Global Sheriff: Using Unilateral Sanctions to Combat Human Trafficking' (2006) 27 *Michigan Journal of International Law* 437–94.

Churchill, R. R., 'The 1982 United Nations Convention on the Law of the Sea' in Donald R. Rothwell, Alex G. Oude Elferink, Karen N. Scott and Tim Stephens (eds.), *The Oxford Handbook of the Law of the Sea* (Oxford: Oxford University Press, 2015) 24–45.

Claeys, P., *Human Rights and the Food Sovereignty Movement: Reclaiming Control* (Abingdon: Routledge, 2015).

Collins, A., *Building a People-Oriented Security Community in the ASEAN Way* (Abingdon: Routledge, 2013).

Collins, A., 'Forming a Security Community: Lessons from ASEAN' (2007) 7 *International Relations of the Asia-Pacific* 203–25.

Commission on Human Security, 'Human Security Now' (Report, 2003), available at www.humansecurity-chs.org/finalreport/index .html.

Comprehensive Security Study Group, 'Sougou Anzenhoshou Kenkyuu Group Houkokusho [Comprehensive Security Study Group Report]' in *Ohira Souri no Seisaku Kenkyuukai Houkokusho [Policy Study Group Reports Commissioned by Prime Minister Ohira]* (Tokyo: Liberal Democratic Party, 1980) 301–44.

Cremona, M. et al., *ASEAN's External Agreements: Law, Practice and the Quest for Collective Action* (Cambridge: Cambridge University Press, 2015).

Crock, M., Saul, B. and Dastyari, A., *Future Seekers II: Refugees and Irregular Migration in Australia* (Sydney: Federation Press, 2006).

Dai, X., 'e-ASEAN and Regional Integration in South East Asia' in Ari-Veikko Anttiroiko and Matti Mälkiä (eds.), *Encyclopedia of Digital Government* (Hershey, PA: Idea Group Reference, 2007) 416–21.

Dalpino, C. and Westmyer, T., 'Southeast Asia: A Measured Nuclear Policy' in Mike M. Mochizuki and Deepa M. Ollapally (eds.), *Nuclear Debates in Asia: The Role of Geopolitics and Domestic Processes* (Lanham, MD: Rowman & Littlefield, 2016) 185–220.

Damrosch, L. F., 'Politics Across Borders: Nonintervention and Nonforcible Influence over Domestic Affairs' (1989) 83 *American Journal of International Law* 1–50.

Daño, E., 'ASEAN's Emergency Rice Reserve Schemes: Current Developments and Prospects for Engagement' (2006) 3 *Women in Action* 35–45.

Davenport, T., 'The Archipelagic Regime' in Donald R. Rothwell, Alex G. Oude Elferink, Karen N. Scott and Tim Stephens (eds.), *The Oxford Handbook of the Law of the Sea* (Oxford: Oxford University Press, 2015) 134–58.

David, P., David, F. and Gallagher, A., *ASEAN Handbook on International Legal Cooperation in Trafficking in Persons Cases* (Jakarta: ASEAN Secretariat, 2010).

Davidson, P. J., 'The Role of International Law in the Governance of International Economic Relations in ASEAN' (2008) 12 *Singapore Year Book of International Law* 213–24.

Dawe, D. (ed.), *The Rice Crisis: Markets, Policies and Food Security* (London and Washington, DC: Earthscan, 2010).

Demeke, M., Pangrazio, G. and Maetz, M., 'Country Responses to the Food Security Crisis: Nature and Preliminary Implications of the Policies Pursued' (FAO, 2009), available at www.fao.org/fileadmin/user_upload/ISFP/pdf_for_site_Country_Response_to_the_Food_Security.pdf.

Desierto, D. A., 'ASEAN's Constitutionalization of International Law: Challenges to Evolution under the New ASEAN Charter' (2011) 49 *Columbia Journal of Transnational Law* 268–320.

Desker, B., 'Energy Security: Southeast Asia Revives Nuclear Power Plans' (Commentary No. 226/2013, S. Rajaratnam School of International Studies, 11 December 2013), www.rsis.edu.sg/wp-content/uploads/2014/07/CO13226.pdf.

Desta, M. G., 'Food Security and International Trade Law: An Appraisal of the World Trade Organization Approach' (2001) 35 *Journal of World Trade* 449–68.

Djiwandono, J. S., *Southeast Asia as a Nuclear-Weapons-Free Zone* (Kuala Lumpur: Institute of Strategic and International Studies, 1986).

Doswald-Beck, L. (ed.), *San Remo Manual on International Law Applicable to Armed Conflicts at Sea* (Cambridge: Cambridge University Press, 1995).

Douglas, J. H. and Schloenhardt, A., 'Combating Migrant Smuggling with Regional Diplomacy: An Examination of the Bali Process' (Research Paper, Migrant Smuggling Working Group, The University of Queensland, February 2012), available at https://law.uq.edu.au/files/6723/Douglas-Schloenhardt-Bali-Process.pdf.

Drifte, R., 'Migrants, Human Security and Military Security' in Harald Kleinschmidt (ed.), *Migration, Regional Integration and Human Security: The Formation and Maintenance of Transnational Spaces* (Aldershot: Ashgate, 2006) 103–19.

Dubner, B. H., *The International Law of Sea Piracy* (The Hague: Martinus Nijhoff, 1980).

Duncan, J., *Global Food Security Governance: Civil Society Engagement in the Reformed Committee on World Food Security* (Abingdon: Routledge, 2015).

East Asia Study Group, 'Final Report of the East Asia Study Group' (adopted at ASEAN+3 Summit, Phnom Penh, 4 November 2002),

available at www.mofa.go.jp/region/asia-paci/asean/pmvo211/re
port.pdf.

Edwards, F. et al., 'Climate Change Adaptation at the Intersection of
Food and Health' 23 (2) *Asia-Pacific Journal of Public Health* 91S–
104S.

Eide, W. B., 'From Food Security to the Right to Food' in Wenche
Barth Eide and Uwe Kracht (eds.), *Food and Human Rights in
Development: Volume I, Legal and Institutional Dimensions and
Selected Topics* (Antwerp: Intersentia, 2005) 67–97.

Elliott, L., 'ASEAN and Environmental Cooperation: Norms,
Interests and Identity' (2003) 16 *The Pacific Review* 29–52.

Emmers, R., 'ASEAN's Search for Neutrality in the South China Sea'
(2014) 2 *Asian Journal of Peacebuilding* 61–77.

Emmers, R., 'Comprehensive Security and Resilience in Southeast
Asia: ASEAN's Approach to Terrorism' (2009) 22 *The Pacific
Review* 159–77.

Emmers, R., *Cooperative Security and the Balance of Power in
ASEAN and the ARF* (Abingdon: RoutledgeCurzon, 2003).

Emmers, R., 'ASEAN and the Securitisation of Transnational Crime
in Southeast Asia' (2003) 16 *The Pacific Review* 419–38.

Emmers, R., 'The Securitization of Transnational Crime in ASEAN'
(Working Paper No. 39, Institute of Defence and Strategic
Studies, Nanyang Technological University, 2002).

Emmers, R., Greener-Barcham, B., and Thomas, N.,
'Institutional Arrangements to Counter Human Trafficking
in the Asia Pacific' (2006) 28 *Contemporary Southeast Asia*
490–511.

European Atomic Energy Community, 'Report on the
Implementation of the Obligations under the Convention on
Nuclear Safety' (presented by the European Commission at the
7th Review Meeting of the Contracting Parties to the Convention
on Nuclear Safety, Vienna, 27 March–7 April 2017), available at

https://www-ns.iaea.org/downloads/ni/safety_convention/7th-re
view-meeting/euratom_nr-7th-rm.pdf.

Ewing-Chow, M. and Slade, M. V., 'A Case Study of Regional Food Security: APTERR' in Michael Ewing-Chow and Melanie Vilarasau Slade (eds.), *International Trade and Food Security: Exploring Collective Food Security in Asia* (Cheltenham: Edward Elgar, 2016) 62–78.

Ewing-Chow, M., Slade, M. V. and Gehuan, L., 'Rice Is Life: Regional Food Security, Trade Rules and the ASEAN+3 Emergency Rice Reserve' in Hitoshi Nasu and Kim Rubenstein (eds.), *Legal Perspectives on Security Institutions* (Cambridge: Cambridge University Press, 2015) 292–307.

FAO, *Regional Overview of Food Insecurity Asia and the Pacific: Towards a Food Secure Asia and the Pacific* (Bangkok: FAO, 2015).

FAO, *State of the World Fisheries and Aquaculture Report 2005* (Rome: FAO, 2005).

FAO, *Trade Reforms and Food Security: Conceptualizing the Linkages* (Rome: FAO, 2003).

Fealy, G. and Thayer, C. A., 'Problematizing "Linkages" between Southeast Asia and International Terrorism' in William T. Tow (ed.), *Security Politics in the Asia-Pacific: A Regional-Global Nexus?* (Cambridge: Cambridge University Press, 2009) 211–27.

Finnemore, M. and Hollis, D. B., 'Constructing Norms for Global Cybersecurity' (2016) 110 *American Journal of International Law* 425–79.

Follesdal, A., 'The Principle of Subsidiarity as a Constitutional Principle in International Law' (2013) 2 *Global Constitutionalism* 37–62.

Food and Agriculture Policy Decision Analysis (FAPDA), 'Country Fact Sheet on Food and Agriculture Policy Trends: Cambodia' (FAO, April 2014), available at www.fao.org/docrep/field/009/i3 761e/i3761e.pdf.

Friedrichs, J., 'East Asian Regional Security: What the ASEAN Family Can (Not) Do' (2012) 52(4) *Asian Survey* 754–76.

Funston, J., *ASEAN and the Principle of Non-Intervention – Practice and Prospects* (Singapore: Institute of Southeast Asian Studies, 2000).

Gallagher, A. T., *The International Law of Human Trafficking* (Cambridge: Cambridge University Press, 2010).

Gallagher, A. T., 'Human Rights and Human Trafficking in Thailand: A Shadow TIP Report' in Karen Beeks and Delila Amir (eds.), *Trafficking and the Global Sex Industry* (Lanham, MD: Lexington Books, 2006) 139–64.

Gallagher, A. T., 'A Shadow Report on Human Trafficking in Lao PDR: The US Approach vs. International Law' (2006) 15 *Asia and Pacific Migration Journal* 525–52.

Gallagher, A. T. and David, F., *The International Law of People Smuggling* (Cambridge: Cambridge University Press, 2014).

Gardiner, R., *Treaty Interpretation* (2nd edn, Oxford: Oxford University Press, 2016).

Garofano, J., 'Power, Institutions, and the ASEAN Regional Forum' (2002) 42(3) *Asian Survey* 502–21.

Geiß, R. and Petrig, A., *Piracy and Armed Robbery at Sea: The Legal Framework for Counter-Piracy Operations in Somalia and the Gulf of Aden* (Oxford: Oxford University Press, 2011).

Gerstl, A., 'The Depoliticisation and "ASEANisation" of Counter-Terrorism Policies in South-East Asia: A Weak Trigger for a Fragmented Version of Human Security' (2010) 3 *Austrian Journal of South-East Asian Studies* 48–75.

Goh, E., 'Great Powers and Hierarchical Order in Southeast Asia: Analyzing Regional Security Strategies' (2007–2008) 32(3) *International Security* 113–57.

Goh, G., 'The "ASEAN Way": Non-Intervention and ASEAN's Role in Conflict Management' (2003) 3(1) *Stanford Journal of East Asian Affairs* 113–18.

Guan, K. C. and Skogan, J. K. (eds.), *Maritime Security in Southeast Asia* (Abingdon: Routledge, 2007).

Haacke, J., 'The ASEAN Regional Forum: From Dialogue to Practical Cooperation' (2009) 22 *Cambridge Review of International Affairs* 427–49.

Haacke, J., 'Myanmar, the Responsibility to Protect, and the Need for Practical Assistance' (2009) 1 *Global Responsibility to Protect* 156–84.

Haacke, J., *ASEAN's Diplomatic and Security Culture: Origins, Development and Prospects* (Abingdon: Routledge, 2003).

Haacke, J., 'The Concept of Flexible Engagement and the Practice of Enhanced Interaction: Intramural Challenges to the "ASEAN Way"' (1999) 12 *The Pacific Review* 581–611.

Häberli, C., 'The WTO and Food Security: What's Wrong with the Rules?' in Rosemary Rayfuse and Nicole Weisfelt (eds.), *The Challenge of Food Security: International Policy and Regulatory Frameworks* (Cheltenham: Edward Elgar, 2012) 149–67.

Häberli, C. and Smith, F., 'Food Security and Agri-Foreign Direct Investment in Weak States: Finding the Governance Gap to Avoid "Land Grab"' (2014) 77 *Modern Law Review* 189–222.

Hafidz, T. S., 'A Long Row to Hoe: A Critical Assessment of ASEAN Cooperation on Counter-Terrorism' (2009) 11 *Kyoto Review of Southeast Asia* online, available at http://kyotoreview.org/issue-11/a-long-row-to-hoe-a-critical-assessment-of-asean-cooperation-on-counter-terrorism/.

Hamilton-Hart, N., 'Terrorism in Southeast Asia: Expert Analysis, Myopia and Fantasy' (2005) 18 *The Pacific Review* 303–25.

Heiduk, F., 'In It Together Yet Worlds Apart? EU–ASEAN Counter-Terrorism Cooperation after the Bali Bombings' (2014) 36 *Journal of European Integration* 697–713.

Heinl, C. H., 'Regional Cyber Security: Moving towards a Resilient ASEAN Cyber Security Regime' (Working Paper No. 263,

S Rajaratnam School of International Studies, 9 September 2013), available at www.rsis.edu.sg/wp-content/uploads/rsis-pubs/WP263.pdf.

Heller, D., 'The Relevance of the ASEAN Regional Forum (ARF) for Regional Security in the Asia-Pacific' (2005) 27 *Contemporary Southeast Asia* 123–45.

Hernandez, C. G., 'Southeast Asia – The Treaty of Bangkok' in Ramesh Thakur (ed.), *Nuclear Weapons-Free Zones* (Basingstoke: Palgrave Macmillan, 1998) 81–92.

High-Level Advisory Panel on the Responsibility to Protect in Southeast Asia, 'Mainstreaming the Responsibility to Protect in Southeast Asia: Pathway towards a Caring ASEAN Community' (Report, 9 September 2014), available at https://r2pasiapacific.org/files/382/mainstreaming-r2p-hlap-report-sep-2014.pdf.

Ho, J. H., 'Enhancing Safety, Security, and Environmental Protection of the Straits of Malacca and Singapore: The Cooperative Mechanism' (2009) 40 *Ocean Development and International Law* 233–47.

Ho, J. H. and Bateman, S. (eds.), *Maritime Challenges and Priorities in Asia: Implications for Regional Security* (Abingdon: Routledge, 2012).

Hodgkinson, S. L., 'The Incorporation of International Law to Define Piracy Crimes, National Laws, and the Definition of Piracy' in Michael P. Scharf, Michael A. Newton and Milena Sterio (eds.), *Prosecuting Maritime Piracy: Domestic Solutions to International Crimes* (Cambridge: Cambridge University Press, 2015) 32–53.

Hong, N., *UNCLOS and Ocean Dispute Settlement: Law and Politics in the South China Sea* (Abingdon: Routledge, 2012).

Hor, M., 'Singapore's Anti-Terrorism Laws: Reality and Rhetoric' in Victor V. Ramraj, Michael Hor, Kent Roach and George Williams (eds.), *Global Anti-Terrorism Law and Policy* (2nd edn, Cambridge: Cambridge University Press, 2012) 271–89.

Hough, P., *Understanding Global Security* (Abingdon: Routledge, 2004).

Hribernik, M., 'Countering Maritime Piracy and Robbery in Southeast Asia: The Role of the ReCAAP Agreement' (Briefing Paper 2013/2, European Institute for Asian Studies, March 2013), available at www.eias.org/wp-content/uploads/2016/04/EIAS_Br iefing_Paper_2013-2_Hribernik.pdf.

Hugo, G., 'Migration in the Asia-Pacific Region' (A paper prepared for the Policy Analysis and Research Programme of the Global Commission on International Migration, September 2005), available at www.iom.int/jahia/webdav/site/myjahiasite/shared/shared/mainsite/policy_and_research/gcim/rs/RS2.pdf.

IAEA, *Objective and Essential Elements of a State's Nuclear Security Regime: Nuclear Security Fundamentals* (Vienna: IAEA Nuclear Security Series No. 20, 2013).

Ikenberry, J. G., *After Victory: Institutions, Strategic Restraint, and the Rebuilding of Order after Major Wars* (Princeton, NJ: Princeton University Press, 2001).

Ikenberry, J. G. and Tsuchiyama, J., 'Between Balance of Power and Community: The Future of Multilateral Security Co-operation in the Asia-Pacific' (2002) 2 *International Relations of the Asia-Pacific* 69–94.

Imperial, N., *Securitisation and the Challenge of ASEAN Counter-Terrorism Cooperation* (Hong Kong: Centre of Asian Studies, The University of Hong Kong, 2005).

International Institute for Strategic Studies (IISS), 'The Shangri-La Dialogue Report 2013' (Conference Proceedings of the 12th Asia Security Summit, Singapore, 31 May to 2 June 2013), available at www.iiss.org/-/media//silos/shangrila/the-shangri-la-dialogue-re port-2013/shangri-la-dialogue-report-2013.pdf.

International Law Commission, 'Draft Articles on the Responsibility of International Organizations' (2011) *Yearbook of International Law* vol. II, Part 2.

Ivanov, K., 'Legitimate Conditionality? The European Union and Nuclear Power Safety in Central and Eastern Europe' (2008) 45 *International Politics* 146–67.

James Martin Center for Nonproliferation Studies, Center for Energy and Security Studies, and Vienna Center for Disarmament and Non-Proliferation, 'Prospects for Nuclear Security Partnership in Southeast Asia' (May 2012), available at www.nonproliferation.org/wp-content/uploads/2014/01/12 0515_prospects_nuclear_security_partnership_southeast_asia .pdf.

Jamnejad, M. and Wood, M., 'The Principle of Non-Intervention' (2009) 22 *Leiden Journal of International Law* 345–81.

Japan International Cooperation Agency, *The Development Study on East Asia: ASEAN Rice Reserve System, Final Report* (Tokyo: Pacific Consultants International, 2002).

Jayagupta, R., 'The Thai Government's Repatriation and Reintegration Programmes: Responding to Trafficked Female Commercial Sex Workers from the Greater Mekong Subregion' (2009) 47 *International Migration* 227–53.

Jervis, R., 'Security Regimes' (1982) 36 *International Organization* 357–78.

Jesus, J. L., 'Protection of Foreign Ships against Piracy and Terrorism at Sea: Legal Aspects' (2003) 18 *International Journal of Marine and Coastal Law* 363–400.

Johnston, A. I., 'The Myth of the ASEAN Way? Explaining the Evolution of the ASEAN Regional Forum' in Helga Haftendorn, Robert Keohane and Celeste Wallander (eds.), *Imperfect Unions* (Oxford: Oxford University Press, 1999) 287–324.

Jones, D. M. and Smith, M. L. R., 'Making Process, Not Progress: ASEAN and the Evolving East Asia Regional Order' (2007) 32 *International Security* 148–84.

Jones, D. M., Smith, M. L. R. and Weeding, M., 'Looking for the Pattern: *Al Qaeda* in Southeast Asia – The Genealogy of a Terror Network' (2003) 26 *Studies in Conflict and Terrorism* 443–57.

Jones, L., *ASEAN, Sovereignty and Intervention in Southeast Asia* (Basingstoke: Palgrave Macmillan, 2012).

Kahler, M., 'Legalization as Strategy: The Asia-Pacific Case' (2000) 54 *International Organization* 549–71.

Kanetake, M., 'Subsidiarity in the Maintenance of International Peace and Security' (2016) 79 *Law and Contemporary Problems* 165–87.

Katsumata, H., *ASEAN's Cooperative Security Enterprise: Norms and Interests in the ASEAN Regional Forum* (Basingstoke: Palgrave Macmillan, 2009).

Katsumata, H., 'Establishment of the ASEAN Regional Forum: Constructing a "Talking Shop" or a "Norm Brewery"?' (2006) 19 *The Pacific Review* 181–98.

Katsumata, H., 'Why Is ASEAN Diplomacy Changing? From "Non-Interference" to "Open and Frank Discussions"' (2004) 44 *Asian Survey* 237–54.

Katsumata, H., 'Reconstruction of Diplomatic Norms in Southeast Asia: The Case of Strict Adherence to the "ASEAN Way"' (2003) 25 *Contemporary Southeast Asia* 104–21.

Keo, C., *Human Trafficking in Cambodia* (Abingdon: Routledge, 2014).

Keohane, R. O., *International Institutions and State Power* (Boulder, CO: Westview Press, 1989).

Khong, Y. F., 'Coping with Strategic Uncertainty: The Role of Institutions and Soft Balancing in Southeast Asia's Post-Cold

War Strategy' in J. J. Suh, Peter J. Katzenstein and Allen Carlson (eds.), *Rethinking Security in East Asia: Identity, Power, and Efficiency* (Stanford, CA: Stanford University Press, 2004) 172–208.

Khoo, N., 'The ASEAN Security Community: A Misplaced Consensus' (2015) 2 *Journal of Asian Security and International Affairs* 180–99.

Kikuchi, T., '*Asia Taiheiyo ni okeru Chiikiseido no Keisei to Doutai: Chiikiseido wo tsuujiteno Hedge Senryaku to Seido wo meguru Bargaining* [The Formation and Dynamics of Regional Institutions in the Asia-Pacific: The Hedge Strategy through Regional Institutions and the Institutional Bargaining]' (2011) 84 *Aoyama Journal of International Politics and Economics* 171–260.

Kittichaisaree, K., 'A Code of Conduct for Human and Regional Security around the South China Sea' (2001) 32 *Ocean Development & International Law* 131–47.

Klein, N., 'Maritime Security' in Donald R. Rothwell, Alex G. Oude Elferink, Karen N. Scott and Tim Stephens (eds.), *The Oxford Handbook of the Law of the Sea* (Oxford: Oxford University Press, 2015) 582–603.

Klein, N., *Maritime Security and the Law of the Sea* (Oxford: Oxford University Press, 2011).

Klekowski von Koppenfels, A., 'Informal but Effective: Regional Consultative Processes as a Tool for Managing Migration' (2001) 39 (6) *International Migration* 61–84.

Kneebone, S., 'The Bali Process and Global Refugee Policy in the Asia-Pacific Region' (2014) 27 *Journal of Refugee Studies* 596–618.

Kneebone, S. and Debeljak, J., *Transnational Crime and Human Rights: Responses to Human Trafficking in the Greater Mekong Subregion* (Abingdon: Routledge, 2012).

Koga, K., *Reinventing Regional Security Institutions in Asia and Africa: Power Shifts, Ideas, and Institutional Change* (Abingdon: Routledge, 2017).

Koga, K., 'Institutional Transformation of ASEAN: ZOPFAN, TAC, and the Bali Concord I in 1968-1976' (2014) 27 *The Pacific Review* 729–53.

Koh, K. L., *Straits in International Navigation: Contemporary Issues* (London: Oceana, 1982).

Koh, T. T. B., 'The Territorial Sea, Contiguous Zone, Straits and Archipelagoes under the 1982 Convention on the Law of the Sea' (1987) 29 *Malaya Law Review* 163–99.

Kongrawd, S., 'Legal Frameworks for Combating IUU Fishing in Thailand' in Vijay Sakhuja and Kapil Narula (eds.), *Maritime Safety and Security in Indian Ocean* (Delhi: Vij Books India, 2016) ch 8.

Koutrakos, P., *The EU Common Security and Defence Policy* (Oxford: Oxford University Press, 2013).

Kraikaew, J., 'Implementation of Nuclear Materials Regulation in Thailand' (2015) 4(2) *International Nuclear Safety Journal* 13–20.

Kranrattanasuit, N., *ASEAN and Human Trafficking: Case Studies of Cambodia, Thailand and Vietnam* (Leiden: Brill, 2014).

Kuijper, P. J., Mathis, J. H. and Morris-Sharma, N. Y., *From Treaty-Making to Treaty-Breaking: Models for ASEAN External Trade Agreements* (Cambridge: Cambridge University Press, 2015).

Kuntjoro, I. A., Jamil, S. and Mathur, A., 'Food' in Mely Caballero-Anthony and Alistair D. B. Cook (eds.), *Non-Traditional Security in Asia: Issues, Challenges and Framework for Action* (Singapore: Institute of Southeast Asian Studies, 2013) 41–65.

Lassa, J. A., 'Brunei's Vision 2035: Can It Achieve Food Self-Sufficiency?' (Commentary No. 34, S Rajaratnam School of International Studies, 2015), www.rsis.edu.sg/wp-content/uploads/2015/02/CO15034.pdf.

Leheny, D., 'The War on Terrorism in Asia and the Possibility of Secret Regionalism' in T. J. Pempel (ed.), *Remapping East Asia: The Construction of a Region* (Ithaca, NY: Cornell University Press, 2005) 236–55.

Leifer, M., 'ASEAN's Search for Regional Order' in Chin Kin Wah and Leo Suryadinata (eds.), *Michael Leifer: Selected Works on Southeast Asia* (Singapore: Institute of Southeast Asian Studies, 2005) 98–110.

Leifer, M., 'The ASEAN Peace Process: A Category Mistake' (1999) 12 *The Pacific Review* 25–38.

Leifer, M., *The ASEAN Regional Forum* (Adelphi Paper No. 302, London: International Institute for Strategic Studies, 1996).

Leifer, M., *International Straits of the World: Malacca, Singapore and Indonesia* (Alphen aan den Rijn: Sijthoff & Noordhoff, 1978).

Leviter, L., 'The ASEAN Charter: ASEAN Failure or Member Failure?' (2010) 43 *New York University Journal of International Law and Politics* 159–210.

Lin, C. H., 'ASEAN Charter: Deeper Regional Integration under International Law?' (2010) 9 *Chinese Journal of International Law* 821–37.

Liss, C., *Oceans of Crime: Maritime Piracy and Transnational Security in Southeast Asia and Bangladesh* (Singapore: Institute of Southeast Asian Studies, 2011).

Loevy, K., 'The Legal Politics of Jurisdiction: Understanding ASEAN's Role in Myanmar's Disaster, Cyclone Nargis' (2015) 5 *Asian Journal of International Law* 55–93.

Loke, B., 'The "ASEAN Way": Towards Regional Order and Security Cooperation?' (2005) 30 *Melbourne Journal of Politics* 8–38.

Lyons, L. and Ford, M., 'Trafficking versus Smuggling: Malaysia's Anti-Trafficking in Persons Act' in Sallie Yea (ed.), *Human*

Trafficking in Asia: Forcing Issues (Abingdon: Routledge, 2014) 35–48.

Mackay, D., *The Malayan Emergency 1948–60: The Domino That Stood* (London and Washington, DC: Brassey's, 1997).

Magpanthong, C., 'Thailand's Evolving Internet Policies: The Search for a Balance between National Security and the Right to Information' (2013) 23 *Asian Journal of Communication* 1–16.

Mahbubani, K. and Sng, J., *The ASEAN Miracle: A Catalyst for Peace* (Singapore: NUS Press, 2017).

Mak, J. N., 'Sovereignty in ASEAN and the Problem of Maritime Cooperation in the South China Sea' in Sam Bateman and Ralf Emmers (eds.), *Security and International Politics in the South China Sea: Towards a Cooperative Management Regime* (Abingdon: Routledge, 2009) 110–27.

Mak, J. N., 'Securitizing Piracy in Southeast Asia: Malaysia, the International Maritime Bureau and Singapore' in Mely Caballero-Anthony, Ralf Emmers and Amitav Acharya (eds.), *Non-Traditional Security in Asia: Dilemmas in Securitization* (Aldershot: Ashgate, 2006) 66–92.

Malley, M. S., 'Bypassing Regionalism? Domestic Politics and Nuclear Energy Security' in Donald K. Emmerson (ed.), *Hard Choices: Security, Democracy and Regionalism in Southeast Asia* (Stanford, CA: Shorenstein Asia-Pacific Research Center, 2008) 241–62.

Maxwell, S., 'Food Security: A Post-Modern Perspective' (1996) 21(2) *Food Policy* 155–70.

McLaughlin, R. and Nasu, H., 'The Law's Potential to Break – Rather Than Entrench – the South China Sea Deadlock?' (2016) 21 *Journal of Conflict & Security Law* 305–37.

Mechlem, K., 'Food Security and the Right to Food in the Discourse of the United Nations' (2004) 10 *European Law Journal* 631–48.

Ministry of Agriculture and Agro-Based Industry (Malaysia), 'Malaysia National Report: Follow-Up of the Implementation of the World Food Summit Plan of Action' (FAO, 2008), available at ftp://ftp.fao.org/docrep/fao/meeting/013/ai699e.pdf.

Morada, N. M., 'The ASEAN Regional Forum: Origins and Evolution' in Jürgen Haacke and Noel M. Morada (eds.), *Cooperative Security in the Asia-Pacific: The ASEAN Regional Forum* (Abingdon: Routledge, 2010) 13–35.

Narine, S., 'ASEAN and the Management of Regional Security' (1998) 71(2) *Pacific Affairs* 195–214.

Nasu, H., 'Revisiting the Principle of Non-Intervention: A Structural Principle of International Law or a Political Obstacle to Regional Security in Asia?' (2013) 3 *Asian Journal of International Law* 25–50.

Nasu, H., 'The Expanded Conception of Security and International Law: Challenges to the Collective Security System' (2011) 3(3) *Amsterdam Law Forum* 15–33.

Nasu, H., 'The Place of Human Security in Collective Security' (2013) 18 *Journal of Conflict and Security Law* 95–129.

Nasu, H. and Rubenstein, K., 'Introduction: The Expanded Conception of Security and Institutions' in Hitoshi Nasu and Kim Rubenstein (eds.), *Legal Perspectives on Security Institutions* (Cambridge: Cambridge University Press, 2015) 1–24.

Nasu, H. and Trezise, H., 'Cyber Security in the Asia-Pacific' in Nicholas Tsagourias and Russell Buchan (eds.), *Research Handbook on International Law and Cyberspace* (Cheltenham: Edward Elgar, 2015) 446–64.

Neuhold, H., 'Common Security: The Litmus Test of International Solidarity' in Rüdiger Wolfrum and Chie Kojima (eds.), *Solidarity: A Structural Principle of International Law* (Berlin and Heidelberg: Springer, 2010) 193–223.

Niksch, L., 'Abu Sayyaf: Target of Philippine-U.S. Anti-Terrorism Cooperation' (Congress Research Service, US Congress, 24 January 2007), available at www.fas.org/sgp/crs/terror/RL31265.pdf.

OECD, 'Cybersecurity Policy Making at a Turning Point: Analysing a New Generation of National Cybersecurity Strategies for the Internet Economy' (OECD Digital Economy Papers No. 211, 2012), available at https://ccdcoe.org/sites/default/files/documents/OECD-121116-CybersecurityPolicyMaking.pdf.

OECD, 'Indonesian Policy Brief: Agriculture' (OECD Better Policy Series, 2015), available at www.oecd.org/policy-briefs/indonesia-agriculture-improving-food-security.pdf.

Ong-Webb, G. G. (ed.), *Piracy, Maritime Terrorism and Securing the Malacca Straits* (Singapore: Institute of Southeast Asian Studies, 2006).

Orakhelashvili, A., *Collective Security* (Oxford: Oxford University Press, 2011).

Ortiz, A., 'Neither Fox nor Hedgehog: NATO's Comprehensive Approach and the OSCE's Concept of Security' (2008) 4 *Security and Human Rights* 284–97.

Osius, T. and Mohan, C. R., *Enhancing India-ASEAN Connectivity* (Lanham, MD: Rowman and Littlefield, 2013).

Palmer, W., 'Discretion in the Trafficking-Like Practices of the Indonesian State' in Michele Ford, Lenore Lyons and Willem van Schendel (eds.), *Labour Migration and Human Trafficking in Southeast Asia: Critical Perspectives* (Abingdon: Routledge, 2012) 149–68.

Parameswaran, P., 'Southeast Asia's Nuclear Energy Future: Promises and Perils' (Project 2049 Institute, 2009), available at https://project2049.net/documents/southeast_asia_nuclear_energy_future.pdf.

Pareja-Alcaraz, P., 'International Law and East Asia's Regional Order: The Strengthening of a Fundamental Institution' in

Matthew Happold (ed.), *International Law in a Multipolar World* (Abingdon: Routledge, 2012) 224–41.

Pati, R., 'Trading in Humans: A New Haven Perspective' (2012) 20 *Asia Pacific Law Review* 135–66.

Pejic, J., 'Armed Conflict and Terrorism: There Is a (Big) Difference' in Ana María Salinas de Frías, Katja L. H. Samuel and Nigel D. White (eds.), *Counter-Terrorism: International Law and Practice* (Oxford: Oxford University Press, 2012) 171–204.

Pempel, T. J., 'Soft Balancing, Hedging, and Institutional Darwinism: The Economic-Security Nexus and East Asian Regionalism' (2010) 10 *Journal of East Asian Studies* 209–38.

Petcharamesree, S., 'ASEAN Human Rights Regime and Mainstreaming the Responsibility to Protect: Challenges and Prospects' (2016) 8 *Global Responsibility to Protect* 133–57.

Phan, H. D., 'The Association of Southeast Asian Nations: International Legal Personality and Its Treaty-Making Power' (2016) 13 *International Organizations Law Review* 273–307.

Prescott, V. and Schofield, C., *Maritime Political Boundaries of the World* (2nd edn, Leiden: Martinus Nijhoff, 2005).

Proulx, V.-J., *Transnational Terrorism and State Accountability: A New Theory of Prevention* (London: Bloomsbury, 2012).

Ramcharan, R., 'ASEAN and Non-Interference: A Principle Maintained' (2000) 22(1) *Contemporary Southeast Asia* 60–88.

Ramraj, V. V., Hor, M. and Roach, K. (eds.), *Global Anti-Terrorism Law and Policy* (Cambridge: Cambridge University Press, 2005).

Ramraj, V. V., Hor, M., Roach, K. and Williams, G. (eds.), *Global Anti-Terrorism Law and Policy* (2nd edn, Cambridge: Cambridge University Press, 2012).

Rees, N., 'EU and ASEAN: Issues of Regional Security' (2010) 47 *International Politics* 402–18.

Roach, K., 'Comparative Counter-Terrorism Law Comes of Age' in Kent Roach (ed.), *Comparative Counter-Terrorism Law* (Cambridge: Cambridge University Press, 2015) 1–45.

Roach, K., *The 9/11 Effect: Comparative Counter-Terrorism* (Cambridge: Cambridge University Press, 2011).

Roberts, C. B., *ASEAN Regionalism: Cooperation, Values and Institutionalisation* (Abingdon: Routledge, 2012).

Robertson, K. A., 'The Evolution of the Nuclear Non-Proliferation Regime: The International Atomic Energy Agency and Its Legitimacy' in Hitoshi Nasu and Kim Rubenstein (eds.), *Legal Perspectives on Security Institutions* (Cambridge: Cambridge University Press, 2015) 205–24.

Roque Jr, H. H. L., 'The Human Security Act and the IHL Law of the Philippines: Of Security and Insecurity' in Victor V. Ramraj, Michael Hor, Kent Roach and George Williams (eds.), *Global Anti-Terrorism Law and Policy* (2nd edn, Cambridge: Cambridge University Press, 2012) 310–33.

Rothwell, D. R. and Klein, N., 'Maritime Security and the Law of the Sea' in Natalie Klein, Joanna Mossop and Donald R. Rothwell (eds.), *Maritime Security: International Law and Policy Perspectives from Australia and New Zealand* (Abingdon: Routledge, 2010) 22–36.

Rothwell, D. R. and Stephens, T., *The International Law of the Sea* (2nd edn, Oxford: Hart Publishing and Bloomsbury, 2016).

Saipiroon, P., *ASEAN Governments' Attitudes towards Regional Security 1975–1979* (Bangkok: Institute of Asian Studies, 1982).

Salim, Z., 'Food Security Policies in Maritime Southeast Asia: The Case of Indonesia' (Trade Network Knowledge Series on Trade and Food Security: Policy Report 1, International Institute for Sustainable Development, 2010), available at www.iisd.org/sites/default/files/publications/food_security_policies_indonesia.pdf.

Santoro, D. and Baker, C., 'Institutionalizing Nuclear Governance in the Asia Pacific: A Conference Report of the Council for Security Cooperation in the Asia Pacific Nuclear Energy Experts Group Meeting' (2013) 13(16) *Issues and Insights* online, available at www.files.ethz.ch/isn/176496/issuesinsights_vol13no16.pdf.

Sarooshi, D., *The United Nations and the Development of Collective Security: The Delegation by the UN Security Council of Its Chapter VII Powers* (Oxford: Oxford University Press, 1999).

Saul, B., 'The Curious Element of Motive in Definitions of Terrorism: Essential Ingredient or Criminalising Thought' in Andrew Lynch, Edwina MacDonald and George Williams (eds.), *Law and Liberty in the War on Terror* (Sydney: The Federation Press, 2007) 28–38.

Saul, B., *Defining Terrorism in International Law* (Oxford: Oxford University Press, 2006).

Schloenhardt, A., 'Trafficking in Migrants in the Asia-Pacific: National, Regional and International Responses' (2001) 5 *Singapore Journal of Comparative and International Law* 696–747.

Schmitt, M. N. (ed.), *Tallinn Manual on the International Law Applicable to Cyber Warfare* (Cambridge: Cambridge University Press, 2013).

Schmitt, M. N. (ed.), *Tallinn Manual 2.0 on the International Law Applicable to Cyber Operations* (Cambridge: Cambridge University Press, 2017).

Seah, D., 'The ASEAN Charter' (2009) 58 *International and Comparative Law Quarterly* 197–212.

Seah, D., 'The Treaty of Amity and Cooperation in Southeast Asia: The Issue of Non-Intervention and Its Accession by Australia and the USA' (2012) 11 *Chinese Journal of International Law* 785–822.

Severino, R. C., *ASEAN* (Singapore: Institute of Southeast Asian Studies, 2008).

Severino, R. C., *Southeast Asia in Search of an ASEAN Community: Insights from Former ASEAN Secretary-General* (Singapore: Institute of Southeast Asian Studies, 2006).

Shulong, C., 'The ASEAN Plus Three Process and East Asian Security Cooperation' in Amitav Acharya and Evelyn Goh (eds.), *Reassessing Security Cooperation in the Asia-Pacific: Competition, Congruence, and Transformation* (Cambridge, MA: The MIT Press, 2007) 155–76.

Simon, S., 'ASEAN and Multilateralism: The Long Bumpy Road to Community' (2008) 30 *Contemporary Southeast Asia* 264–92.

Slaughter, A.-M. and Burke-White, W., 'The Future of International Law Is Domestic (or, the European Way of Law)' (2006) 47 *Harvard International Law Journal* 327–52.

Song, Y.-H., 'Regional Maritime Security Initiative (RMSI) and Enhancing Security in the Straits of Malacca: Littoral States' and Regional Responses' in Shicun Wu, Keyuan Zou and Tim Benbow (eds.), *Maritime Security in the South China Sea: Regional Implications and International Cooperation* (Abingdon: Routledge, 2009) 109–34.

Sorel, J.-M. and Eveno V. B., '1969 Vienna Convention: Article 31 General Rule of Interpretation' in Olivier Corten and Pierre Klein (eds.), *The Vienna Conventions on the Law of Treaties: A Commentary* (Oxford: Oxford University Press, 2011) 804–37.

Sotharith, C., 'Maritime Security in Cambodia: A Critical Assessment (Working Paper No. 21, Cambodian Institute for Cooperation and Peace, 2007), available via www.cicp.org.kh.

Stanslas, P. T., 'Transborder Human Trafficking in Malaysian Waters: Addressing the Root Causes' (2010) 41 *Journal of Maritime Law & Commerce* 595–606.

Stubbs, R., 'ASEAN Plus Three: Emerging East Asian Regionalism?' (2002) 42(3) *Asian Survey* 440–55.

Su, Y.-Y., Weng, Y.-H. and Chiu, Y.-W., 'Climate Change and Food Security in East Asia' (2009) 18 *Asia-Pacific Journal of Clinical Nutrition* 674–78.

Sukma, R., 'The ASEAN Political and Security Community (APSC): Opportunities and Constraints for the R2P in Southeast Asia' (2012) 25 *The Pacific Review* 135–52.

Sukma, R., 'ASEAN and Regional Security in East Asia' in Wilhelm Hofmeister (ed.), *Security Politics in Asia and Europe* (Singapore: Konrad-Adenauer-Stiftung, 2010) 109–20.

Suryadinata, L., 'Indonesia: Continuing Challenges and Fragile Stability' in Daljit Singh and Chin Kin Wah (eds.), *Southeast Asian Affairs 2004* (Singapore: Institute of Southeast Asian Studies, 2004) 89–103.

Symon, A., 'Southeast Asia's Nuclear Power Thrust: Putting ASEAN's Effectiveness to the Test?' (2008) 30 *Contemporary Southeast Asia* 118–39.

Tan, S. S., 'A Tale of Two Institutions: The ARF, ADMM-Plus and Security Regionalism in the Asia Pacific' (2017) 39 *Contemporary Southeast Asia* 259–64.

Tan, S. S., 'The ADMM-Plus: Regionalism That Works?' (2016) 22 *Asia Policy* 70–5.

Tan, S. S., *Multilateral Asian Security Architecture: Non-ASEAN Stakeholders* (Abingdon: Routledge, 2015).

Tan, S. S., 'The Institutionalisation of Dispute Settlements in Southeast Asia: The Legitimacy of ASEAN in De-Securitising Trade and Territorial Disputes' in Hitoshi Nasu and Kim Rubenstein (eds.), *Legal Perspectives on Security Institutions* (Cambridge: Cambridge University Press, 2015) 248–66.

Tan, S. S., 'Indonesia among the Powers: Should ASEAN Still Matter to Indonesia?' (National Security College Issue Brief No. 14, Australian National University, 2014), available at http://nsc.anu.edu.au/documents/Indonesia-Article14.pdf.

Tan, S. S., *The Making of the Asia Pacific: Knowledge Brokers and the Politics of Representation* (Amsterdam: Amsterdam University Press, 2013).

Tan, S. S., '"Talking Their Walk"? The Evolution of Defence Regionalism in Southeast Asia' (2012) 8(3) *Asian Security* 232–50.

Tan, S. S., 'From Talkshop to Workshop: ASEAN's Quest for Practical Security Cooperation through the ADMM and ADMM-Plus Processes' in Bhubhindar Singh and See Seng Tan (eds.), *From 'Boots' to 'Brogues': The Rise of Defence Diplomacy in Southeast Asia* (Singapore: S. Rajaratnam School of International Studies, 2011) 28–41.

Tay, S. S. C., 'The ASEA Charter: Between National Sovereignty and the Region's Constitutional Moment' (2008) 12 *Singapore Year Book of International Law* 151–70.

Teng, P. and Morales, M. C. S., 'Food Security Robustness: A Driver of Enhanced Regional Cooperation?' (Policy Brief, S. Rajaratnam School of International Studies, 2014), available at www.rsis.edu.sg/wp-content/uploads/2014/07/PB140331_Food_Security_Robustness.pdf.

Teo, S., Singh, B. and Tan, S. S., 'South Korea's Middle Power Engagement Initiatives: Perspectives from Southeast Asia' (2016) 56 *Asian Survey* 555–80.

Tey, Y. S., 'Malaysia's Strategic Food Security Approach' (2010) 17 *International Food Research Journal* 501–7.

Thampapillai, D., 'The Food and Agriculture Organization and Food Security in the Context of International Intellectual Property Rights Protection' in Hitoshi Nasu and Kim Rubenstein (eds.), *Legal Perspectives on Security Institutions* (Cambridge: Cambridge University Press, 2015) 269–91.

Thayer, C. A., 'Managing Security Tensions in the South China Sea: The Role of ASEAN' in David Brewster (ed.), *Indo-Pacific*

Maritime Security: Challenges & Cooperation (Canberra: National Security College, Australian National University, 2016) 24–30.

Thayer, C. A., 'Vietnam's Strategy of "Cooperating and Struggling" with China over Maritime Disputes in the South China Sea' (2016) 3 *Journal of Asian Security and International Affairs* 200–20.

Thayer, C. A., 'ASEAN, China and the Code of Conduct in the South China Sea' (2013) 33(2) *SAIS Review of International Affairs* 75–84.

Thayer, C. A., 'ASEAN's Code of Conduct in the South China Sea: A Litmus Test for Community-Building' (2012) 10 (34) *The Asia-Pacific Journal* No. 4.

Thayler, C. A., 'Reinventing ASEAN: From Constructive Engagement to Flexible Intervention' (1999) 3(2) *Harvard Asia Pacific Review* 67–70.

Thomas, N., 'Cyber Security in East Asia: Governing Anarchy' (2009) 5 *Asian Security* 3–23.

Tow, W. T. and Taylor, B., 'What Is Asian Security Architecture?' (2010) 36 *Review of International Studies* 95–116.

Treves, T., 'Historical Development of the Law of the Sea' in Donald R. Rothwell, Alex G. Oude Elferink, Karen N. Scott and Tim Stephens (eds.), *The Oxford Handbook of the Law of the Sea* (Oxford: Oxford University Press, 2015) 1–23.

Trybus, M. and White, N. D. (eds.), *European Security Law* (Oxford: Oxford University Press, 2008).

Tsagourias, N., 'Security Council Legislation, Article 2(7) of the UN Charter, and the Principle of Subsidiarity' (2011) 24 *Leiden Journal of International Law* 539–59.

Tsagourias, N. and White, N. D., *Collective Security: Theory, Law and Practice* (Cambridge: Cambridge University Press, 2013).

UN Conference on Trade and Development (UNCTAD), *Review of E-Commerce Legislation Harmonization in the Association of Southeast Asian Nations* (New York, NY and Geneva: United Nations, 2013).

Vannarith, C., 'Cambodia: Maritime Security Challenges and Priorities' (Working Paper No. 32, Cambodian Institute for Cooperation and Peace, 2010), available via www.cicp.org.kh.

von Hoesslin, K., 'Piracy and Armed Robbery against Ships in the ASEAN Region: Incidents and Trends' in Robert C. Beckman and J. Ashley Roach (eds.), *Piracy and International Maritime Crimes in ASEAN: Prospects for Cooperation* (Cheltenham: Edward Elgar, 2012) 119–38.

von Tigerstrom, B., *Human Security and International Law: Prospects and Problems* (Oxford and Portland, OR: Hart Publishing, 2007).

Walter, C., 'Defining Terrorist in National and International Law' in Christian Walter, Silja Vöneky, Volker Röben and Frank Schorkopf (eds.), *Terrorism as a Challenge for National and International Law: Security versus Liberty?* (Berlin: Springer, 2004) 23–44.

Wattanapruttipaisan, T., 'A Brief on ASEAN Economic Integration' (Bureau for Economic Integration and Finance Studies Unit Paper No. 07/2006, ASEAN Secretariat, 2006), available at www.asean.org/uploads/archive/STU_Paper_07–2006-Brief_on_ASEAN_Economic_Integration.pdf.

Woon, W., *The ASEAN Charter: A Commentary* (Singapore: NUS Press, 2016).

Yoshimatsu, H., *Comparing Institution-Building in East Asia: Power Politics, Governance, and Critical Junctures* (Basingstoke: Palgrave Macmillan, 2014).

Yturriaga, J. A. de, *Straits Used for International Navigation: A Spanish Perspective* (Dordrecht: Martinus Nijhoff, 1991).

Yusran, R., 'The ASEAN Convention against Trafficking in Persons: A Preliminary Assessment' (2018) 8 *Asian Journal of International Law* 258–92.

Zou, K., 'The South China Sea' in Donald R. Rothwell, Alex G. Oude Elferink, Karen N. Scott and Tim Stephens (eds.), *The Oxford Handbook of the Law of the Sea* (Oxford: Oxford University Press, 2015) 626–46.

Zou, K., *China-ASEAN Relations and International Law* (Oxford: Chandos Publishing, 2009).

Piracy, 112–13, 117, 137–8
Plan of Action for Cooperation on
　Immigration Matters
　(2000), 167
Plan of Action to Combat
　Transnational Crime (1999),
　83, 85, 167
Plan of Action to Strengthen the
　Implementation of the Treaty
　on the Southeast Asian
　Nuclear Weapon-Free Zone
　(2007), 59–60, 72 3
Plan of Action to Strengthen the
　Implementation of the Treaty
　on the Southeast Asian
　Nuclear Weapon-Free Zone
　(2013), 63, 74–5, 215
PRC. *See* People's Republic of
　China (PRC)

Ramos, Fidel, 82
Razak, Datuk Seri Najib Tun, 102
ReCAAP Agreement. *See*
　Regional Cooperation
　Agreement on Combating
　Piracy and Armed Robbery
　against Ships in Asia (ReCAAP
　Agreement) (2004)
ReCAAP Information Sharing
　Centre, 120, 129
Regional Cooperation Agreement
　on Combating Piracy and
　Armed Robbery against Ships
　in Asia (ReCAAP Agreement)
　(2004), 120, 127–8, 129–30
Regional Cooperation Framework
　(2011), 177–9

Regional Ministerial Conference on
　People Smuggling, Trafficking
　in Persons and Related
　Transnational Crime (2011),
　176–9
Regional security. *See* Security
　institution, ASEAN as
Regional Support Office, 178–9
Republic of Korea
　in ASEAN Plus Three, 42–4
　counter-terrorism and, 86, 110
　EAS and, 48
　maritime security and, 114
Rithauddeen, Tengku Ahmad, 56–7
Rohingyas, killing of, 39–41
Rusatom Overseas, 67, 70–1
Russia
　Bangkok Treaty and, 59
　Cambodia, assistance to, 71
　counter-terrorism and, 86, 110
　EAS and, 48
　maritime security and, 114
　TAC and, 23
　Vietnam, assistance to, 68

SAARC Convention on Preventing
　and Combating Trafficking in
　Women and Children for
　Prostitution (2002), 173–4
Sabah dispute, 3
Security institution, ASEAN as.
　See also Legal authority of
　ASEAN; *specific treaty, entity,*
　or country
　overview, 10–11, 14–15
　ARF, role of, 17–20
　broader security issues and, 220–1